SAVAGE MESSIAH

SAVAGE MESSIAH

How Dr. Jordan Peterson Is Saving Western Civilization

JIM PROSER

ST. MARTIN'S PRESS NEW YORK

First published in the United States by St. Martin's Press,
an imprint of St. Martin's Publishing Group

For information, address St. Martin's Publishing Group,
120 Broadway, New York, N.Y. 10271.

www.stmartins.com

The Library of Congress Cataloging-in-Publication Data is available upon request.

ISBN 978-1-250-25142-8 (hardcover)
ISBN 978-1-250-25143-5 (ebook)

First Edition: January 2020

10 9 8 7 6 5 4 3 2 1

For Adoley, my one and only

CONTENTS

FOREWORD

There is a famous Jewish legend that holds that, at any given time, there are thirty-six righteous people in the world. Thanks to these people the world continues to exist; were it not for them, humanity would collapse into such evil that it would consume itself and essentially cease to exist.

Neither we nor they know who these individuals are.

I do not take this legend literally—I assume there are more than thirty-six righteous people in the world. But I do take it seriously. Its point is entirely accurate. We all know the power of the truly evil to wreak havoc on Earth. Therefore, some truly good people have to counterbalance them.

The deck is stacked against the good. It is far easier for one individual to do great evil than for one individual to do great good. Any pathetic soul can murder dozens of people; but other than some physicians, how many people can save dozens of lives?

Jordan Peterson is one of those rare people.

Needless to say, if you know anything about the man, you know that he would scoff at this idea. Once, when I asked him at a public dialogue if he believed in God, he answered that he didn't think he was good enough to be able to say he did. In his view, to believe in God is so morally demanding, he cannot imagine who can truly say they believe in God.

I can only say, as one who does believe in God, that while Jordan may not be certain he believes in God, I am certain God believes in Jordan. At the end of each day in the Genesis creation story, it says

"And God saw it was good." Only after creating the human being does the text say, "And God saw it was *very* good."

Jordan Peterson is one of those rare people who wants to be very good. I think he is. Not just a very good psychologist, husband, and father, but a very good human being.

But what distinguishes Jordan most is the rarest of the good traits: courage. Many people are ethical, have integrity, and regularly show kindness, but few good people have courage. Jordan does.

It was his courage that brought him to the public's attention. He refused to be cowed by the Orwellian bullies of Political Correctness, who in the province of Ontario have passed laws governing what pronouns a person must use when speaking or addressing people.

Decent man that he is, Jordan Peterson would never intentionally insult a person. As he has repeatedly made clear, if someone looks and dresses as a female, and has a female name, he will refer to this person as "she," whether the person is transgender or not. Likewise, if a person looks and dresses as male, and has a male name, he will refer to this person as "he." But if a bearded person wearing a skirt demands to be referred to as "she," Jordan might not acquiesce, and will not allow Ontario to tell him he must.

Such a stance takes courage today—especially in the least open and most intolerant institution of our time, the university.

As a result of his remarkable ability to intellectually, rationally, and coolly respond to hostile interviewers the world over, Jordan became an international sensation, particularly among young people.

And why is that?

There is no definitive answer to that question but allow me to suggest a few.

No generation in modern history has been deceived by their elders as much as the past two generations have, especially in the English-speaking countries. Most young people do not realize this. How could they? If the people who present reality to you—most particularly your teachers and the news and entertainment media—tell you the Earth is flat, why would you assume it is round?

But many young people suspect they haven't heard the whole truth. At the very least, many of them realize that they have not been exposed to any other view of the world, of good and evil, or of Western civilization. So when an obviously decent, honest, erudite, intellectual came along and spoke to them about good and evil, about meaning in life, and how to be a more fulfilled and ultimately happier person, millions of them responded with enthusiasm.

Young people need adults to provide a model and to provide wisdom. Jordan Peterson has become that adult for millions of them. And he has especially touched young men, because too many adult men since as far back as the 1970s have chosen not to become men but to remain boys. Combined with the deliberate emasculating of a generation of men by feminists (of both sexes), countless boys and men are lost.

The subtitle of this biography is "How Dr. Jordan Peterson Is Saving Western Civilization."

It is not overstated. That is how important Jordan Peterson's life and work are.

—Dennis Prager

Dennis Prager is cofounder of Prager University, which garners more than a billion views a year, a nationally syndicated radio talk show host, syndicated columnist, and author of nine bestselling books, including the first two volumes of *The Rational Bible,* a projected five-volume commentary on the Torah.

INTRODUCTION

I discovered Jordan Peterson on YouTube and was immediately captivated by his use of language. There was a musicality to it. He spoke in a rush of barely comprehensible scientific concepts taken to a crescendo, and then stopped in a long, unexpected silence. He was speaking some form of elevated Canadian English. I stopped that first video and took a moment to digest what I'd just heard. I thought he was warning me about something called *postmodern Neo-Marxism*—whatever that was. I restarted the video from the beginning.

I saw that Peterson's long, unexpected silences were spontaneous moments of introspection, often in the middle of bursts of scientific observations. He was parsing his words, not to make them more palatable or to protect himself, but the opposite. He was making them more precise and frequently more inaccessible. He used phrases like "the proper level of analysis" and, "Agreeableness is one of the traits associated closely with creativity." This was definitely over my head, but he challenged me to keep up by interjecting a Will Rogers–style, plainspoken reflection:

> So what the hell's going on here, exactly? And why are we damn near at each other's throats?

He spoke in terms of psychometrics, an area of science that measures psychological responses. He colored scientific facts with his unique understanding of human nature learned from great minds like Carl Jung, Friedrich Nietzsche, and Jean Piaget. He added the wisdom of great writers like Aleksandr Solzhenitsyn and Fyodor Dostoevsky. He shared his own pain openly without shame.

But finally, it was his profound sensitivity to human suffering and insights into the evil in every human heart that made Jordan Peterson's message in this video unique and vital. I hope you will find here some solace in his words of wisdom, some inspiration from his heroic stand against overwhelming enemies, and some relief from the undeserved suffering in your life.

—Jim Proser
Sarasota, Florida
2019

CHAPTER ONE

DESCENT INTO HELL

The very fact that a general problem has gripped and assimilated the whole of a person is a guarantee that the speaker has really experienced it, and perhaps gained something from his sufferings. He will then reflect the problem for us in his personal life and thereby show us a truth.

—CARL GUSTAV JUNG, FOUNDER OF ANALYTICAL PSYCHOLOGY

He studied the neck of the young man, a fellow student, sitting in front of him. The fine hairs and gentle swell of the vertebrae were nauseating—something about their fragility and weakness. His compulsion to attack welled up, threatening to spill into the real world this time. He was suddenly in a rage, blinding and bloodthirsty. His heartbeat quickened, and his focus narrowed onto the curve of the fragile, downy hairs, fine as baby's hair, that wrapped around from the vulnerable jugulars on each side to the precise center of the delicate neck vertebrae. There they merged into a dark, vertical line that marked dead center of the spinal nerve.

Obviously, the hairs would be no protection at all in an attack like the one he was considering. In fact, they were pointing to prime targets and underlining the broad band of muscle where the tip of his pen would find bloody satisfaction. Somewhere inside his head a voice close to his own was perhaps saying something like, *Doesn't he understand that the entire world is about to be wiped out in a nuclear war? Well, he and everybody else in this stupid class will bloody well wake the hell up when I'm done!*

He sat there, stewing in his plot of revenge for his classmates' ignorance, while he imagined world leaders preparing to vaporize them all in uranium fires of 150 million degrees Fahrenheit, six times hotter than the core of the sun! He had no way to think about this. He knew there was no logic to it, there was no religion or philosophy that could explain it. There was nothing but the obvious and endless examples of barbarity that had happened everywhere, every day, time and time again since the beginning of the world.

The tormenting question of, How did evil—global, eternal evil—operate in the world? had lately been ricocheting around inside his skull like a glowing tracer bullet, shattering his thoughts, denying him sleep, and shuttering him silently away in his room. He knew he was slipping away, now even publicly. But there was no guide rail to grip, no North Star to guide him as he stumbled down his own shadowy mineshaft toward hell and insanity.

Jordan Peterson had entered the mineshaft of his own fears seven years earlier. At the age of thirteen he was already scoffing at the fairy tales being taught in his Christian confirmation class. *The virgin birth,* yeah, right. *Jesus rose from the dead,* oh, come on! He bristled even against the idea of this nonsense being taught in a classroom, as if it were truly education and not just a bunch of old fantasies. He believed in science. Small for his age and weighing around a hundred pounds, just being around these quiet and obedient Christian kids was enough to get him kicked out of the cool crowd—the tough guys who swore, got drunk, told raunchy and highly insulting jokes, and pissed on gravestones. He didn't want to even be seen with these religious nerds.

In spite of the hope of his mother, Beverley, that he would find comfort and guidance in her Christian faith, she was losing him. His father, Walter, a high school principal and teacher, was little help since he never had much to say on the subject. Although young Jordan loved and trusted his mother completely, he just couldn't believe in a god that turned a woman into a pillar of salt, or that his only *son,* an ordinary man, could walk on water.

It was as if the twinge of anxiety in rejecting his mother's faith, the first hairline crack of adult separation from her, pushed his already overactive, nearly manic curiosity into high gear. If the Bible was baloney, what was the truth? Now he had to find out. He probably couldn't even hint at such a nerdy idea with his friends. It was his only, as if he had stepped into his own, personal echo chamber of debate and closed the door behind him. Alone then, he plunged ahead into a sort of vision quest, into the realm of heroes searching for the golden fleece, the Holy Grail, or the Great Spirit itself. With only a vague notion of direction he turned his back on his mother's walled garden of Eden and ran headlong toward a personal knowledge of good and evil.

He knew it was somewhere down at the bedrock of human reasoning and science—it had to be. And he was in a hurry. But he already had all the knowledge about good and evil he could ever use.

He'd been absorbing it through the hundreds of science fiction and adventure novels he'd read, one a day on average, since he was a small boy. He recognized a bad guy instantly with just a few words of introduction, and naturally hoped they would pay for their evil deeds in the end. He'd been figuring out good and evil since he could read a newspaper at age six. In 1968, it started with the horror of the My Lai Massacre that year. Then he began to learn of the stories about the millions killed in recent world wars that filled popular books and movies. In 1975 at thirteen years old, he read of the killing fields of the Khmer Rouge in Cambodia that would eventually be filled with 1.8 million political outcasts, most killed with pickaxes to save bullets. He'd already read about the tens of millions of corpses from the world wars, and knew that evil people routinely operated in the open, while good people often seemed to hide in fear. *God is dead,* he'd heard. *And religion is the opiate of the people,* he'd heard. Religion was for obedient nerds, not tough guys who knew the score. *Religion* is *evil,* he'd heard.

And so young Jordan, barely a teenager, challenged his confirmation class minister by asking how the man could possibly believe the Bible story of Genesis in light of the modern scientific theories of the big bang and evolution? Apparently there was no satisfactory answer, only the musings of a devoted follower of Jesus Christ. This disgusted the rebel, the about-to-be fallen angel. What he was thinking was blasphemy and he knew it. But who cared? There was no Jesus or God to punish him anyway.

He already knew that evil was something that came from outside, like the space monsters of his science fiction books and the black-hatted gunslingers of his Western adventures who slouched into town looking for trouble. What he didn't know was that a special, personal evil already had deep roots inside him and was growing quickly. The religious wisdom that he'd scoffed at, that might have helped him deal with it, would not be earned for many years and only after much suffering to the point of insanity and near death.

It seemed like the only guidance young Jordan followed from his trusted, devoted mother was to pursue his vision quest through the books he continued to consume by the dozen. Fortunately, she had just started as a librarian at near by Fairview College. She was a rising star on campus, attracting students and faculty and amusing her colleagues with her fun-loving, prankster personality. Everyone soon fell for her almost as completely as Jordan had. With help from her colleagues, she was able to advise her precocious high-schooler about college-level books and lectures concerning his new fascination with global politics and social issues.

She was aided by Sandy Notley, Jordan's high school librarian and very influential mentor who introduced him to the newest books of social and political commentary from George Orwell, Aldous Huxley, Aleksandr Solzhenitsyn, and Ayn Rand. Sandy also introduced Jordan to Canada's emerging socialist politics. She was married to Grant Notley, the leader of the socialist Alberta New Democratic Party. The NDP was even more liberal than Canada's ruling Liberal

Party. Welcomed into the party by Grant, Jordan soon became an advocate for the NDP's socialist policies. With his ambition, gritty work ethic, and gift for argument, he helped push the party's advancement in Canadian politics.

As he stuffed mailing envelopes and built hand placards for protest marches, he was becoming more inspired toward revolution in solidarity with oppressed laborers, farmers, and factory workers around the world. He was now proudly part of the global collective, the proletariat, who were abused and cheated in every nation on Earth.

These new words, *collective* and *proletariat,* could barely be understood by the uninitiated. But he, Jordan Peterson, thirteen years old, was certain he'd found the path from religious ignorance toward the answer to the question that now fully possessed him—How and why does evil exist?

He wanted to know how political evil overtook entire countries and apparently everyone in them. Why were some countries consistently wealthy and their people happy and successful, while others were always poor, miserable, and then overtaken by evil? Why were NATO and the Soviet Union always on the brink of self-annihilating nuclear war? How could ordinary Germans have become Nazis? How could they have committed such obviously evil acts, and so blithely, as just following orders?

He peppered the Notleys with questions and challenged his young comrades in the NDP to debate him. But his comrades, the low-level volunteers like him, seemed annoyed that things weren't already solved, like all questions would be answered "come the revolution." It couldn't happen fast enough for them. They complained constantly as they stuffed voter outreach letters alongside him, always seeming to be "peevish and resentful."[1] They complained constantly that the people, the *lumpenproletariat,* as some disdainfully referred to them, were not sufficiently motivated, weren't out marching in the street or even fighting the police. They just weren't sufficiently revolutionary for these soft-handed sons and daughters of Canada. This crew seemed like cloud-headed whiners, just as lazy intellectually but even more annoying than his former Christian classmates. At least the Christians didn't expect people to find Jesus on their own, and then complain about it when they didn't. They knew people were struggling through a fallen world. These younger Marxists were peeved that people just didn't get it when it was all so obvious.

Everything was not at all that obvious or easy to Jordan, so he began to steer clear of the complainers. Huge questions, questions that might save humanity from catastrophe, were yet to be answered. The simple answer, as they all read in Marx and Engels's *The Communist Manifesto,* was economic injustice. That was the root of all evil; not money, but the lack of it and the power that went with it for working-class people. That is what caused all the suffering in the world. But, to Jordan's mind, it didn't even come close to explaining how a brilliant medical researcher from a wealthy German family could become the infamous Dr. Josef Mengele in Auschwitz. Economics had nothing to do with that. There was obviously something much deeper, much more evil, going on.

With his mind firmly fixed on the utopian vision of an end to evil, somehow, through a global worker's paradise, he joined the struggle of all laborers and began his work in the real world. He strode into the workforce, he may have imagined, like a muscular, hammer-wielding colossus in the Soviet revolutionary posters—hammer held high in defiance, upturned face set heroically toward the future. Actually, he was a not-very-muscular dishwasher in a small, local restaurant with a head full of desperately important questions in need of answers.

Always a hard worker and a pleasant if somewhat reserved young man, he soon graduated to short-order cook where he experienced the first faint indications of oppression. Not class oppression, because as far as he could tell everyone in Fairview was of the same class, but from the constant demands of the job itself that allowed him no time to read. He moved on to pumping gas at a local gas station where he could get his hands dirty like a real working-class Ivan and manage to read a few pages between customers. He was learning skills and discipline as a worker, but the oppression in his small, close-knit community of Fairview must have seemed hard for him to find. Everyone was a worker, even the bosses. But there was no lack of oppression according to the NDP. The political bosses in Ottawa were always up to chiseling the farmers out of something, or cheating the oil workers with some scheme. The problem was the NDP just couldn't get many people interested and continued to flounder, out of power, until Notley rose to leadership of the party in 1968 and then gained a seat as a member of Alberta's legislative assembly in 1971. When Jordan answered the call to action in 1975, the NDP was still a minority party in the provincial government with very little real power. But it was a group where he was able to mold his youthful enthusiasms into refined concepts of social justice while learning grassroots political organizing.

Just after high school, at seventeen, he moved sixty miles to Grand Prairie and took up undergraduate studies at Grand Prairie Regional College. He thought he'd like to be a lawyer, someone who protected the innocent and punished the wicked. His choice of studies was to prepare him for a career in the courtroom.

Politics still captivated him, particularly the left-wing politics that was popular among his new classmates. Strident Marxism seemed to be a semi-turnoff since most students were trying so hard to be cool. It was a bit pushy and a bit dorky to march about and shout slogans wearing nerdy little Trotsky eyeglasses or commie worker's caps, so intense beer-and bong-fueled debates in dorm rooms were the cooler alternative. Particularly in a world that thrived on coolness—cool jazz, cool clothes, cool chicks, and cool guys. Marxism was a bad fit for Jordan.

He was a roughneck, a frontier cowboy from the lonely Alberta oilfields. He talked fast and thought faster. He grew up fighting for his place in a wolf pack of tough guys, so what he lacked in physical stature, he made up for in smackdown ridicule.

People who know about cowboys say the most dangerous animal in the world is a 150-pound cowboy. Jordan was now one of those—but even smaller and with a little provocation, ornery as hell. Around him you quickly learned to watch what you said. No lazy or weak argument went unchallenged, and no veiled insult went untopped. He wasn't very cool. He was serious. He was intense. He was in a hurry.

As a younger man he'd read about the fictional worlds of ruling-class oppression in George Orwell's *1984* and Aldous Huxley's *Brave New World* with the help of Sandy Notley. But when he eventually found the shocking and real world of Aleksandr Solzhenitsyn's *The Gulag Archipelago,* it was like he got hit in the chest with a salt miner's shovel. As he read the hundreds of pages detailing the disgusting and monstrous evils of the modern Soviet Union, the luster quickly dimmed on his dreams of a utopian worker's paradise. The Marxists were no better, in fact, horribly worse than the capitalists! Marx said that religion was the opiate of the people that lulled the workers to sleep, but the communists were the heroin that killed them outright.

For a quicksilver mind and trusting heart like his, on a sacred quest for the truth, this was a crushing revelation. He'd been a fool. He'd been betrayed by trusted family friends Sandy and Grant Notley.

He'd been a young fool shooting his mouth off like a smart-aleck lawyer using big words he didn't completely understand. He was outraged. Liars!

His utopia on the horizon crumbled in his mind's eye as he watched, stupefied by his foolishness. It collapsed like Solzhenitsyn's inmates who, that very day, were being worked and starved to death in the gulags. The inmates he had helped enslave. Yes, he himself. All his big talk had only justified a corrupt system that humbled these miserables, exiled them, and then murdered them. *There was no way around that one, bucko!* The realization must have been shattering.

There was no way around it, and no way forward. Ignorance, humiliation, and deception lay in every direction. All he could do was retreat. He became resentful of those who had tricked him and those, like him, who had let themselves be tricked. He became angry at himself and all the other dummies around the world who were promoting this blatantly evil system. And finally, to ease his pain, he swallowed the bitter drug of nihilism, the belief that life was meaningless and people were just mindless drones. Vaguely hellish thoughts of violence began seeping into the void where his dreams used to be. He may not have even understood the word *nihilism* yet, but the devil, as his mother might have explained if he'd shown enough respect to listen to her, had many obscure names. He'd soon learn them all.

After some weeks, as he processed the devastating realization, as the shock and nausea subsided, he still felt the collectivist idea of everybody sharing everything must still hold some value. It was just common sense. It couldn't all be thrown out the window. He *felt* the truth of it. The Russians obviously got it wrong somehow, were corrupted somehow.

Working people were being treated like indentured servants everywhere, that much was obvious. Rich people didn't care about them, politicians didn't care, the Church didn't really care—or they would have done something about it by now.

Maybe they had all been undermined, probably even the Russian Marxists, by the capitalists who were constantly attacking them with propaganda and were ready to protect their profits with nuclear bombs if necessary. It was clear both sides were part of an insane system. It was the system that was wrong, not Marx's theory. It had to be the system. Something deep within the system, something hidden from the lazy and corrupted thinkers.

In any case, he couldn't just slip away from Marxism as he'd done from Christianity. When he stopped showing up for bible classes, no one had even noticed. But this was different. He'd made his mark and taken a position. The humiliation of backing away would be fatal, socially. He knew he could square this round peg if he just had enough time to think it through. He'd just have to work harder to find the flaw that had snared Solzhenitsyn and his fellow inmates.

It must have been hard to march on, hiding his humiliation, but he had no choice. He had to redeem himself. The nuclear clock was ticking. Nuclear war wasn't even being called *war* anymore, it was now called *mutually assured destruction,* or MAD in political speak. Total, global annihilation. It didn't even matter who launched first; the Russians would hit the United States and wipe out Canada as well—for 24,000 years! But the world would end long before that in nuclear winter and mass starvation, so said the Soviet KGB propaganda fiction that decimated American political will.[2] This lie about nuclear winter was so effective that when community fire whistles were tested on weekends all across America and Canada, no one, particularly teenagers with overheated imaginations like Jordan Peterson, could be 100 percent certain it wasn't actually the alarm announcing incoming missiles and the end of the world.

Humiliation for his naivete and the prospect of starving to death in a nuclear winter like Solzhenitsyn's inmates in Siberia kept the pressure building inside him. He obviously didn't truly understand even some basic political realities. It wasn't a question that beer, bongs, and chitchat with the cool kids could answer. And how could he even get to the answers if there weren't any adults he could rely on?

He hoped for guidance among the socialist leaders on campus and apparently found a few that were worthy of his respect. But the whiners, just like NDP volunteers, who "had no career, frequently, and no family, no completed education—nothing but ideology. They were peevish, irritable, and little, in every sense of the word."[3]

The dead in Solzhenitsyn's story clawed away at his peace of mind. They whispered to him when girls watched him and giggled at parties. They woke him up in stuffy classrooms when the thud of an eraser on a blackboard became a pick striking a seam of white rock in a salt mine. They never left him alone for long.

He drove himself harder, determined to find out where he'd gone wrong. What had he missed while chasing utopia? He stayed with the generally left-leaning politics on campus since that's where things were happening. Things like the iconic novelist and totem of the youth culture, Kurt Vonnegut, speaking at Bennington College:

> It isn't moonbeams to talk of modest plenty for all. They have it in Sweden. We can have it here. Dwight David Eisenhower once pointed out that Sweden, with its many Utopian programs, had a high rate of alcoholism and suicide and youthful unrest. Even so, I would like to see America try socialism. If we start drinking heavily and killing ourselves, and if our children start acting crazy, we can go back to good old Free Enterprise again.[4]

Closer to home, Soviet KGB agent Yuri Bezmenov had defected to Canada years earlier and been spilling the beans on Russia's twenty-year plan to support left-leaning students like Jordan and undermine the West, saying,

> The main emphasis of the KGB is not in the area of intelligence at all . . . 85 percent is a slow process which we call either ideological subversion . . . or psychological warfare. What it basically means is to change the perception of reality of every American (and Canadian) to such an extent that despite the abundance of information no one is able to come to sensible conclusions in the interests of defending themselves, their families, their community, and their country.[5]

Of course, almost no one but conservatives (whose hair instantly caught on fire) ever heard of Bezmenov, but everybody had heard of

Vonnegut. With growing conflict in his mind, idealist Jordan Peterson knew he could at least hang out among the left-wing students, even though he didn't admire them, while he pounded away at the same old questions of good and evil that were beginning to drive him crazy.

It was time to take action. He set his sights to run for the position of student representative on Grand Prairie Regional College's Board of Governors. He'd learned how to campaign for Grant Notley, now he would campaign for himself. He plunged ahead into politics and won a seat on the Board of Governors thinking it would be a direct confrontation with the conservative enemy. On the board were successful local businessmen, conservative, like most Albertans, generally agreeable and tolerant of the young socialist in their midst. Jordan became annoyed that he couldn't find a shred of oppressive sentiment in the group. What the hell was there to fight against? It annoyed him even more that he actually began to admire them. At least they didn't whine about the state of the world like his socialist colleagues. Their world was actually thriving and it made him somewhat more confused and miserable.

As he mentions in his first book, *Maps of Meaning*, at the time he had a similarly cynical college roommate who had had

> skepticism regarding my ideological beliefs. He told me that the world could not be completely encapsulated within the boundaries of socialist philosophy. I had more or less come to this conclusion on my own, but had not admitted so much in words.[6]

Soon in his reading, he came upon George Orwell's *The Road to Wigan Pier*, a book that cleared up his confusion about why his socialist colleagues were such insufferable losers, and in the process pointed to at least one major flaw in socialism that he'd been desperately searching for. He said about this book:

> Orwell did a political-psychological analysis of the motivations of the intellectual, tweed-wearing middle-class socialist and concluded that people like that didn't like the poor; they just hated the rich . . . I thought, Aha! That's it: it's resentment.[7]

He found not only resentment, but the downward winding staircase into hell itself. He found that resentment led to hatred. And hatred led to revenge. And revenge led to the footstool of the Prince of Darkness himself: demonization. Once a person is demonized, his humanity is erased. He becomes inhuman and subject to all inhumanities. Then any evil, even murder, even genocide, that is dealt to him becomes merely housekeeping and banal.

That is how a friendly German baker becomes an untroubled guard at Auschwitz, bringing children to the once-brilliant medical researcher who had transformed himself into the merciless Dr. Mengele. They are then both proud, loyal Germans, contentedly in the employ of the Prince.

As Jordan realized that resentment and atrocity lay at either end of a straight line, he also realized that this could not just be true for socialists. It was the human condition. It was the way of the world. And so, any advocate for any cause, even he himself, should be regarded with suspicion. Every belief seemed then to be valueless, since no one could be trusted to live by it.

But at least now he had a direction. He took the first step down the winding staircase into darkness. He could no longer recognize who, including himself, including his own family, was good and who was bad; what to believe or not to believe. From this terrible dilemma, the pressure inside him apparently escalated and increased his isolation.

The next step down was obscure, and he was cautious. More thinking and more reading would have to be done. For the moment, he could still fake his way through his pre-law courses and duties on the Board of Governors, but politics and law began to lose their attraction. He was losing his points of reference, so he lingered on the top step of the staircase, believing in nothing and no one.

The next step down the staircase would be his discovery: resentment. It was not something that came naturally to him; he was not a resentful person and found it an unattractive quality. Since everyone seemed equally untrustworthy, there was no one in particular he resented. Not yet. There would soon be many opportunities in the direction he was going, and the Prince was already tapping his slippered foot impatiently.

CHAPTER TWO

THROUGH THE UNDERWORLD

The adventure [of the archetypal hero] is always and everywhere a passage beyond the veil of the known into the unknown; the powers that watch at the boundary are dangerous; to deal with them is risky. . . .

—JOSEPH CAMPBELL, *THE HERO WITH A THOUSAND FACES*

It had been raining for a few days in Edmonton, the industrial heartland of Alberta, Canada, when Jordan Bernt Peterson was born on June 12, 1962. For his arrival, the rain clouds blew away and the early summer sun warmed the freshened air. As Wally and Beverley Peterson's first child, Jordan's safe arrival was an enormous relief and life-changing celebration all rolled into one. The sun was shining, the birds were singing, and they were now a real family. They'd been blessed.

On the seven-hour drive north, back to their home in Hines Creek, population around 380 or so, hypervigilant Wally no doubt focused all his attention on safety, driving carefully with a keen eye trained on any odd movement of approaching cars and trucks. Beverley naturally must have paid almost no attention to the road, the joy in her heart focused entirely on inspecting every tiny detail of her beautiful new baby.

For Jordan, growing up in the tiny, frontier village of Hines Creek was like being part of an isolated tribe. With only 150 families living together in the northern oilfields of Alberta, it was an extremely tight-knit community that had the basics of modern life but not much more. When his younger brother and sister arrived, they all enjoyed essentially the same rural lifestyle that children of prairie pioneers had lived for a hundred years. They were fed, clothed, and educated, but for entertainment they were generally on their own to make up games and run wild outdoors.

Especially during the six long, frigid months of winter, when one's own imagination was the only movie playing. For that half of the year when night fell early and stayed seemingly forever, board games or reading were usually the only entertainment.

It seemed young Jordan was well suited to the spartan, somewhat cloistered aspects of Hines Creek. He was safe under his father's rather serious but loving attention and buoyed by his mother's playfulness. With few distractions, he developed a keen awareness of the world around him and the ability to study it in an orderly way from his educator father. He remembers learning to read at the age of three, and quickly polished off all the Dr. Seuss books. His father remembers,

> He could read damn near anything. We went to visit his great-grandmother out on the coast when he was about five and she couldn't get over it. She'd give the kid the newspaper and he'd read the newspaper to her.[1]

Hines Creek's unspoiled northern plains landscape with its meticulous, reassuring order and sudden, explosive chaos, properly fascinated and frightened the boy. It formed the bedrock survival trait of watchful respect that helped harness his emerging, blazing intellect that tended to shoot off into fantasy. With his father's patient guidance, he explored nature, learning to fish and hunt, and to pay proper respect as well for those gruesome sacrifices.

But Jordan didn't share his father's patience or his mother's quiet resolve. He was an emotional whirlwind. His reading often produced outbursts of questions with tears of frustration filling his eyes as he waited for the answer. Even the excitement of childhood games could produce an emotional earthquake that soon drew teasing from other childhood friends that only made things worse. His emotions seemed to be amplified by his intelligence, like certain ideas came with sharp edges. It was a trait that would stay with him throughout his life.

Hines Creek was within walking distance of huge Lake George a little over a mile north, five miles north of the Sand Lake Nature Area, and just thirteen miles east of the Peace River and the Dunvegan West wilderness area. He learned of the roving tribes of Cree, Beaver, and Chipewyan natives who had hunted buffalo for thousands of years on those northern plains, far from the rich forests and easy summers of the south.

Books held all the stories, all the pictures of this other kind of people. They did everything differently; they spoke a different language, they didn't have jobs. They wandered the plains following the buffalo herds, dragging their tents of sticks and animal skin behind them. They were even a different color. But they were almost all gone, and the buffalo with them. It was a mystery and almost too fascinating for him to manage. He needed more books.

More books explained the local gold rush, the coming of the railroad (Hines Creek being the farthest point north of the Canadian Pacific line), the discoveries of oil, then diamonds in the province. Then came the laws and treaties that gave the tribes land but not enough to hunt on like in the old days. The buffalo had all been wiped out by that time, so they had nothing to hunt anyway. Professional hunters from the cities had killed them all for money.

For money? His young mind that was just beginning to grasp the inner workings of a real and troubling world must have paused at this idea. All the buffalo were wiped out *for money*? In his books there were images of massive piles of bleached buffalo bones—three times the height of a man—and railroad flat cars stacked high with hides. This was not respect like he'd been taught. The lessons of his father and mother were clear—if you killed an animal you'd bloody well better be ready to eat it, bucko. Every hunter knew that. To kill an animal and not eat it was a sin. A big sin.

And if those hunters hunted just for money, why did they have to kill *all* the buffalo? This and an endless stream of other questions demanded answers that his parents did their best to answer. They spoke of greed and a kind of blindness inside city people that only created more questions. He knew it was some kind of sin, but that was all he knew. He returned to his reading with a sense of urgency and now, some sorrow.

The family, prompted by Beverley, attended the United Church of Canada, a collaboration of Presbyterian, Methodist, and other Christian protestant churches. It must have seemed like torture to hyperactive Jordan. For the longest time, he didn't even know what the minister at the front of the church was talking about, but just had to pretend like he knew because he couldn't ask any questions.

Sometimes it was about Jesus who got tortured to death by bad guys. They had a scary statue of him bleeding and nailed to a wooden cross hung up at the front of the church. Sometimes it was about people who God liked or didn't like because they did certain things. There was this gigantic book that explained it all but it was in some weird, old language that he could hardly understand. It was just a nightmare, the whole thing—stand up, sit down, kneel down, stand up again, listen to the man tell a story about something—for an hour! There was no way out. He got the eye from this father and a tug on the sleeve from his mother if he even fidgeted or poked his little brother for fun. It was a disaster.

At ten, Jordan and his family moved from the little frontier village of Hines Creek fifteen miles south to the town of Fairview, population around three thousand. Fairview had high school baseball and ice hockey teams, hotels, movie theaters, and all kinds of fairs and parades. They had lots of oil patch roughnecks as in Hines Creek, but they also had farmers, cowboy ranchers, and small businessmen who made it seem like a big city.

The only problem with the place was that now he had to go to Sunday School where he sat behind a desk for an hour and listened to a minister talk. The man told Bible stories that were sometimes interesting and taught different prayers to memorize. When he got home, only his mother seemed interested in what he learned. Otherwise, religion wasn't ever discussed in his house.

Since he had skipped a grade, he had only one year of elementary school left before he entered high school. As his classmates were beginning to shoot up in height and broaden into teenage bodies, Jordan remained small and thin for his age. His being a year younger made his small stature even more noticeable. Adolescent socialization with its ever-present threat of embarrassment, even ostracism, was beginning to take hold, shredding childhood friendships and forming alliances against attack. The cult of cool was coming but Jordan had no friends in the area to vouch for his coolness or ease his introduction into junior society. He would have to find a niche, an approving social group, and act fast to survive socially.

High school arrived without fanfare and he soon found himself spending time exploring Fairview with new friends. He wasn't good at sports and so didn't really fit in that group. He wasn't particularly interested in art, so that group was out. Because he was physically small he began compensating by finding ways to prove his toughness. He was drawn to the misfits, the tough guys who tended to talk loud and play rough. Since this crew had no organized activity to help focus their energies, they tended to roam Fairview after school as a pack, finding mischief where they could. They wasted no time knocking the smaller Jordan into line.

A favorite pastime was hanging him, kicking and cursing, by his shirt collar in a hall locker. Another favorite was catching him on the stairway and tossing him back and forth from one boy to another. They soon found out that Jordan was small but extremely strong. They also learned that even though he was normally slow to enter the conversation, he commanded a remarkable range of opinions about their mothers' sexual habits. He'd been well prepared by his father's spare but insightful advice on dealing with large and small antagonists: "If something is bothering you, you don't want to sit on it and let it sour you."[2]

This rough treatment was the sort of swaggering, combative fun that won him his proper place in the tough guy gang, even though his eyes still occasionally filled with tears of emotion. In spite of his tears, he made the cut and happily ran with this crowd as just another one of the loudmouth boys looking for anything to pass the time in their little prairie town.

More than most Fairview preteens, Jordan was troubled about the world beyond his small-town pranks. The *Fairview Post* newspaper was full of obscure horrors and scandals from around the world, but he didn't have enough context about these events to generate much interest. The who, what, and where just didn't make much sense to him. Instead, he turned to books.

As fate would have it, his first books were science fiction. Extremely popular at the time was the brilliant Isaac Asimov, an admirer of Tolkien's The Lord of the Rings series. Asimov had created the Lucky Starr young adult science fiction series that were thrilling adventure stories like The Lord of the Rings but instead of European mythology, Asimov's stories were grounded in factual science. As Asimov said at the time,

> I want science fiction. I think science fiction isn't really science fiction if it lacks science. And I think the better and truer the science, the better and truer the science fiction.

The connection sparked between imagination and the real world! Jordan began to borrow five or six library books at a time through his avid supporter Sandy Notley. Asimov's complete and fascinating worlds provided all the context needed, unlike the brief stories in the newspaper, so that Jordan could discover who was good, who was bad, and why. He was suddenly enthralled by science and its many connections to the workings of the human heart.

The year before his burgeoning mind was set spinning into other worlds of science fiction, Asimov's publisher also published *The Working Brain,*[3] a popular book by pioneering Russian neuropsychologist Alexander Luria. Jordan may well have stumbled upon, or been given, this work in his stacks of science-oriented borrowed books. His later references to Luria in lectures indicate the seminal place of Luria's work somewhere in his formative years. As a precocious youngster, well aware of his own overactive brain, he could easily have comprehended the three basic systems of a working brain presented in the short book—the Attentional, or sensory system, the Mnestic, or memory system, and the Energetic maintenance system. Luria was also the likely precursor to Jordan's enduring attraction to Russian literature and thought.

Now with his head full of spellbinding science fiction and fact, his withdrawal from frustrating Christian theology accelerated dramatically. But there was still the matter of maternal tyranny that controlled his Sunday school attendance. There was nothing for it but capitulation. He dutifully put on the mask of obedient son and learned how to endure boredom.

Jordan set out to master his own rioting brain by first increasing his memory in a practice called The Memory Palace found in Luria's earlier, popular short book *The Mind of a Mnemonist.*[4] The Memory Palace, Roman Room, or Method of Loci (*places* in Latin) is a technique popular since ancient Greece that uses visualized physical locations, such as shops on a street, to collect and recall information.

The book was written like a detective novel about a real person, Solomon Shereshevsky, a Russian journalist. Shereshevsky was of average intelligence, but had an awe-inspiring talent for memorization. Luria interviewed him soon after Shereshevsky got into an argument at his newspaper. At an editorial meeting, the journalist was pointedly criticized for not taking any notes. He shocked fellow journalists and editors when he instantly recalled the entire meeting verbatim! The unassuming reporter was also shocked to realize that no one else could do the same.

The story unfolds as Shereshevsky is asked to memorize ever more complex mathematical formulas, huge intersecting matrix charts, and even foreign language poems. He memorized them all, flawlessly, in a matter of minutes.

Luria diagnosed Shereshevsky with synesthesia in which the stimulation of one of his senses produced a reaction in the others. If Shereshevsky heard a musical tone he saw a color, the texture of an object would trigger a taste, and so on. When thinking about numbers Shereshevsky said,

> Take the number 1. This is a proud, well-built man; 2 is a high-spirited woman; 3 a gloomy person; 6 a man with a swollen foot; 7 a man with a moustache; 8 a very stout woman—a sack within a sack. As for the number 87, what I see is a fat woman and a man twirling his moustache.

This was now real life appearing to be science fiction and was irresistibly magnetic to young Jordan Peterson. He was in; 100 percent passionately committed to exploring his own and other human minds. Perhaps in that moment, his life's course was set.

Jordan practiced The Memory Palace diligently. It would prove to be a fundamental tool to help store the increasing volume of raw information and ideas now filling up every corner of his mind. His mind, always on a fast idle, now shifted into overdrive. He practiced the memory technique every spare moment when he wasn't reading his extracurricular book a day, on top of his regular schoolwork.

On his frequent hunting and fishing trips with his father, his broadened mind could now make more complex observations of the natural world and how at least one human being acted in it. His father, being an introvert, demonstrated many fundamentals of wilderness survival without the need for conversation. A quiet and observant composure, regardless of the situation, was his baseline quality. High technical competency particularly as a gunsmith and a profound reliance on intuition, a sixth sense, the ability to think like a prey animal, completed his profile as a highly competent hunter. As a human being, his father's respect for all life, animals, and plants, filled the spiritual place left empty by Christianity in Jordan's life.

With ample quiet time to ponder his observations, Jordan may have noticed the similarities between his father and the heroes in his science fiction worlds. The planets and bad guys changed, but the good guys always acted in the same ways. Bad guys were always chaotic and cynical. Good guys were orderly and idealistic. He was beginning to gain firsthand insight into human nature and with it the wisdom to possibly affect the human condition.

In the critical year 1975, at the age of thirteen, Jordan had had enough of the Christian fables and refused to attend church or Sunday school any longer. Beverley recognized the futility of arguing with her headstrong son, and the subject was no longer discussed. Although his mother continued to attend church regularly with his younger brother and sister, Jordan's Sundays could now be devoted to other activities including his new, inspiring volunteer work for the National Democratic Party run by his trusted mentors and neighbors Sandy and Grant Notley.

Other activities included drinking heavily and smoking cigarettes. These habits were acquired in order to maintain his place in the wolf pack of his tough friends—teenagers who often dropped out of high school to work in the oilfields. The first Middle Eastern oil embargo of 1973 had quadrupled the price of oil and caused a market boom that offered inflated wages for new oil workers. It drew thousands of able-bodied Canadians into the fields and Jordan soon followed, becoming a drill bit re-tipper.

His drinking, smoking, and lack of regular exercise, other than skiing for pleasure and the occasional wrestling match with his buddies, soon ballooned his small frame into an overweight, physically weakened, and generally unhealthy body. It wouldn't be until twelve years later, at the age of twenty-five, when he managed to quit his teenage habits and force himself into a gym that he regained his health. With impressive personal discipline, he spent a year lifting weights that trimmed fat while adding thirty new pounds of muscle.

But at the age of thirteen and for the next five years through 1978, while his health deteriorated, a mental rot that could not be as easily reversed had also begun to set in. By the time his fervent, teenage dedication to Grant Notley's political career had turned to complete disillusionment, and he saw that Notley's socialist philosophy was really just a murderously naive mental trap, the psychological damage to Jordan had been done. He had been steadily losing confidence in the Notleys, the NDP, Marxism itself, and in his own judgment.

He had been preparing in his first two years of college at Grand Prairie to become a lawyer, to heroically right the wrongs and punish the bad guys of the world. But that dream crashed and burned by age eighteen. He seemed to be just another fool in a long line that stretched back seventy years—"a useful idiot" in Soviet socialist words and indeed in his own mind. He was not going to be someone who could help anyone.

Yet, while increasingly undermined by self-doubt, he still managed to do well in his studies and in his position on Grand Prairie's Board of Governors. Under the surface, his shadow side was filling the hole in his soul left by his rejection of God, any god. Coincidentally, his comfortable, familiar personality began rotting away.

His social skills also began to rot as well, turning his usual hesitancy to join in conversation into a stony silence. He had nothing to offer, his beliefs had become meaningless. He thought people, obviously including himself, would believe whatever they bloody well needed to believe to climb the hierarchies of the world, even the corrupt hierarchies like Marxism. At that moment, as he would later learn, his life began to parallel the life of Roquentin, the fictitious main character in Jean-Paul Sartre's seminal work on nihilism, the Nobel Prize–winning novel *Nausea.*

Roquentin's nauseating realization, like Jordan's, was that life and his role in it were meaningless. This was a common sentiment when the novel was published in 1938, particularly in Europe, as the world was being drawn into a second world war just twenty years after the first one had devastated modern civilization. Many writers, particularly the French like Sartre and Louis-Ferdinand Céline (quoted on the flyleaf of *Nausea*), correctly observed that the next stop after nausea was total despair, and despair then led directly to a belief in nothing, or nihilism. What Sartre and Céline couldn't know at the time was that this growing nihilism, when combined with the different forms of Marxism that they both promoted, would soon produce as yet unimaginable evil in Germany, and then after the war in Russia. To his credit, only Sartre saw that the flash of recognition that produced this existential nausea was necessary to an individual's development and would eventually lead to "a release from disgust into heroism."

Jordan's release from disgust wouldn't come for years, until he had endured the complete rotting away of his life's meaning and lingered at the nihilistic edge of insanity at age twenty.

At eighteen, when his belief in becoming a lawyer, "so I could learn more about the structure of human beliefs,"[5] had evaporated, he transferred to the University of Alberta three hundred miles away in his birthplace of Edmonton, and focused on political science. Logically, this may have been to pursue his undergraduate degree at a more prestigious school. It could also have been to escape from the now loathsome Marxists or others, like the conservative lawyers and prosperous business owners on the Board of Governors, in front of whom he may have felt embarrassed.

After receiving his bachelor of arts degree in political science in one additional year of study, Peterson took a year off to work as a driver for various social and community service groups in Europe. He said of this time,

> All my beliefs—which had lent order to the chaos of my existence, at least temporarily—had proved illusory; I could no longer see the sense in things. I was cast adrift; I did not know what to do or what to think.[6]

In country after country he saw, firsthand, the devastating aftereffects of World War II. His endless curiosity and avid reading led him to the foundations of the nihilism that had destroyed a generation and now threatened nuclear annihilation of the entire world. The threat was never more real or pressing than it was now. According to *The New York Times,* the Doomsday Clock from the Chicago Atomic Scientists was said to be set at seven minutes to midnight, i.e. time to hit the panic button.

The fear level had been critical for years, almost thirty-five in fact. The Doomsday Clock was the same in 1982 as it was in 1947 when it was created. Even during the Cuban Missile Crisis in 1962, from development of the crisis, through the climax, and on to the resolution, the clock never moved. It didn't really have to; people were terrified, argumentative, or, like Jordan, retreating into anonymity. No one was really checking. In fact, the designer of the cartoon for the cover of *Bulletin of the Atomic Scientists,* artist Martyl Langsdorf said she drew the Doomsday Clock at seven minutes to midnight "because it looked good to my eye."

The Atomic Scientists of Chicago, who reset the clock when they felt it needed it, were not really from Chicago. They were an international group of physical scientists, including several Soviet citizens, who had virtually no credentials in international affairs, but did have an office at the University of Chicago. As an accurate depiction of the probability of nuclear war, the Doomsday Clock was completely useless. But as a possible tool to advance destabilizing psychological warfare, it was exceptionally effective.

Under the usual threat of annihilation, Jordan urgently studied the psychological origins of the Cold War and twentieth-century European totalitarianism through the works of Carl Jung, Friedrich Nietzsche, Aleksandr Solzhenitsyn, and Fyodor Dostoevsky.

Not the most cheerful selection, it could only have created a deeper dread of nihilism and its effects. Yet, he was a nihilist. He had identified some part of his affliction but had no idea how to cure it. And by the appearance of things and the current situation, he might have felt it was too late to do anything about it.

But further reading and what he picked up from talking to the people he drove all over Europe revealed that nihilism didn't die in the war with everything else—it got stronger. It grew a new branch called *postmodernism* among the French in the 1950s. Most postmodernists believed that truth was always contingent on context and subjective rather than being absolute and universal. They generally believed that truth was also partial, never complete or certain. Even without the truth, they believed they could build a better, more equitable world; a global, shared world. Everyone would work together and everyone would have enough, so there would be nothing to fight about. The natural results would be peace everywhere, and war would end. At the worst, it couldn't possibly be any worse than living in a permanent nuclear nightmare.

Postmodernism was a hit in the art world where writers, musicians, and painters flocked to its promise of peace and freedom. It was a hit among the young, attracting tens of thousands of students who shared a growing mistrust of traditional Western civilization and an increasing taste for revolutionary ideals. It was a hit in academia, where university administrators were always keen to accommodate their young customers and prospects. The utopian promise of Marxism, at the core of postmodernism, was the rage.

Postmodernism had become the lingua franca of cool. The Morse Code of hip. It was fashion. And fashion according to postmodernists was, charitably, dour. Like its designers, the peevish sort of Marxian apparatchiks Jordan had disliked since adolescence, the art of postmodernism was infused with the grim, the soulless, and the banal. He heard it clearly in the voices of the Russian writers. Tantalizing views of its psychological roots were found in the writings of Freud and Nietzsche.

Particularly Frederich Nietzsche, who personally suffered a similar crisis of meaning as Jordan, became an important early guide. On the cusp of the blood-stained twentieth century, Nietzche correctly foresaw the coming catastrophes of mankind. He saw that Europe had largely abandoned or "killed" their traditional Abrahamic God who had provided meaning and value for over a thousand years. His most famous quote, "God is dead,"[7] reflected this observation rather than his personal belief, as is often misunderstood. He believed that God was being replaced by the despair that comes from believing that nothing is sacred, and therefore life in general lacked a motivating purpose. This was another life-changing observation that perfectly described to Jordan the foundations of despair and nihilism, including his own. Jordan would later write,

> What people valued, economically, merely reflected what they believed to be important. This meant that real motivation had to lie in the domain of value, of morality. The political scientists I studied with did not see this, or did not think it was relevant.[8]

Nietzsche was turning him away from politics toward psychology as the best way to find the answers to avoid a meaningless life that resulted in meaningless wars, including the pending nuclear one promising global self-extermination. Nietzsche summed it up, writing,

> A nihilist is a man who judges that the real world ought not to be, and that the world as it ought to be does not exist. According to this view, our existence (action, suffering, willing, feeling) has no meaning: this "in vain" is the nihilists' pathos—an inconsistency on the part of the nihilists.[9]

Certainly concerning to Jordan was Nietzsche's remedy—Christianity. The philosopher wrote that Christianity was an antidote to the despair, the nausea, of meaninglessness, or Western Buddhism as he called it, the belief that separating oneself from will and desire reduced suffering.

To Jordan, this meant rethinking everything back to the very beginning, the earliest lessons of childhood. Even so, Nietzsche egged him on, challenging him to consider the Christian God as a savior, as the bringer of order and peace. All the things Jordan had heard over and over in Sunday school but in other words.

Nietzsche seemed to be speaking directly to Jordan, giving the young pilgrim no place to hide from his own internal crisis. A more complete excerpt of his famous "God is Dead" quote reveals the true sorrow and trepidation behind it:

> God is dead. God remains dead. And we have killed him. How shall we, murderers of all murderers, console ourselves? That which was the holiest and mightiest of all that the world has yet possessed has bled to death under our knives. Who will wipe this blood off us? With what water could we purify ourselves?[10]

Nietzsche clearly feared the coming battles for mankind's soul. His fear would be justified by the hideously bloody world wars of the coming twentieth century. Jordan had been fully engaged in his own private battle over the death of God for seven years at this point. He'd been steadily weakening under each new revelation of the meaningless, capricious, and malevolent world around him. He felt cut off from life and was losing hope.

In Portugal, realizing the full cost of Nietzsche's premonition and seeing its many dismal outcomes throughout Europe, he made a small move back toward tradition. He bought a traditional Portuguese shepherd's wool cape and the leather boots to go with it. This must have been an extravagance on his meager driver's salary but even so, he then owned an excellent outfit for herding sheep in the nineteenth century. Maybe it was just profound fashion blindness. Or maybe it was a subtle signal of his fondness for his European passengers or respect for their history. But it certainly wasn't going to help him connect with his own crowd, young people in their colorful, tight-fitting polyester doing the jungle boogie in overheated European discos to "Nasty Girl," "Sexual Healing," and "I'm So Excited." No, 1982 was not a big year for traditional shepherd's capes.

Clearly in his earlier reading of Solzhenitsyn's *The Gulag Archipelago,* he saw the end stages of a rampaging disease of the soul that had dehumanized, then murdered fifty million Russian citizens. That book made such a shocking impression on young Jordan not only because of the scale of the evil, but because it was undeniably true. The author actually lived, and lived to tell, the story of his own journey through the Marxist nightmare to the gulags.

Jordan then stumbled upon the beginning of Solzhenitsyn's trek in Fyodor Dostoevsky's *Crime and Punishment,* a meticulous dissection of the Russian society that led up to the gulags. In this book, nihilist Rodion Raskolnikov, an impoverished ex-student like Jordan, finds himself overwhelmed with confusion, paranoia, and disgust for a murder he has committed. His nihilistic rationalizations for the crime disintegrate into Sartre's familiar nausea as he confronts the horror and the real-world consequences of what he has done. Raskolnikov then joins the tens of millions of other Russian victims in the precursors of later gulags. With a few small adjustments of circumstance, Raskolnikov could be Jordan Peterson.

Finally, Dostoevsky's *Demons* outlined the catastrophe of political and moral nihilism on everyone in an entire fictional town. The town descends into chaos as it suffers through an attempted revolution by nihilists. These characters are portrayed as the accomplices of "demonic" forces that come to possess the town, another reference to Marxism by way of Christian theology.

Although the Russian writers clearly indicated Christianity was the most likely possible salve for modern madness, Jordan was in no way ready to concede this. The fairy tale world of the Bible still seemed ridiculous. Maybe it worked for older people or those traumatized in the war, but for him, no, it didn't work. His logical mind wouldn't allow it. Even though he had no alternative, he couldn't stop looking for another answer.

He sank further into isolation. Having cut himself off from friends, family, and even new friends by dressing in old-fashioned, unattractive clothes, all he could think to do was bear down even harder on the questions about evil that still haunted him. No one was coming to help him, to guide him, or to reassure him this time.

Understanding the Russian writers, it was now obvious that the problem couldn't be in the externals like politics or economics. It couldn't be a changeable class or social situation. The problem of intrinsic evil existed at all levels of humanity. It was internal, the Russians had shown that clearly. The problem was in everyone.

Logically then, the problem was also in him. He embodied the problem; it was actually *his* problem. This was observably true because he was the one who didn't know what to make of the world, he was the one isolated from life, he was the one who had gotten himself, somehow, into his own personal hell.

Jordan's hell at the age of twenty may have felt something like Dante's *Inferno*. The true sinner, someone who had repeatedly denied God as Jordan had, was not burning in fire and brimstone, that was just the preparation on the way down through the top eight circles. At the bottom, in the ninth circle of hell, the sinner was frozen up to his waist in ice—isolated, immobilized, in agony, and forever without companionship or love. Jordan knew very little about mythology at this point. He was a pure scientist. All he knew for sure was that he and many people he met were isolated and often in agony, and he was still mystified as to why.

Later, to a lecture hall of his students, recalling this lonely period in his life when he first realized the unbelievable horrors people had committed, with emotion cracking his voice, he said,

> I read a lot about the terrible things that people have done to each other. You just cannot even imagine it, it's so awful . . . There's this idea that hell is a bottomless pit and that's because no matter how bad it is, some stupid son of a bitch like you could figure out a way to make it a lot worse. So you think, well, what do you do about that?
>
> Well, you accept it. That's what life is like. It's suffering. That's what the religious people have always said, life is suffering. You have to look for . . . that little bit of sparkling crystal in the darkness when things are bad. You have to look and see where things are still beautiful and where there's still something that's sustaining . . . be grateful for what you have, and that can get you through some very dark times and maybe even successfully if you're lucky.[11]

But at this moment in his young life, Jordan didn't understand suffering like he would later. He didn't understand the mythological hero's journey that he was on in order to gain such wisdom. He was Orpheus descending into hell to bring back his wife, the love of his life; he was Odysseus traveling through the land of the dead to learn of his future; he was Jason on his dangerous voyage with the Argonauts to bring back the golden fleece of knowledge.

He also didn't know he was entering the most dangerous part of his particular journey. He had completed his descent into hell and crossed the River Styx into the land of the dead. Fifty million Russians and seventy million Europeans and others killed in the war now spoke to him from the pages of Solzhentisyn. Ghosts routinely went about their normal business in the shadows of villages across Europe. On market days, they shopped in sunny plazas with their still-living mothers who, inside, would never stop weeping for them. They stared mutely at the young Canadian from the dark corners of his desolate *pensiones*. By the time Jordan ended his year in Europe and returned to Canada, one might say that he was truly possessed by them.

CHAPTER THREE

INTO THE BELLY OF THE BEAST

The idea that the passage of the magical threshold is a transit into a sphere of rebirth is symbolized in the worldwide womb image of the belly of the whale. The hero, instead of conquering or conciliating the power of the threshold, is swallowed into the unknown and would appear to have died.

Dragons have now to be slain and surprising barriers passed—again, again, and again. Meanwhile there will be a multitude of preliminary victories, unsustainable ecstasies and momentary glimpses of the wonderful land.

—JOSEPH CAMPBELL, *THE HERO WITH A THOUSAND FACES*

Clinically, Jordan Peterson might have been diagnosed as suffering from neurasthenia, more commonly known as a nervous breakdown, when he entered the University of Alberta in 1983 to study psychology. This condition was sometimes attributed to the stresses of modern civilization, such the constant threat of nuclear annihilation.

Carl Jung, the creator of analytical psychology, suffered from apparently the same condition in 1913, as World War I approached. At that time the condition was called *hysteria*. He experienced a horrible "confrontation with the unconscious." He hallucinated visions and heard voices. He felt "menaced by a psychosis."[1]

Jung had been seeing ghosts since he was a young boy. His mother also saw spirits who came to visit her at night. On one particular night, young Carl saw a ghostly, glowing figure coming from her room with a head detached from the neck and floating in front of the body.[2]

Sigmund Freud, who had experienced a similar period of hysteria after the death of his father, became an enthusiastic collaborator and supporter as Jung advanced as a practicing psychiatric clinician and writer.

Early in Jordan's first year Introduction to Psychology course he read Freud's *The Interpretation of Dreams* and was relieved that at least dreams were taken seriously. But he didn't believe that his nightmares were subconscious wish fulfillments, or coming from a repressed sexual desire. Like Jung, who eventually split from his mentor over this same subject, Jordan felt his dreams were more closely related to a religious experience. He knew Jung had worked extensively on the concepts of myth and religion, and even though his professors generally viewed dream interpretation skeptically, he didn't have that luxury. He probably felt he was steadily losing his mind and Jung might be the only one who could guide him through his underworld of nightmares.

It was tough going. Jung's concepts were hard to understand, even the language he used, or the translation of it from his native Swiss-German dialect had terms and phrases that weren't clear. They needed context and related concepts to begin to make sense. Jordan pressed on. He had no choice, he was beginning to suffer hallucinations of a "voice" that criticized him constantly.

Occasionally, Jung offered a glimmer of hope as in his observation,

> It must be admitted that the archetypal contents of the collective unconscious can often assume grotesque and horrible forms in dreams and fantasies, so that even the most hard-boiled rationalist is not immune from shattering nightmares and haunting fears.[3]

The phrase "archetypal contents of the collective unconscious" was one of those puzzling phrases that needed more investigation but clearly Jung was on Jordan's wavelength and at least indicating a direction for him. He continued scouring Jung's writings for more clues.

He found that Jung was an adventurer who freely explored the new and often obscure topics of his time. He studied physics, sociology, and vitalism, the belief discussed among biologists of the time that "living organisms are fundamentally different from non-living entities because they contain some non-physical element or are governed by different principles than are inanimate things."[4]

That "non-physical element" that Jung and several biologists believed in and hoped could be scientifically proven was commonly called the *soul*. They were never successful in proving the existence of a soul. He went even further into unscientific areas like alchemy, astrology, Eastern and Western philosophies, literature, and the arts. To many, Jung was considered a mystic and not a scientist at all. In spite of this, he went on to establish several revolutionary concepts in psychology including synchronicity, archetypal phenomena, the collective unconscious, and the persona.

Jordan said of his first encounter with Jung's writings around the time he returned from Europe,

> I read something by Carl Jung, at about this time, that helped me understand what I was experiencing. It was Jung who formulated the concept of persona: the mask that "feigned individuality." Adoption of such a mask, according to Jung, allowed each of us—and those around us—to believe that we were authentic.[5]

What Jordan was referring to was Jung's quote,

> When we analyse the persona we strip off the mask, and discover that what seemed to be individual is at bottom collective; in other words, that the persona was only a mask of the collective psyche.

> Fundamentally the persona is nothing real: it is a compromise between individual and society as to what a man should appear to be . . . The persona is a semblance, a two-dimensional reality, to give it a nickname.[6]

Jordan realized that not only was he isolated in his own dark thoughts, but that his thoughts weren't really even his own. He was not actually a nineteenth-century Portuguese shepherd any more than he was a tough guy from the far north oilfields. Those were just masks he put on, like the mask of the dutiful son that allowed him to be an acceptable member of his immediate family or a social gang in school. He was, in fact, no one. The pain of this thought deepened his crisis even further. He began to have truly terrifying, gruesome nightmares.

Two or three times a week he would wake up exhausted from a dream so vivid and horrifying that he soon began to fear going to sleep at all. Generally, the dreams had to do with his primary fear of nuclear war. The worms of hysteria had by now burrowed so far into his subconscious that they were affecting his physical health as well. He had no remedy, no weapon to defend himself as his terrified soul began to vomit images.

> I was sitting in the darkened basement of this house, in the family room, watching TV, with my cousin Diane, who was in truth—in waking life—the most beautiful woman I had ever seen. A newscaster suddenly interrupted the program. The television picture and sound distorted, and static filled the screen. My cousin stood up and went behind the TV to check the electrical cord. She touched it, and started convulsing and frothing at the mouth, frozen upright by intense current.
>
> A brilliant flash of light from a small window flooded the basement. I rushed upstairs. There was nothing left of the ground floor of the house. It had been completely and cleanly sheared away. . . . Red and orange flames filled the sky, from

> horizon to horizon. Nothing was left as far as I could see, except skeletal black ruins sticking up here and there: no houses, no trees, no signs of other human beings or of any life whatsoever. . . . Some dogs emerged, out from under the basement stairs. . . . They were standing upright, on their hind legs. . . . They were carrying plates in front of them, which contained pieces of seared meat. . . . I took a plate. In the center of it was a circular slab of flesh four inches in diameter and one inch thick, foully cooked, oily, with a marrow bone in the center of it. Where did it come from?
>
> I had a terrible thought. I rushed downstairs to my cousin. The dogs had butchered her, and were offering the meat to the survivors of the disaster.[7]

Outwardly, Jordan Peterson seemed to be a friendly, well-adjusted if perhaps slightly eccentric college student. There was no hint of his inner turmoil except for a somewhat obsessive focus on books of psychology having to do with dreams. He picked up jobs off-campus in a plywood mill and on the Canadian Pacific railroad that demanded his total concentration and physical effort. He had little room to speculate about nuclear war or the public's apparent lack of concern about it if he wanted to avoid being mauled by a steel saw or crushed under a locomotive. This physical exercise and complete focus on tasks in front of him may have been the only rest his fragile mind got for over a year.

As James Joyce's character and alter ego, Stephen Dedalus (Dedalus being the mythological holder of knowledge) said in the author's novel *Ulysses,* "History is a nightmare from which I am trying to awake."[8]

Jordan echoed Joyce, saying of this time in his life,

> For me, history literally was a nightmare. I wanted above all else at that moment to wake up and make my terrible dreams go away. . . . I became very depressed and anxious. I had

> vaguely suicidal thoughts, but mostly wished that everything would just go away. I wanted to lie down on my couch, and sink into it, literally, until only my nose was showing—like the snorkel of a diver above the surface of the water. I found my awareness of things unbearable.

And then things got worse.

> I dreamed that I was running through a mall parking lot, trying to escape from something. I was running through the parked cars, opening one door, crawling across the front seat, opening the other, moving to the next. The doors on one car suddenly slammed shut. I was in the passenger seat. The car started to move by itself. A voice said harshly, "There is no way out of here." I was on a journey, going somewhere I did not want to go. I was not the driver.

Jordan began to feel that there were two planes of his existence. One was the normal, sunlit world of everyday events that he shared with other first-year students in his classes. Here, everyone appeared to have complete self-control. The second was his private shadowy world of secret horrors and crushingly intense emotions where he had no control. This second plane seemed to be behind the first one, the one that everyone accepted as completely real. The one where everyone went about their daily lives assured that they were real people in a real world. But he knew he couldn't be the only one who lived in two worlds. That was impossible.

And if everyone was just a two-dimensional persona, an image called *student* or *professor* so they could fit into their mutual invention called *university,* was that any more real than the images that made Jordan's heart race and his head feel like it was splitting open? Was the fact that they could blithely ignore impending nuclear war any more real, any more logical, than the fact that he couldn't?

He was beginning to fracture along the fault line that was currently called schizophrenia. The world of the living was fading into the distance the longer he continued to drift through the underworld of the dead.

> My interest in the Cold War transformed itself into a true obsession. I thought about the suicidal and murderous preparation of that war every minute of every day, from the moment I woke up until the second I went to bed.

As the academic year wore on and Jordan became engaged with students and professors in discussions and debate, activities that he'd always enjoyed, he began to feel odd. It was his voice or something about the words he was using that began to annoy him. Soon, he couldn't bear to hear himself talk. The criticizing voice hallucination inside his head suddenly spoke up and cut him off, sometimes in midsentence, with a pair of bored, patronizing comments, *You don't believe that,* or *That isn't true.*

The voice interrupted nearly every phrase he spoke until he was forced to drop out of conversations completely. This jolted Jordan out of his hysteria and confusion about the world he was living in. It forced him to focus instead on this new enemy and, if he was to survive, to prepare for war with it.

The voice was a challenge from the underworld, like the song of the Sirens, that beckoned Jason and his Argonauts toward submerged rocks and death. If Jordan failed and could not somehow defeat the voice, he could lose his battle against madness and remain mute forever—a lonely schizophrenic hounded by voices in his head.

The voice seemed to be a direct attack against his tough guy persona that had heroically fought its way to acceptance in high school using Jordan's sharp tongue, his primary weapon. He decided he was not going to surrender his only reliable weapon and the persona, real or not, that wielded it, to some patronizing bully from who knows where. As in the ancient stories, an angel, a spirit guide, arrived with a strategy to defeat the voice.

Without any understanding of the primal forces at work, Jordan was suddenly guided by the creative force represented by Athena, the goddess of war, wisdom, and protector of mortal men like Jason and his Argonauts. In the modern world Athena was called Jordan's feminine aspect. In keeping with her feminine character, Athena would distract and undermine rather than attempt to overpower his enemy. She would envelope the critical, masculine voice in clouds of absolute truth, confusing and denying it any chance to speak. Gradually with disuse, the voice would lose power, weaken, and die. Jordan's battle position was to stay firmly within the truth. He swore an oath to himself, he thought, that from this moment on, he must never, even for a moment, step away. He must scrutinize every word he intended to say and if he strayed from the truth, even a half step toward exaggeration, he must stop and fight his way back. In this battle, there would be no quarter given. Someone was going to die.

Jordan later wrote,

> This meant that I really had to listen to what I was saying, that I spoke much less often, and that I would frequently stop, midway through a sentence, feel embarrassed, and reformulate my thoughts. I soon noticed that I felt much less agitated and more confident when I only said things that the "voice" did not object to. This came as a definite relief. . . . Nonetheless, it took me a long time to reconcile myself to the idea that almost all my thoughts weren't real, weren't true—or, at least, weren't mine.[9]

This hard-won habit of truth telling gave him his first small victory against chaos and impending madness. It was then set as a cornerstone of his life. In his future live lectures this practice of stopping midsentence, silently thinking through what he intended to say next and often reformulating it in the moment, persisted. To his students and later his public audiences, this demonstrated his authenticity and exciting spontaneity. In his second book, *12 Rules for*

Life: An Antidote to Chaos, he devoted an entire chapter to this principle called Tell the Truth, or At Least Don't Lie. It is number eight on his list of twelve fundamental rules for living a more meaningful, less distressing life.

He wrote more about this experience in that book:

> I started to practice only saying things that the internal voice would not object to. I started to practice telling the truth—or, at least, not lying. I soon learned that such a skill came in very handy when I didn't know what to do. What should you do, when you don't know what to do? Tell the truth.[10]

Truthfulness would prove its absolutely essential value over and over in later years in his clinical practice.

In 1983, while his battle over the truth was still raging inside, he found himself in the deepest part of the beast's belly. He was surrounded by dozens of paranoid, schizophrenic, and deeply depressed murderers, rapists, and armed robbers near the weight room of the Edmonton Institution, a maximum security federal prison in the northeastern suburbs of the city. It was his first field assignment as a psychology student.

He had accompanied a somewhat eccentric adjunct professor who, when he wasn't filling in for full professors at the university, was supposed to provide full psychological care to some of Canada's most violent criminals.

Jordan and the professor must have made quite a distinct impression on the convicts considering that Jordan may have appeared to be also somewhat eccentric dressed, as he again was, in his Portuguese cape and tall leather boots. The professor rather inconveniently disappeared without telling Jordan, leaving the young, caped visitor soon surrounded by large and sinister-looking men. One muscle-bound inmate had a sloppily carved scar running from his collarbone to his midsection, something possibly made with an ax or butcher's knife. Like most of the prisoners, he was dressed in a thin, ragged uniform, so the Portuguese cape instantly became an item of intense interest. Several of the men immediately offered to trade their clothes for Jordan's cape, and/or his boots.

With typical dead-pan humor Jordan later recalled, "This did not strike me as a great bargain, but I wasn't sure how to refuse."

A short, skinny, bearded man, a demon, arrived just as negotiations were becoming less collegial. The small man said that the professor had sent him. Jordan gratefully escaped from the unplanned swap meet as the two moved outside into the prison yard. The man chatted innocently about everyday things in the low whisper of certain longtime convicts as Jordan continued to glance over his shoulder toward the weight room hoping to see no one else coming. Not soon enough, the absentminded professor appeared and motioned Jordan toward a private office. The small man disappeared as quietly as he had come.

In the office, Jordan's unsteady guardian mentioned that the little man was a multiple murderer. He had murdered two police officers. According to his detailed court confession, he had calmly watched over them, perhaps chatting idly as he'd just done with Jordan, as the two policemen dug their own graves. One officer pleaded for his life. He had two small children and begged the pleasant little man to spare him for the children's sake. The little man, brandishing his pistol, suggested that the officer keep digging. When the graves seemed deep enough, the pleasant little man shot the young father and his partner several times to make sure they were both dead. He then went about the relatively easy task of covering them both with the loose dirt of their shallow graves.

Jordan controlled his panic as images of the heartless murder played in his head. It was as if a flock of harpies, the half vulture, half beautiful woman creatures of mythology, had suddenly appeared and were beating their bony wings around him. Panic swelled and subsided like the tide as he saw his friendly little escort become a towering monster shooting fire and death down on terrified men.

How could this be? How could this same innocuous, friendly man who had just saved him from a crowd of dangerous convicts also be a merciless killer? How did that work? It was the same old question of evil. But instead of reading about it or being nauseated by the effects of it forty years after the fact, he'd just been saved by it, chatted with it, and was thankful it had saved him.

The impatiently tapping, slippered foot of the Prince stopped and rested quietly on his footstool for a moment. The Prince stood at his shadowed throne and greeted Jordan. Finally, they'd had an opportunity to meet and chat comfortably about everyday things. At least now they were on speaking terms.

That's when the compulsion began. Perhaps it was the Prince's small test of their new friendship. In the amphitheater lecture halls where first-year psychology students sat in semicircular rows above and behind each other, Jordan was always behind some unwitting classmate usually half listening to a professor speak. Casually in the everyday course of his daydreaming, the urge to stab the point of his pen into the neck of the student in front of him flickered by and then disappeared. It was disturbing but not terribly alarming, nothing to discuss, really. He was a good person, a thoughtful person. He'd never been aggressive in his life. But it did set his teeth on edge. After all, he was still wrestling with the demeaning voice that usually kept him carefully watching his words among friends, and was still being shaken awake several nights a week by horrifying, bloody dreams of being roasted alive in a nuclear fire.

This new compulsion seemed to be a psychological flea and easily flicked away. But like an actual flea, it had many relatives who kept up the irritation. His compulsion to attack an innocent classmate increased almost imperceptibly day after day, as if someone was egging him on, probing for a moment of weakness.

About a month later, his classwork took him back to the prison. He found that two prisoners had held down a *rat,* an informer, and pulverized the bones in one of his legs with a lead pipe. Shocking brutality was a bit less shocking by this time, and the budding psychologist thought he was ready for his own thought experiment.

He would imagine, down to the smallest detail of action and emotion, pulverizing another man's bones with a pipe. The physical action was clear enough but the feel of worn denim under one hand and cold lead in the other required concentration, and time. The screams of pain would have to be muffled, so an accomplice would be needed, someone strong and equally merciless who would stuff a rag into the victim's mouth, preferably something foul and sickening. The revolting smells of terror-made sweat and fresh blood would need to become routine, even welcoming to him as he set about destroying a man's leg with righteous satisfaction. He worked for days on the scenario. From hating the rat in the depths of his soul, to maintaining a neutral or even friendly mask toward him, to snatching him at exactly the right moment in exactly the right spot. It was a chore of criminal planning that took time to visualize accurately. Then there was holding the rat down and breaking the easily bruised, extremely pain-sensitive shin bone with a fierce blow. The second, third, and fourth strikes would shatter the large bone pieces into small, sharp fragments that tore open the muscle and arteries. The rat might bleed to death, die of shock, or choke to death on his own vomit. Either way, he'd never walk on that leg again without pain. Then, of course, would be the deep satisfaction from a job well done and the accolades from the other cons who appreciated a guy willing to uphold the code of silence with violence.

As Jordan focused on becoming a sadist, the nausea felt for classmates who happened to be sitting in front of him became nearly overwhelming as the empathy for them receded. He was now seeing that stabbing the tip of his pen into a fat, complacent neck was a reasonable and forgivable little crime that would provide the tiny taste of evil he needed to end his exhausting theorizing. Then he could finally sleep through the night.

As his visualizations became clearer and his motivations deepened, the time in this altered state of mind stretched from hours, into days, and then over a week.

Finally, eureka! His bloody revenge attack against some nauseatingly weak-minded classmate wouldn't even be a challenge! He realized with a shock of recognition that it would be easy, and so satisfying. When you get right down to bedrock, he knew he was no different than the friendly little man who had murdered two policemen in cold blood. He could easily manage this.

But there was still the problem of the voice. It was beginning to squawk again, *That's not right. That's not true. Blah, blah, blah.* Annoying little bastard. Always shutting him up, ruining his plans. Who the hell was this little shit, anyway?

Whatever grace or luck or strength of character that kept his vicious hand from actually striking, it probably saved his life. Over the next few hours, Jordan felt his compulsion to attack his fellow classmates gradually fade. It was as if an infection had been lanced and was draining.

Instead of going about with his gaze downcast in a conversation with the shadowed part of himself, he felt himself stand a bit straighter with his gaze again on the world in front of him. With no more inner chatter about the ways and costs of doing evil, his redeeming voice gradually fell silent. This battle was over but its aftermath was not. He was on edge and upset. Clinically, this may have been a condition that was recently renamed *post-traumatic stress disorder,* but until a few months earlier had been called *battle fatigue.*

Thinking back on this moment in his life as an experienced clinical psychologist, he wrote,

> The behavioral urge had manifested itself in explicit knowledge—had been translated from emotion and image to concrete realization—and had no further "reason" to exist. The "impulse" had only occurred, because of the question I was attempting to answer: "How can men do terrible things to one another?" I meant other men, of course—bad men—but I had still asked the question. There was no reason for me to assume that I would receive a predictable or personally meaningless answer.[11]

Mythologically, he had passed another more dangerous and more difficult test on his journey through the underworld, just as Jason and the Argonauts had passed through the clashing rocks with only the stern end of their ship getting smashed in the passage—a small, but permanent scar and reminder of the price of failure.

Spiritually, it might be said that he had tasted evil and very nearly swallowed it. Personally, he now had one concrete answer to his endless questions about evil. He had the internal scar to prove that this particular answer would never be found in books or lectures. It had to be earned, personally.

But the Prince apparently did not take Jordan's rejection lightly. He'd been patient with the young man who was so bright and seemed so enthusiastic. But now, well, the Prince was quite disappointed.

The college drinking party was roaring and Jordan was drinking heavily, as usual. He yelled over the music about God and war and love and other things he didn't know a lot about, but with great confidence. At some point he noticed that he was embarrassing himself. No one was listening. Everyone was drunk and hoping to have sex with someone hopefully drunker than themselves.

He staggered home disgusted with himself and angry. What an idiot he'd made of himself. After all he had seen and all he had realized, still no one much cared.

Fucking moron. Even though he could now tell firsthand stories about meeting the devil face to face, no one gave a shit. *Worthless clod.*

He stumbled into his dorm room, slapped up a canvas, and grabbed some paints. *Big mouth.* He sketched a wobbly, crude picture of a crucified Christ, "glaring and demonic—with a cobra wrapped around his naked waist, like a belt." He later wrote,

> The picture disturbed me—struck me, despite my agnosticism, as sacrilegious. I did not know what it meant, however, or why I had painted it. Where in the world had it come from?[12]

The Prince may have smiled at that thought. He had made his point and left his calling card. For the evening, the Prince abandoned his drunken prospect to suffer in his well-deserved vomit and crushing hangover. Very soon Jordan had to lay down and rest his throbbing head on the floor.

The next day Jordan was not only hungover but mystified. What the hell was that painting about? He hadn't thought about Christ on the cross for years. So what exactly *was* he thinking? He hid the painting under a pile of old clothes in a closet and then sat cross-legged on the floor for a moment.

It became pretty obvious at this time, in spite of his drunken proclamations of the night before, that he didn't really understand very much about himself or anyone else.

> Everything I had once believed about the nature of society and myself had proved false, the world had apparently gone insane, and something strange and frightening was happening in my head.[13]

CHAPTER FOUR

RETURN OF THE HERO

> **Rejection of the unknown is tantamount to "identification with the devil," the mythological counterpart and eternal adversary of the world-creating exploratory hero. Such rejection and identification is a consequence of Luciferian pride, which states: all that I know is all that is necessary to know. This pride is totalitarian assumption of omniscience—is adoption of God's place by "reason"—is something that inevitably generates a state of personal and social being indistinguishable from hell.**
>
> **—JORDAN PETERSON, *MAPS OF MEANING: THE ARCHITECTURE OF BELIEF***

At twenty-one, still plagued with self-doubt, Jordan returned to his family home in Fairview for the summer break. He had decided to continue his education in psychology in the fall at McGill University in Montreal, and awaited their reply to his application.

Meanwhile, he rested among his family and childhood friends. One of his oldest friends and earliest romantic crush, Tammy Roberts, still lived just across the street from his parents' house. They were childhood playmates and adventurers who could play rough outdoors like boys, or whisper naughty secrets and laugh like girls with equal ease. They'd gone their separate ways during their tumultuous teenage years but now as young adults seemed to share a growing attraction.

Tammy was a warmhearted and unpretentious character, quite different from some of the frivolous sorority girls Jordan had encountered at University of Alberta. She was more like the plainspoken pioneer women of the northern plains but with a vicious sense of humor. She particularly loved crushing his chances at croquet by sending his croquet ball into the far reaches of the prairie with one mighty blow, followed by a merciless taunting. He laughed at her fiendish glee in beating him so soundly.

As the fireflies rose in the early evenings, she was quietly intent on his muted recollections of the terrible events and inner trials he'd gone through. She listened to his continuing battle with good and evil, a familiar theme since childhood. Jordan was a slightly quieter version of his young self—intense, popping with ideas, shy, and polite like many prairie cowboys and with an easy smile whenever she wanted to divert him.

She reminded him of a time when they were eleven or twelve years old. He'd just gotten a pair of horn-rimmed prescription eyeglasses and was quite proud to show them off, parading out into their street so everyone could admire them and him. Tammy came out of her house and inspected his new fashion accessory closely as he asked, "What do you think of these?" with great pride.

She stepped back to view his full face and thought for a moment before replying, "I think you look really funny in those." She pointed at him and ran back into her house.

Now, in the gentle prairie evening ten years later, Tammy finally admitted that she had wanted glasses too and was jealous. She teased him instead of swelling his head even more. A wavy half smile stretched across Jordan's face, and his dark mood disappeared.

At McGill, he began formal training to become a clinical psychologist. Although Freud and Jung had validated his symptoms and theorized solutions for his postmodern nausea, and Solzhenitsyn and Dostoevsky had provided their personal solutions in Christianity, he still had his doubts, recalling, "I could not distinguish the basic elements of Christian belief from wishful thinking."[1]

It was 1984, the year of Orwell's imagined dystopian society. Ironically, totalitarian socialism was gaining a foothold throughout Western culture and particularly on American and Canadian college campuses. Senior Russian KGB agent and recent defector to Canada, Yuri Bezmenov, elaborated on Russian psychological warfare or "active measures" that were presumably a large part of the reason for this activity,

> It takes from fifteen to twenty years to demoralize a nation. Why that many years [is] because this is the minimum number of years which [is required] to educate one generation of students in the country of your enemy exposed to the ideology of the enemy.
>
> In other words, Marxism Leninism ideology is being pumped into the soft heads of at least three generations of American students without being challenged or counterbalanced by the basic values of Americanism, American patriotism. The result you can see [in] most of the people who graduated in [the] sixties, dropouts or half-baked intellectuals are now occupying the positions of power in the government, civil service, business, mass media, educational system. You are stuck with them, you cannot get rid of them, they are contaminated, they're programmed to think and react to certain stimuli in a certain pattern. You cannot change their mind even if you expose them to authentic information, even if you prove that white is white and black is black, you still cannot change the basic perception and the logic of behavior.[2]

In spite of the fact that at this point Jordan had only contempt for "soft-headed" socialist students and the apparatchiks in the National Democratic Party, the movement was growing all around him. Apparently, as Bezmenov said, "they [the soft-headed students] are contaminated, they're programmed to think and react to certain stimuli in a certain pattern."

This was apparently accurate since, in spite of their belief in it, socialism was collapsing in front of their eyes. Even the Chinese Communist Party recently repudiated their founder, Mao Tse-tung, and his Cultural Revolution. In 1966, they called the Cultural Revolution, "a great revolution that touches people to their very souls and constitutes a deeper and more extensive stage in the development of the socialist revolution in our country." Now, eighteen years later, they were saying, "The Cultural Revolution was responsible for the most severe setback and the heaviest losses suffered by the Party, the country, and the people since the founding of the People's Republic."[3]

Yet five-pointed red stars on clothing and red fists of solidarity on posters were popping up all over college campuses at the usual grim events promoting solidarity with the oppressed. The KGB and perhaps even the reformed Chinese communists were making steady progress in the West.

Content to ignore these Marxist "useful idiots" on campus, Jordan returned to his studies buoyed by his flirtation with Tammy and relieved of his compulsion to attack fellow students. But bloody dreams still haunted his nights and a deep-seated fear of nuclear war shadowed his days.

His advanced psychology studies at McGill quickly brought him to another lonely island of lost souls like the prisoners at Edmonton Institution. Originally filled with hundreds of people suffering from all types of debilitating mental illnesses, the sprawling Douglas Mental Health University Institute, a teaching hospital affiliated with the university, now housed only the most severely mentally ill. In the late 1960s, the advent of antipsychotic drugs and government mandates "freed" most of Douglas's patients to a dangerous, unforgiving life on the streets.

> Those who remained were strange, much-damaged people. They clustered around the vending machines scattered throughout the hospital's tunnels. They looked as if they had been photographed by Diane Arbus or painted by Hieronymus Bosch.[4]

As Jordan and a young female classmate were standing together waiting for the humorless director of Douglas's clinical training to issue their assignments, a fragile, older woman approached and asked the classmate in the voice of an innocent, friendly child, "Why are you all standing here? What are you doing? Can I come along with you?"

The classmate, a cautious type, turned to Jordan for help: "What should I say to her?" Both students were at a loss for words in front of someone so trusting and obviously in need of a friend. They didn't want to say the wrong thing and hurt the poor woman any further than she had obviously already been.

They were novices, in no way prepared to deal with an actual mental patient in need. But she was just asking them for information and wondering if they could be friends. Was a white lie appropriate? Would that calm and divert the woman, or would she see through that and be driven back into her eternal nightmare?

Jordan thought he could spin a reasonable white lie, *We can only take eight people in our group,* that would avoid hurting her feelings. But maybe he heard the faint echo of the voice that had saved him from madness just a few months ago. He told the woman that they were new students in training to become psychologists. And so, she couldn't join them.

His answer hurt. The woman was clearly dejected and hurting along some old and private wound. The moment hung heavily in the air between them. Then, in a moment of grace, she understood, accepted the truth, and everything was suddenly all right. The voice inside Jordan's head had stayed silent. In his first unofficial therapy session, a nightmare had been temporarily checked by the unadorned truth. It became item number one in his clinician's mental notebook.

Not only did truth telling become a bedrock personal principle, but, like a surgeon's scalpel, the truth would become his best clinical instrument to cut through a person's natural defenses and reveal the problems of a damaged psyche. This would be particularly true when dealing with future paranoid and dangerous clients who were, "hyper-alert and hyper-focused. They are attending to non-verbal cues with an intentness never manifest during ordinary human interactions."[5]

In other words, they could smell a lie and tended to severely punish any authority figure who lied to them. The truth would become his shield as well as his sword.

With only the truth as his weapon against several twentieth-century demons, he'd fought them to a draw and so had earned a meeting with the Queen Goddess of the World. In the daylight world, she was called Tammy Roberts. He would now have to earn her love to survive in hell and someday, if he was brave and strong enough, fight his way back to the daylight and present her with the golden fleece of wisdom and protection.

But while still in his private hell, a legion of doubts, like small, fiendish imps, descended on him prodding, confusing, and laughing at him as he tried to fight his way back to the world. But there was no fighting them, they were too fast, too small. The truth had no effect on them; they just laughed. They flew in his ear, whispering insults and nonsense. They sat for a moment in his mind chattering and laughing, distracting him, drawing his anger, and then vanishing, leaving only their echo of doubt.

He challenged and cursed them. He began to doubt himself for having doubts. He got drunk to drown them out, but it was hopeless. He had no weapon against them and could only run. Mythologically, it might be said he was attempting to recross the River Styx from hell back toward the daylight world of the living. But he was crossing in defeat and surrender. As in Dante's vision of hell, perhaps he was wading through the river up to his waist as the river was beginning to freeze. Unless he could find an ally or summon the power of the gods somehow, he would be locked in ice in the ninth level of hell forever.

Clinically, being pursued and wading against a current or through mud was often a patient's hellish image of clinical depression. Extending back to his grandfather, depression was a constant in the Peterson line. Compounded by the lack of sunlight during the long, empty winters at the subarctic tip of the North American prairie, Jordan's grandfather had suffered severely from depression. Once an energetic and powerful blacksmith, after the death of his own father, Jordan's grandfather never again walked more than half a block. Only forty-five years old at that time, Jordan's grandfather spent the rest of his life practically frozen in ice, laying on the couch in his darkened living room, smoking. This sudden collapse had a nightmare effect on Jordan's father who eventually left his own successful career as a teacher and school administrator because of depression. Young Jordan would also not be spared. Perhaps depression was behind his lifelong obsession with bad guys, political oppressors, and eventually the common demons of mental illness. Neither would Jordan's daughter be spared.

In the daylight world, he appeared to be his usual focused and diligent self. Perhaps a bit more intent in his studies, a bit more moody in the local bars, but on the whole, quite normal. Inside however, he was frantic. If he didn't resolve his nagging doubts, everything he had learned, everything he had built, and everything he was, could suddenly vanish into a sinkhole of doubt and depression. He still had not found his bedrock to build on. The voice of truth inside him seemed solid, but how could he be sure it would always be? He needed to find the foundational source behind the voice. He needed to find objective truth, not his truth, *the* truth, the bedrock and the only hope for heaven.

He found his rescuing ally in an ancient book once condemned as black magic by the Catholic Church. Three hundred and forty-three years earlier in Holland, perhaps also driven by depression after the death of his five-year-old daughter, French philosopher René Descartes dared to write his *Meditations on First Philosophy*. In it, Jordan found the magic words that could dispel doubt by systematically challenging everything he was taught and, so, everything he believed. It was pure heresy and exactly the weapon Jordan needed. He could scatter the imps of doubt and dig down to bedrock and certainty where he would build his tower out of hell.

Descartes argued that all humans were born with a spark of God-given knowledge that could not be learned. It simply existed, had always existed, and therefore would always exist, whether men ever understood it or not. It was outside of humankind, behind and beyond the world they lived in. It was in fact God himself, the Word that had been spoken across the waters in the beginning and had created the world.

It was known to every civilization of mankind and fundamental to their understanding of themselves. Different cultures had different mythologies around it, but they all referred to the existence of a god or gods just as mythology and psychology described identical phenomena in different terms through time. Nonetheless, the book begins with a method to severely test all these beliefs, and an admonition to discard any that weren't absolute certainties. He went on to reduce even the activity of human belief to its essence. He wrote in *Meditations,* in Latin because it was intended for the learned classes of Europe, *"Cogito ergo sum,"* translation: "I think, therefore I am," implying that humans were not primarily their physical bodies in a physical world, but were fundamentally "thinking things" connected to a physical body, but existing primarily in an ephemeral world with God. Descartes reveals his thinking on doubts in the first lines of *Meditations* that may have captured Jordan's attention:

> Several years have now elapsed since I first became aware that I had accepted, even from my youth, many false opinions for true, and that consequently what I afterward based on such principles was highly doubtful; and from that time I was convinced of the necessity of undertaking once in my life to rid myself of all the opinions I had adopted, and of commencing anew the work of building from the foundation.

Descartes was a devoted Catholic, probably even more so after the recent cruel death of his young daughter, so God was then probably fixed in his mind. Jordan was a lapsed Catholic, brimming with doubts and resentments about the state of humanity, and so wasn't ready to accept even the existence of God. The philosopher's Hyperbolic (Extreme) Doubt method was a four-step process:

- **Accept only information you know to be true (i.e., beyond any and all possible doubt).**
- **Break down these truths into smaller units.**
- **Solve the simple problems first.**
- **Make complete lists of further problems.**

It quickly becomes obvious that this is a huge amount of mental work that only a person consumed with doubt or compelled by unanswerable questions would want to attempt. It is an exhaustive mental exercise intended to build a reliable belief system from the ground up, exactly what Jordan was looking for. We can hear echoes of this disciplined, meticulous approach to the truth in Jordan's certainty about his beliefs:

> Suffering is real, and the artful infliction of suffering on another, for its own sake, is wrong. That became the cornerstone of my belief. Searching through the lowest reaches of human thought and action, understanding my own capacity to act like a Nazi prison guard or a gulag archipelago trustee or a torturer of children in a dungeon, I grasped what it meant to "take the sins of the world onto oneself."[6]

In his reference to the distinctly Christian idea to "take the sins of the world onto oneself," it seems certain that Jordan at least recognized some of the value of Descartes's bedrock belief in God. But he never, at least as of this writing, came to Descartes's certainty. He came only as far as to accept the value of believing in God. In later years, in answer to the often-repeated question, "Do you believe in God?," he was able to answer, "I can't really say . . . but I act as if there is a God."

In 1985, at least then certain about some of his beliefs and perhaps inspired by Descartes, he began writing his first book, *Gods of War,* a philosophy of religion and belief. In it, he explored *ideological possession,* calling it a pathology that replaces a person's individuality with his or her belief in an ideology such as Nazism, communism, or Western democracy. His use of the word *possession,* of course, evoked the still powerful Christian belief of demonic possession. Attesting to the enduring grip of demonic possession on the public imagination, the film *The Exorcist* had been released over a decade earlier to huge commercial and critical success, which continued for decades after to become one of the highest grossing films of all time, and was entered into the Library of Congress as being "culturally, historically, or aesthetically significant."

Demonic possession was still a powerful current in the sea of human affairs. In *Gods of War,* Jordan argued that when individual reason is sublimated to any ideology, it emerged in genocidal impulses so profound, so demonic, that even an annihilating global nuclear war seemed reasonable. In this, he struck the first blow against his own lifelong demonic possession by the specter of nuclear war. He was now on the offensive, armed with the truth and a few unshakable beliefs. He was building his tower out of hell.

But the Prince was not amused. He still owned the night and filled Jordan's dreams with more bloody terrors. He struck at Jordan's Achilles' heel, depression, sending the young graduate student tumbling down into the freezing, numbing mud of social withdrawal, like his father and grandfather before him. Days and weeks passed with Jordan slogging through psychic, frozen mud, unable to rest at night and sleepwalking through his days. Only his extraordinary personal energy and dogged commitment to fight off his depression allowed him to continue in his studies and write *Gods of War* at night. He would work for the next thirteen years writing the book, saying, "I am writing my book in an attempt to explain the psychological significance of history—to explain the meaning of history."[7]

At McGill University, Jordan began his advanced studies in psychology by examining substance abuse, alcohol-induced aggression, addiction, and behavior modification. He studied primarily under Professor Robert O. Pihl, an American who was celebrated for his world-changing work on children with learning disabilities. Using analysis of the children's hair, he had found high levels of lead and cadmium in children who had problems learning. This influenced the US Congress to ban lead in all paint beginning in the 1970s. He went on to find similar levels of the toxins in the hair of violent criminals.

His work with environmental toxins and violent criminals led him into further study of human aggression from other toxins including alcohol. When Jordan arrived at McGill, Pihl had most recently published "Effects of Alcohol and Behavior Contingencies on Human Aggression"[8] and was a codirector of the Alcohol Studies Group at the Douglas Institute.

Pihl's study of aggression was closely related to Jordan's interests in social conflict and psychological pathologies. Jordan and Pihl began an eight-year working relationship that continued through the completion of Jordan's master's degree, PhD in Clinical Psychology, and postdoctoral fellowship at the Douglas Institute until June of 1993.

Jordan would witness quite a bit of human aggression in his years at Douglas Institute including several potentially dangerous encounters with patients who shared violent and bloody nightmares like his own, who harbored serious depression like his own. He used Leo Tolstoy's account of depression in his *Maps of Meaning* to describe the condition that he and his patients continued to suffer from:

> It had come to this, that I, a healthy, fortunate man, felt I could no longer live: some irresistible power impelled me to rid myself one way or other of life. I cannot say I *wished* to kill

> myself. The power which drew me away from life was stronger, fuller, and more widespread than any mere wish. It was a force similar to the former striving to live, only in a contrary direction. All my strength drew me away from life. The thought of self-destruction now came to me as naturally as thoughts of how to improve my life had come formerly.[9]

Jordan's ongoing depression was so painful that even years later recalling the cost of depression to himself and his family brought instant tears to his eyes. As he counseled an online follower about the depression-driven suicide of the follower's daughter, he broke down and cried, yet managed to recover his composure and continue his counsel for her:

> FOLLOWER: Our daughter ended her life at 24 due to depression. If someone is determined to end their life how can one change their mind?
>
> JORDAN: Oh well first of all that's . . . I'm very sorry about that. That's a terrible thing. Look I had this friend her . . . [*he begins to cry*] . . . sorry. There's been a lot of depression in our family so it's a question that cuts close to the bone.[10]

In his earliest work on depression as a suspected precursor to alcohol addiction and aggression, he and Professor Pihl focused first on a new antidepressant as possibly the quickest way to address potentially life-threatening depression.

Fluoxetine, a selective serotonin reuptake inhibitor, or SSRI, had been developed in the 1970s and was the most recent antidepressant being used in clinical trials. But first, they had to try cognitive therapy, essentially their own therapeutic advice, to lead suffering patients back from the brink of self-destruction, a path Jordan himself was walking. The first step was to gain the patient's absolute trust. Jordan describes this process in a YouTube video:

> One of the things I do with my clients all the time especially if they're really in trouble is to tell them, "Look, I don't know exactly what's going to help you." But [I] don't arbitrarily throw out any possibilities because you might not have that luxury.[11]

He gives an example in his book *12 Rules for Life*,

> I had a client who was paranoid and dangerous. Working with paranoid people is challenging. They believe they have been targeted by mysterious conspiratorial forces, working malevolently behind the scenes. . . . They make mistakes in interpretation (that's the paranoia) but they are still almost uncanny in their ability to detect mixed motives, judgment, and falsehood.
>
> You have to listen very carefully and tell the truth if you are going to get a paranoid person to open up to you.
>
> I listened carefully and spoke truthfully to my client. Now and then, he would describe bloodcurdling fantasies of flaying people for revenge. I would watch how I was reacting. . . . I told him what I observed. I was not trying to control or direct his thoughts or actions (or mine). I was only trying to let him know as transparently as I could how what he was doing was directly affecting at least one person—me. . . . I told him when he scared me (often), that his words and behaviour were misguided, and that he was going to get into serious trouble.
>
> He talked to me, nonetheless, because I listened and responded honestly, even though I was not encouraging in my responses. He trusted me, despite (or, more accurately, because of) my objections. . . . He was paranoid, not stupid. . . . There was no chance of understanding him without that trust.[12]

After earning their trust, he developed a standard list of questions based on his studies with Pihl, and also, presumably, from his own experience. To help sort through the many possible reasons for depression, he would often probe into the orderliness of the person's life since many depressives are simply overwhelmed by the disorder in their lives. He asks, "Do you have a job?" He explains why that question is important:

> If you don't have a job you're really in trouble in our society. . . . Sometimes you see people who are depressed, they have no job, they have no friends, they have no intimate relationship, they have an additional health problem, and they have a drug and alcohol problem. My experience has been if you have three of those problems it's almost impossible to help you. You're so deeply mired in chaos that you can't get out because you make progress on one front and one of the other problems pull[s] you down.[13]

Then he digs a little deeper: "Let's figure out what your aims are, you've got to have some aims." And he explains a possible solution,

> They might say, well, I'm so depressed I don't have any aims. And then I say, "Well, pick the least objectionable of the aims and act it out for a while and see what happens."[14]

In this method, he was gently nudging his depressive patients back on track toward a meaningful life. But this early in his studies, he hadn't yet found the primary importance of meaning in a human life. His manuscript-in-progress was still called *Gods of War*, but was not yet the book *Maps of Meaning*. He explains, as an older man, what he was soon to discover about meaning and human suffering:

> Once I started studying these mythological stories and I got this idea about the fact that life can be meaningful enough to

justify its suffering, I thought, God, that's such a good idea!, because it's not optimistic exactly.

You know some people will tell you that you can be happy. It's like, those people are idiots. I'm telling you, they're idiots! There's gonna be things that come along that flatten you so hard you won't believe it, and you're not happy then. . . . Well, in those situations what are you doing? Why even live? . . . If you're happy, you're bloody fortunate and you should enjoy it, you should because it's the grace of God.[15]

CHAPTER FIVE
SAVAGERY

Wealth signified oppression, and private property was theft. It was time for some equity. More than thirty thousand kulaks were shot on the spot.

Many more met their fate at the hands of their most jealous, resentful, and unproductive neighbors who used the high ideals of communist collectivism to hide their intent.

—JORDAN PETERSON, *12 RULES FOR LIFE: AN ANTIDOTE TO CHAOS*

In 1962, the year Jordan was born, the United States and the Soviet Union were locked in a warlike failure of morality called the Cold War that suggested both could never live together on the same planet. The best moral solution the Americans could manage was to settle on a war policy called MAD (mutually assured destruction) that promised both could die on the same planet. In reaction, the Doomsday Clock stayed frozen at seven minutes to Armageddon as did the rest of mankind. For the next eleven years the world remained on the brink, not out of caution or sensible reconsideration, but because no one could even imagine a shared moral resolution.

In 1983, just a month before Jordan entered McGill University, US president Ronald Reagan recognized that the Soviet Union was collapsing economically just as communist China had. He rolled the dice in the world's first all-or-nothing crap game for existence and announced the Strategic Defense Initiative, a research program into ballistic missile defense against what he considered to be the Evil Empire. This was a coup de grace designed to bankrupt and destroy the Soviet Union. It succeeded by shattering Soviet counterpart Yuri Andropov's "peace offensive" and prompted Andropov to say,

> It is time [Washington] stopped thinking up one option after another in search of the best way of unleashing nuclear war in the hope of winning it. To do this is not just irresponsible. It is madness.[1]

Apocalyptic psychoses then being nearly universal, this drove a terrified population even further into panic. Twenty-one-year-old Jordan soldiered on somehow, containing his fear enough to focus on his studies with Professor Pihl. In the midst of this devilish new premonition of fire and brimstone, he shouldered the awesome responsibility of administering psychological therapy to about twenty severely mentally damaged patients per week at the Douglas Institute under Pihl's supervision. He was now frequently distracted from his terrors and may even have felt the first small waves of solace in finding a deeper meaning for his life by helping others in such dire need.

Up to this time, Jordan had found temporary relief from anxiety in his practice of weightlifting. He realized as his studies intensified that the semi-solitary discipline also helped to clear his mind as it energized and calmed him. At thirteen, he'd begun lifting weights as the proverbial hundred-pound weakling with the added bonuses of being flabby and a chain smoker. He immediately mastered a bench press of fifty pounds. In spite of the humiliation of being offered assistance by weightlifters doing multiple sets of one-arm curls of fifty pounds, Jordan persevered. By the age of twenty-two, he had lost the flab and added thirty-five pounds of muscle. His weightlifting was now causing him to eat four or five meals a day that were costing him a large part of his graduate student income. It was also taking hours away from his studies, and that he truly couldn't afford.

He dropped his weights and continued to lift his books. His anxiety was further helped by his work with Pihl in alcohol aggression. He realized his customary relaxation of binge drinking to the point of stumbling and babbling nonsense wasn't helpful, so he began to cut down on the booze as well.

At about this time, just as defected KGB agent Yuri Bezmenov said it would, the full twenty years of psychological warfare required to demoralize a society was beginning to bear the forbidden fruit of resentment against the West, and academia had taken a big bite. Inside universities across the UK, Canada, and the United States, professors who had been unwitting Soviet activists as students twenty years ago in the 1960s were actively undermining Western values to Jordan's generation. Colleagues of these proletarian professors had achieved prominent positions in media, politics, and journalism. Suddenly, they were the "me" generation dancing to the disco inferno of the 1980s. They were everywhere, and the West would never be rid of them, as Bezmenov had foretold.

While Jordan was busy building his tower out of hell, a Western cornerstone of capitalism was taking a beating. It had become little more than the "compulsory hedonism of unplanned and irresponsible economic growth,"[2] according to Michael Harrington.

In 1982, Harrington, the handsome, Kennedy-esque Yale Law graduate created the Democratic Socialists of America from a merger of the New American Movement (NAM), a coalition of intellectuals from the New Left movements of the 1960s, and former members, like Max Shachtman, of the Old Left socialist and communist parties. Shachtman was an American Marxist, associate of Leon Trotsky and mentor of senior assistants to AFL–CIO president George Meany. He convinced Harrington to cooperate with Meany's union workers in penetrating the Democratic Party and pushing the Democrats to the left. This strategy was known as *realignment.*

Harrington was so successful at realigning the Democratic Party to the left that Democratic senator Ted Kennedy said at a party honoring Harrington, "I see Michael Harrington as delivering the Sermon on the Mount to America," and "Among veterans in the War on Poverty, no one has been a more loyal ally when the night was darkest."[3]

Harrington summed up his contribution to America in an interview cited in his *New York Times* obituary:

> Put it this way. Marx was a democrat with a small d. The Democratic Socialists envision a humane social order based on popular control of resources and production, economic planning, equitable distribution, feminism and racial equality. I share an immediate program with liberals in this country because the best liberalism leads toward socialism. I'm a radical, but as I tell my students at Queens, I try not to soapbox. I want to be on the left wing of the possible.[4]

If one of Jordan's guiding lights, Aleksandr Solzhenitsyn, an eyewitness to the horrors of Marxism who was then living in Vermont was aware of Harrington's interview occurring a few hundred miles south in New York, he may have been somewhat unnerved by it. But if he read the review of Harrington's most popular book, *The Other America: Poverty in the United States,* published by the Woodrow Wilson Institute that summarized Harrington's view on American society by saying, "Values and moral responsibilities that once bound people together have given way to relativistic codes, all encouraging an unhealthy individualism,"[5] he may well have panicked. It was then obvious that Marxism had fully infiltrated the West, claiming an emerging minority party in Canada, Jordan's alma mater the National Democratic Party, and one of the two major political parties in the United States and England. It then boldly declared its collectivist condemnation of "unhealthy individualism."

Jordan Peterson had no idea who was coming for him. At McGill, as at hundreds of other universities, neo-Marxists sprang up in the humanities and social science departments. They were determined to fight against oppressors—oppressors of women, brown and black people, poor people, working people, indigenous people, and homosexual people. Further fragmenting and codifying these fragments of society, feminist scholar Kimberlé Crenshaw developed the social theory of intersectionality that identified major social strata including class, race, sexual orientation, age, religion, creed, disability, and gender as overlapping oppressed identities. In years to come, gender would be divided even further into fifty-two separate sub-identities, each demanding its own unique, new pronoun. That's when Jordan, an obscure college professor at the time, would return fully from his private hell to lead the battle for Western civilization. That was coming, and *they* were coming.

But until then, as a humble psychology student with a growing use for religious and mythological archetypes, Jordan found himself suddenly facing these identities like the multi-headed Hydra of Hercules's trials in the underworld. He immediately recognized the familiar strains of resentment in student arguments and professors' lectures, and may have recognized this emerging resentment as Jung's "shadow," the dark side of human consciousness that allowed all evils free rein.

Campus demonstrations for civil rights, human rights, gay rights, workers' rights, and women's rights became more frequent and more heated. These new Marxists armed themselves with Mao's little red book; they raised clenched fists of solidarity and swore obedience in slogans like, "One world, one people!" as their belief in a just and perfect world turned slightly more strident. They rejected the highly effective peaceful revolutionaries like Dr. Martin Luther King Jr. and Mahatma Gandhi, and embraced the ruthless heroes of violent Marxist revolution like Huey P. Newton, former leader of the Black Panthers, and Fidel Castro and Ernesto "Che" Guevara of the Cuban Revolution.

Particularly Guevara, whose handsome, long-haired image became a universal icon and fashion totem of Marxist revolutionaries, held the new Marxists in sway. They called him by the familiar name "Che." Che was deeply feared in Cuba for convicting intellectuals in mock trials and assassinating them by firing squad the same day. Yet, even with his power of life and death over all Cubans, he was deeply resentful after the Soviets backed away from nuclear war with the United States during the Cuban Missile Crisis. He said the cause of socialist liberation from global "imperialist aggression" would have been worth "millions of atomic war victims."[6]

With each passing day it seemed like the new Marxists were adopting a slightly more militant, more malevolent stand. Jordan Peterson had only met this type of people in books. He had no idea they'd soon be his antagonistic colleagues in real life.

Tammy was well into her studies, also in psychology, at Jordan's former school, the University of Alberta in Edmonton. Edmonton was over two thousand miles west of Montreal, so their courtship floated along, progressing slowly and primarily by telephone.

Holiday trips home were rare for Jordan due to the travel expense and nearly overwhelming demands of his research, his doctoral studies, and clinical practice. But it was a committed courtship. As he later happily confessed, "I think I fell in love with her from the first moment I saw her, although I don't think the feeling was necessarily mutual and so I was about, like, seven, I think."[7]

He also recalled that a bit later at age twelve,

> I was sitting with her on this big armchair in our living room and she was sitting beside me on the armchair which I was pretty damn thrilled about. . . . And so anyway she left and I told my Dad that I was going to marry her. I remember that and he told that story at our wedding which was quite cute.[8]

And at thirteen or fourteen,

> I also delivered [the newspaper] to her house and one day she was there with another of her friends who was kind of a cute chick too, and I liked her quite a bit and they were sitting around talking about . . . how they were feminists, roughly

> speaking . . . that neither of them were going to take their husband's last name when they got married. And Tammy said to her friend, "Well, that really means I'm gonna have to find some wimp and marry him." And she turned around and looked at me and smiled evilly and said, "Hey, Jordan, do you want to get married?" And of course I had heard the whole conversation and, you know, she knew I liked her obviously, and so that was a nice little comical date. She has a very vicious sense of humor.[9]

The comfort of their courtship was restorative and a welcome constant in Jordan's life. As he grew closer to, gained stability, and drew power from Tammy, his personal, mythological Queen Goddess of the World, his challenges changed to match his circumstances.

His work on alcohol addiction under Pihl from 1985 to 1989 brought him face to face with dozens of Jekyll and Hyde monsters of the daylight world. Even at home, after work, the lost souls of alcoholism waited for him, including one of hell's angels.

Jordan lived in a poor district of Montreal apparently with just enough money to clothe and feed himself. His landlord, a powerful, aging, former hell-raising president of the local Hell's Angels, lived next door. Denis was a French Canadian and had spent time in prison as a young man, but then married and settled down as he matured. Over many years of married life he had moderated his drinking to a point where it was no longer a problem. He ran a small electronics business out of his apartment and tended to the repairs of his old building enough to keep his few tenants mostly satisfied. This provided a stable and sufficient income for him and his wife. Yet trouble was apparent in the various wounds from self-cutting that marked his wife's arms and hands. If you believe such things, Denis's demons who had created a king of hell-raisers, an angel of chaos, visited the domesticated Denis in his tidy, complacent new life. They were intent on exacting retribution for his betrayal.

His wife committed suicide, and Denis suddenly had no kingdom, nor any purpose. He was now just an old, gray landlord—abandoned and heartbroken. Whatever money he had was now given over to numbing alcohol. Within days he was back to drinking a case, or more, of beer a day.

At the witching hour, three a.m., the hallway outside Jordan's door rang with the clash of battle. Denis's curses, shouting, and roars of pain echoed throughout the building. Again, if you believe in such things, the demons had the old, blind-drunk king surrounded. He howled at his little dog, his one remaining friend, then laughed with his tormentors at the sheer joy of hell-raising again. Perhaps he would kill the dog, just for good measure. He hissed between his teeth, became incoherent, and finally passed out in humiliation.

Sometimes in the morning after a great battle, he would greet Jordan pleasantly in the hallway as they both began their day as if nothing had happened. He made an effort to befriend his young tenant, inviting him out for a night to one of his old haunts. Jordan accepted, in sympathy, and perhaps thinking he could offer the man some relief from his new store of clinical knowledge about alcoholism.

The night came and they climbed onto Denis's 1200cc Honda with "the acceleration of a jet plane." They charged into the night, Jordan clinging on for dear life and wearing only Denis's wife's tiny helmet perched uselessly on top of his head for protection.

In the dive bar, with the usual imps and minor demons lounging among the weakened souls, Denis sat impotent, reveling silently in his youthful atrocities as the beer loosened his inhibitions. Jordan drank with his grieving landlord in friendliness and compassion, until as innocently and naturally as walking, the old man magically transformed back into the king of Hell's Angels. Adopting Jordan as his one and only subject, now to be protected, he attacked anyone incautious enough to say anything displeasing. No doubt some industrious imp of the underworld sat in the old king's ear interpreting seemingly innocent comments for him. Soon, the screams of the wounded erupted in satisfying choruses as the king wore their blood once again in triumph.

With help, Jordan dragged his grieving landlord from the bar and somehow, Denis managed to navigate his motorcycle back over the icy streets of Montreal to home without killing them both. From then on, Jordan declined invitations but continued to help Denis through his suffering by remaining his friend.

Back behind the relatively safe and orderly walls of the university, Jordan continued his apprenticeship under Dr. Pihl. The abstract to their first paper together reads as follows:

> Acute alcohol intoxication produces changes in the cognitive functioning of normal individuals. These changes appear similar prima facie to those exhibited by individuals who sustain prefrontal lobe damage during adulthood. In order to test the validity of this observation, and to control for the confounding effects of expectancy, 72 male subjects were administered a battery of neuropsychological tests, within the context of a balanced-placebo design. Each subject received one of three widely different doses of alcohol. Analysis of the results of the cognitive test battery demonstrated that a high dose of alcohol detrimentally affects a number of functions associated with the prefrontal and temporal lobes, including planning, verbal fluency, memory and complex motor control. Expectancy does not appear to play a significant role in determining this effect. The implications of this pattern of impairment are analyzed and discussed.[10]

After receiving her degree from the University of Alberta in psychology, Tammy began working as a massage therapist in Ontario, expressing her caring and sensitive nature, rather than pursuing the high-pressure life of a clinical psychology practice, academic research, and advanced degrees like Jordan. An empathetic healer, she remained grounded in the simple acts of listening and physical touch. She and Jordan shared the traits of empathetic healers, forging their personal bonds, Tammy in the physical world and Jordan in the world of the mind.

Fortunately, the debilitating depression and anxiety that had colored much of Jordan's life and compelled him ever further into the darkest reaches of the human mind for their root causes, held little sway over Tammy. She was able to maintain the stabilizing counterbalance Jordan had come to rely on, both as one his oldest friends and now his committed girlfriend. Their long-distance courtship soon progressed to a love affair in spite of Jordan's punishing schedule since Tammy had cut the distance between them from two thousand to just over five hundred miles by settling in Ontario.

In 1989 Jordan and Tammy were married in Fairview at the Peterson family's St. Paul's United Church. At the wedding, Jordan's father, Wally, recounted the afternoon in the Peterson family living room fifteen years earlier, when he came upon Tammy and Jordan squeezed into a big chair, pressed against each other's sides. The living room was empty otherwise. A large couch, open carpet area, and other chairs offered other places to rest, but there they were, wedged in, almost snuggling but not quite. Wally noted their comfortable connection without comment but spent a moment with them until Tammy got up and left for home, perhaps feeling the grown-up intrusion on an intimate moment. Wally turned to his twelve-year-old son and asked, "You kinda like that girl, don't ya?" Jordan looked at his father and answered with typical seriousness and said, "I'm going to marry her."

Now having secured the love of his life, a vital achievement in any mythological hero's journey, Jordan gained her clear and grounded view toward everything in his crowded mind, but lost any refuge he may have allowed for old weaknesses. He no longer had to rely on his own skewed and emotional responses to get a clear perspective on things, but Tammy's X-ray moral vision allowed no compromise.

In a sense, he had finally fitted the last cornerstone into the foundation of his tower out of hell. He had a partner in the work ahead, and Tammy had found the focus of her life of caring. The couple shared Jordan's small apartment in Montreal next to Denis whom Tammy grew fond of and protective toward. The young couple immediately set to work, building the tower walls on the foundation Jordan had laid. Tammy's first challenge as queen of their small realm came with a gentle knock on the apartment door late one night after the orderly daylight world had gone to bed.

Denis, bearing recent wounds of battle, stood unsteadily in the doorway, offering his toaster for cash. Up to this point, Jordan had been helping Denis out, he thought, by buying various appliances from him. This was a blind spot in Jordan that Tammy immediately recognized. Obviously, the man had drunk all of his money away and was selling his appliances so he could keep drinking. She demanded that Jordan face Denis, drunk and dangerous as he was, and stand his ground for what was right. Jordan dutifully accepted the command and stood in the doorway facing Denis after two a.m., trying to find the right words to avoid any violent reaction.

> I said that he had told me he was trying to quit drinking. I said that it would not be good for him if I provided him with more money. I said that he made Tammy, whom he respected, nervous when he came over so drunk and so late and tried to sell me things.
>
> He glared seriously at me without speaking for about fifteen seconds.
>
> That was plenty long enough. He was watching, I knew, for any micro-expression revealing sarcasm, deceit, contempt or self-congratulation. . . . Denis turned and left. Not only that, he remembered our conversation, despite his state of professional-level intoxication. He didn't try to sell me anything again. Our relationship, which was quite good, given the great cultural gaps between us, became even more solid.[11]

Tammy's first edict as queen proved the wisdom and courage of her vision. Jordan, humbled before her, recommitted himself to telling the truth, banishing even little white lies to avoid discomfort. They began then in earnest to build their tower walls with truth and courage, as the walls of Jordan's old enemy, totalitarian socialism, were beginning to crumble.

Following China's lead, the Marxist experiment in Russia was coming to an end. In 1988, just months before Jordan and Tammy were married, Russian head of state Mikhail Gorbachev began poking holes in Stalinist state secrecy with his policy of *glasnost,* or openness. Russia's wall of isolation soon collapsed and freedom of speech flooded into Russia for the first time in decades.

On July 19, American musician Bruce Springsteen bravely performed a live concert in Soviet-controlled East Berlin where he addressed a crowd of three hundred thousand, carefully parsing his words in German so as not to trigger a reaction from the still-active East German secret police, the feared Stasi: "I'm not here for or against any government. I've come to play rock and roll for you in the hope that one day all the barriers will be torn down."

Springsteen's carefully phrased hope was the fifty-year-old prayer of the free world. It was realized in November 1989 as the first sections of the Berlin Wall, officially known as the Anti-Fascist Protection Rampart between free and Marxist-enslaved Germany, were torn down.

It was a euphoric moment for the Petersons, and an end to madness for generations around the world raised under the specter of nuclear war. Karl Marx's godless utopia died three days before Christmas with the signing of the Alma-Ata Protocol and was buried the day after at 7:32 p.m., December 26, 1991, when Stalin's flag, the communist hammer and sickle that had flown over the murder of tens of millions, was lowered for the last time. Nine days later, the Peterson's first child, a daughter, was born on January 4, 1992. They named her Mikhaila in honor of the Russian leader who had begun to lift Russia out of hellish Marxism and set an example for the rest of the world to follow.

CHAPTER SIX

TEMPTATION

The devil led him up to a high place and showed him in an instant all the kingdoms of the world. And he said to him, "I will give you all their authority and splendor; it has been given to me, and I can give it to anyone I want to. If you worship me, it will all be yours."

—LUKE 4:1–13, NIV

It was 1992. Jordan was twenty-nine years old, a new father in his young, healthy prime, relatively financially stable, and in love with the love of his life. His reputation was advancing as research papers written with Pihl and others were being well received and widely cited. His career track seemed set, and Tammy was an adoring, affectionate mother and wife. His demons were often down to just a whisper.

He could imagine his future, laid out before him as if he'd been led up to a high place and was overlooking a valley that contained all that the world had to offer. A promise seemed to be implicit in this vision. He could have it all, everything he ever wanted. All he had to do was drift into the comfortable folds of academia and settle in for a long, quiet cruise up to tenure. *Just be quiet, believe in the vision, worship it.* The rest would take care of itself. It was very, very tempting.

At first it was just a tremor. Barely noticeable. The world was at peace. The missiles of Armageddon had been set aside to rust in their silos; the armies of renegade tyrant Saddam Hussein had been easily crushed after invading Kuwait; and the People's Republic of China had signed on to the Treaty on the Non-Proliferation of Nuclear Weapons. The United States, Canada, and a coalition of over forty nations that had just rescued Kuwait from dictator Hussein now stood united, astride the globe as a colossus of peace and prosperity.

But the recent, sudden collapse of the West's mortal enemy, the Soviet Union, was like a sudden crack in the tectonic plates under everyone's feet. Just a little wobble. Nothing to worry about. The ripples from communism's collapse were lost in the general relief of world peace, except in certain circles.

Certainly in Russia it became a catastrophe. President Yeltsin stood in the ashes of communism desperate for a plan to restore his shocked nation. He grasped for the *shock therapy* of American economist Jeffrey Sachs to jump-start a free market economy. Prices on nearly all consumer products would be allowed to rise to market levels, but there would be no immediate rise in wages and few if any regulations on capital and investment. It was the wild west of free markets. It was radical surgery without anesthesia.

But instead of being seen as a catastrophe among global communists, as David Horowitz points out in his book *The Black Book of the American Left*,

> In articles, manifestoes and academic texts, leftists the world over claimed that the Marxist economies they had supported and defended did not represent "real socialism" and were "not what they had meant to defend."[1]

In Europe, Jutta Ditfurth, a member of Germany's Green Party, made it plain there was nothing to learn from recent events:

> There simply is no need to re-examine the validity of socialism as a model. It was not socialism that was defeated in Eastern Europe and the Soviet Union because these systems were never socialist.[2]

Revered British historian Eric Hobsbawm remained unfazed. He reflected on the inspiration that set the course of his life and was still available for all true believers even in the wreckage of the Marxist experiment:

> The months in Berlin made me a lifelong Communist, or at least a man whose life would lose its nature and its significance without the political project to which he committed himself as a schoolboy, even though that project has demonstrably failed, and as I know now, was bound to fail. The dream of the October Revolution is still there, somewhere inside me.[3]

In the United States, Samuel Bowles, a professor of economics at the University of Massachusetts Amherst, bravely admitted among all the denial that some "rethinking about socialist economies but little about capitalist economies,"[4] was needed. Like George Orwell, who denigrated the herds of resentful British socialists in his *The Road to Wigan Pier*, Jordan may have also recognized that socialists didn't really love socialism, they just hated capitalism. Their true motivation wasn't to help the poor, it was to destroy the rich.

And so the abject, universal failure of Marxism was not going to be a problem for the new or neo-Marxists. Of course, to almost everyone else, including Jordan, Marxism as a belief system and socialism as an economic system were provable nonsense. Yet Hobsbawm, being in his eighties and too old to change, did his best to restart the fires of social and economic justice:

> Capitalism and the rich have, for the time being, stopped being scared. Why should the rich, especially in countries like ours where they now glory in injustice and inequality, bother about anyone except themselves? What political penalties do they need to fear if they allow welfare to erode and the protection of those who need it to atrophy? This is the chief effect of the disappearance of even a very bad socialist region from the globe.[5]

Hobsbawm's proof was that Russia was adapting poorly to American-imported shock therapy for its economy. President Boris Yeltsin found himself presiding over the wholesale plunder of national assets by wealthy investors using gangster tactics to gain control of entire industries such as oil and gas production. Again capitalism, not Yeltsin's imprudence, was blamed for this piracy of Russian wealth. This fueled even greater resentment of the West, particularly of America.

But the fracturing of the old world order wasn't over. It was just beginning. A second crack formed at the very foundation of human social life that sent a shock wave out from academia to every part of the world. This signaled the beginning of radical or third-wave feminism, fueled again by the trademark of revolutionary Marxism: resentment disguised as compassion for the oppressed. More than anything else, this movement would embroil Jordan in a clash of cultures for decades to come.

Radical feminist Gerda Lerner, a onetime communist in the 1930s and pioneer of the new movement, was a professor of history at the University of Wisconsin when she wrote one of the movement's defining works, *The Creation of Patriarchy*. As Horowitz noted in his *The Black Book of the American Left, Volume II*, the recent fall of the Soviet Union prompted her to reflect on her past:

> I have striven to lead a conscious, an examined life and to practice what I preach. It now appears that, nevertheless, I failed in many ways, for I fell uncritically for lies I should have been able to penetrate and perceive as such.[6]

But, like Hobsbawm, this realization did nothing to dissuade her from promoting the trademark of all Marxist revolutionaries, overwhelming emotion.

> Like all true believers, I believed as I did because I needed to believe: in a utopian vision of the future, in the possibility of human perfectibility. . . . And I still need that belief, even if the particular vision I had embraced has turned to ashes.[7]

At this time, another fracture suddenly split Western society, particularly in America, that would soon bedevil Jordan as well. It snaked out from the Crown Heights neighborhood in Brooklyn, New York, on August 26, 1991, when "the most serious anti-Semitic incident in American history"[8] killed 2 people and sent 152 police officers and 38 civilians to the hospital. One hundred and twenty-two blacks and 7 whites were arrested.

Resentment had festered in the mixed black/Jewish neighborhood for years until it erupted into a frenzy of race hatred. Conditions in the government-subsidized housing of black neighbors had become intolerable and oppressive when compared to the tidy private homes and thriving businesses of their Orthodox Jewish neighbors. It was a cauldron of resentment that devolved into violence when a Jewish driver accidentally hit and killed one and injured a second young Guyanese child in the neighborhood. This touched off three days of rioting.

In his eulogy at the children's funeral, the Reverend Al Sharpton further enflamed black resentment by referring to Jewish neighbors as "diamond dealers" and then, typically, disguised this resentment behind a curtain of compassion for black residents by referring to the Jewish ambulance service that had attempted to save the children's lives by saying, "It's an accident to allow an apartheid ambulance service in the middle of Crown Heights."[9]

Not far from his podium, a banner was raised confirming that Sharpton had achieved his goal to lead the movement against black oppression. It read, HITLER DID NOT DO THE JOB.[10]

This third crack in civilization soon exploded across academia. The magazine *Race Traitor* was founded just a few months later by Harvard students and alumni under the blatantly racist motto "Treason to whiteness is loyalty to humanity." Even decades later, as a testament to its enduring destructiveness, an Amazon reviewer wrote, "The journal *Race Traitor* began in 1992 with one lofty ambition: 'to serve as an intellectual center for those seeking to abolish the white race.'"[11]

And so the bloody wheel of social revolution turned again, powered by the inexhaustible resource of human resentment. The new middle-class leaders of the oppressed again demanded equality, liberty, and brotherhood as their forebears had in Paris, St. Petersburg, and Beijing. They rushed in a wave toward the compassionate promises of Marxism for a just and equal society. Jordan Peterson knew the promises of Karl Marx were obvious and murderous lies, but the new wave was headed right for him as well. If he spoke up against it, his own future, his family's future, and all that he had achieved might easily be swept away.

As a postdoctoral fellow at McGill's Douglas Hospital with a new daughter, twenty clinical patients per week, a soon-to-be peer-reviewed research paper in the works, and three hours a day dedicated to writing *Gods of War,* Jordan didn't have a lot of spare time. His life was necessarily quite orderly. Practically every minute and every dollar was assigned to one good purpose or another. He did, however, encounter chaos every day in the lives of his clinical patients and even in his own deep-seated personal depression, but it was, for the time being, manageable. At least until chaos knocked again on his front door. This time it was not Denis but Jordan's high school buddy Chris, in Montreal for a visit all the way from Fairview.

> He (Chris) was a smart guy. He read a lot. He liked science fiction of the kind I was attracted to (Bradbury, Heinlein, Clarke). He was inventive. He was interested in electronic kits and gears and motors. He was a natural engineer. All this was overshadowed, however, by something that had gone wrong in his family. I don't know what it was. His sisters were smart and his father was soft-spoken and his mother was kind. The girls seemed OK. But Chris had been left unattended to in some important way. Despite his intelligence and curiosity he was angry, resentful and without hope.[12]

Jordan welcomed his old friend into the apartment. It was soon apparent that things had not improved much for Chris over the twelve years since high school, and that he'd traveled over two thousand miles from Fairview not just for a friendly visit but seeking help. Jordan offered a sympathetic ear and hours of his precious time to his old friend. Maybe now that they were older and Jordan had some practical experience sorting out wrecked psyches, some of Chris's problems could be sorted as well. He certainly wasn't looking for more work, but as a committed healer Jordan naturally wanted to help, especially an old friend. Tammy had also been friendly with Chris in high school so the troubled young man got a warm, small-town welcome into the tiny Peterson home.

The days rolled out and often after Tammy and one-year-old Mikhaila had gone to bed, the talks between the two old friends stretched into the late hours. There was hope that a fresh start in Montreal would bring Chris out of the aimless, drifting life he'd fallen into. The visit stretched into weeks.

But even after all the talks, the laughs, the dinners, and recalling old times and adventures together, there it was. At rock bottom of Chris's dissipated and chaotic life resentment swirled like a black hole consuming everything. All of Jordan's precious time, all of Tammy's kindnesses, all the love shown to Chris and even whatever pitiful respect and love he could muster for himself, weren't enough to overcome the psychological gravity.

> Chris started by hating men, but he ended by hating women. He wanted them, but he had rejected education, and career, and desire. He smoked heavily, and was unemployed. Unsurprisingly, therefore, he was not of much interest to women. That made him bitter. I tried to convince him that the path he had chosen was only going to lead to further ruin. He needed to develop some humility. He needed to get a life.[13]

But the only life Chris saw was a pit of cruelty and barbarism, something to be despised and avoided. It was once again Sartre's nausea, Nietzsche's nihilism, and Marx's world of oppression. It was philosophers Jacques Derrida and Michel Foucault's postmodern, deconstructionist view of a world drained of meaning and without possibility of spiritual redemption. It was 180 degrees opposite of Jordan's emerging worldview. It was the approaching cross of Chris's crucifixion.

The gaping black hole of chaos that Jordan had let into his home in friendship began to shake the orderly, loving life he'd built with so much sacrifice and effort. Jordan liked Chris and knew him as well as he knew any of his old friends. They were so close in interests and temperament, they'd spent as much time together as almost anyone outside of his immediate family. Yet, Chris had already slipped beyond reach.

> One evening, it was Chris' turn to make dinner. When my wife came home, the apartment was filled with smoke. Hamburgers were burning furiously in the frying pan. Chris was on his hands and knees, attempting to repair something that had come loose on the legs of the stove. My wife knew his tricks. She knew he was burning dinner on purpose. He resented having to make it. He resented the feminine role (even though the household duties were split in a reasonable manner; even though he knew that perfectly well). He was fixing the stove to provide a plausible, even creditable excuse for burning the food. When she pointed out what he was doing, he played the victim, but he was deeply and dangerously furious.
>
> Part of him, and not the good part, was convinced that he was smarter than anyone else. It was a blow to his pride that she could see through his tricks.[14]

Tammy was tiring of Chris but Jordan continued to hope for the best, perhaps allowing himself to be flattered by Chris's deference or worse, allowing himself the arrogance of thinking he could resolve his friend's issues. In either case, the demands of family life and career on the Petersons allowed Chris to avoid the normal alarms and permit a guest in their house. This was the perfect condition to low Chris's stunted ambition to survive intact; no one was challenging him or watching too closely. And so, from the chaos of human potential, Chris chose to continue his slide hellward while the Petersons continued, obliviously, to live a near perfect life.

At Christmas that year, 1994, Jordan's brother, Joel, and his wife arrived to celebrate the holiday. Although Chris knew the couple, their arrival meant fresh eyes on his situation, new scrutiny, more humiliation. They were intruding on his space.

For fun, everyone decided to take a walk through old, charming downtown Montreal. Christmas joy sparkled everywhere and traditional music, sights, and treats livened everyone's spirits, except Chris's. He trudged along, mostly mute, clad in funereal black from head to toe. Back at the apartment, the light and warmth of Christmas seemed to leak out of the apartment from every crack as a deathly stillness settled in. Their festive dinner ended, conversation waned, and everyone said goodnight, settling into their beds, all snug, well-fed, and thinking of happy Christmases past. But no one would sleep that night. Something very like murder was afoot.

> Something wasn't right. It was in the air. At four in the morning, I had had enough. I crawled out of bed. I knocked quietly on Chris's door and went without waiting for an answer into his room. He was awake on the bed, staring at the ceiling, as I knew he would be. I sat down beside him. I knew him very well. I talked him down from his murderous rage. Then I went back to bed, and slept. The next morning my brother pulled me aside. He wanted to speak with me. We sat down. He said, "What the hell was going on last night? I couldn't sleep at all. Was something wrong?" I told my brother that Chris wasn't doing so well. I didn't tell him that he was lucky

> to be alive—that we all were. The spirit of Cain had visited our house, but we were left unscathed. Maybe I picked up some change in scent that night, when death hung in the air.[15]

Jordan wasn't speaking metaphorically. He had been aware of Chris's scent for some time and noted it well.

> Chris had a very bitter odour. He showered frequently, but the towels and the sheets picked up the smell. It was impossible to get them clean. It was the product of a psyche and a body that did not operate harmoniously. A social worker I knew, who also knew Chris, told me of her familiarity with that odour. Everyone at her workplace knew of it, although they only discussed it in hushed tones. They called it the smell of the unemployable.[16]

A few months later, after Chris had left their home, a letter arrived from him. Jordan saved it and quoted it in full years later in *Maps of Meaning*. In the letter, we can glimpse a promising young man's mind at the end of the twentieth century in the midst of being torn apart by the received wisdom of that age. Chris would never recover from his *ideological possession* as Jordan would come to call it. Chris wrote,

> I hope you will have patience while I unburden myself on you, because I need desperately to confess my sins to someone. . . .
>
> Imagine if you can a grown man who harbors in his heart the most vicious resentment for his fellow man, his neighbor, who is guilty of nothing more than embodying a superior consciousness of what it means to be a man. When I think of all the black, scathing thoughts I have directed at those who I could not look in the eye, it is almost unbearable.[17]

It may be worth noting below the similar murderous resentment in the journal entries of Columbine mass killer Eric Harris. It seems that postmodern social disintegration was effecting young white men in particular. Harris wrote,

> One big fucking problem Is people telling me what to fuckin do, think, say, act, and everything else. I'll do what you say IF I feel like it. But people (I.E. parents, cops, God, teachers) telling me what to just makes me not want to fucking do it! thats why my fucking name is REB!!! no one is worthy of shit unless I say they are, I feel like GOD and I wish I was, having everyone being OFFICIALLY lower than me.[18]

Chris continued, detailing the mile markers on the road to hell that were all too familiar to Jordan.

> I equated independence and success with egotism and selfishness, and it was my fondest hope, my highest ambition, to witness and participate in the destruction of everything that successful, independent people had built for themselves. This I considered a duty. In fact there was a decidedly fanatical element in my urge to cleanse the world of what I perceived to be selfishness. . . . It makes me wonder that I have even one friend in this world. But of course I had friends before. Anyone with enough self-contempt that they could forgive me mine.
>
> I was sitting and thinking about what course my life should be taking . . . to the point where it was unacceptable to consider any career at all because just by being alive I would contribute to the destruction of the planet . . . so one is then faced with the need to accept on faith that things will turn out for the better with some luck and perseverance. And being a fine upstanding modern mouse with an enlightened rational mind, I have no use for faith and other such religious sounding claptrap and nonsense. Faith is obviously irrational, and I'll not have any irrationality influencing my behavior.[19]

Chris closed by acknowledging Jordan's guidance and the cost of ignoring it,

> Your ideas are starting to make sense to me now—at least I think they are. Faith in God means faith in that which kindles one's interest, and leads one away from the parental sphere out into the world. To deny those interests is to deny God, to fall from heaven and land squarely in hell, where one's passions burn eternally in frustration.[20]

For years afterward, in spite of his glimpse of Jordan's path to redemption, Chris continued to drift from one menial job to the next, never finding the relief or a compelling meaning that could sustain him through the predictable catastrophes in every life. Even so, Jordan never abandoned Chris over the years.

Chris called Jordan the day before his fortieth birthday and the two spoke hopefully about the possible publication of Chris's writing in a local paper. Things were looking up. Maybe the fires of youth had died out and progress could now be made.

The following day, on his fortieth birthday, Chris drove his battered pickup truck to the edge of the empty prairie outside of Fairview, ran a hose from the exhaust pipe of the running engine through the driver's side window, climbed in, closed the cab door, and smoked a cigarette while he waited for the end.

It had been eight years since Jordan began writing his book *Gods of War,* his attempt "to explain the meaning of history." He'd committed himself to writing three hours a day, seven days a week—a huge commitment that he protected fiercely even through his marriage, demanding career, and birth of two children—Mikhaila and his new son, Julian. Soon after he began the work, he quit drinking beyond an occasional social beer, sacrificing most of his social life. His full focus was on integrating his clinical work, research, wide reading, and life experiences into a concise story about how evil continued to thrive in the modern world. Now his manuscript was nearly complete and he found the work trending toward a conclusion. His final chapter, "The Hostile Brothers," seemed to zero in on the individual and societal cost of a postmodern godless and perceived hostile universe. It seems more than possible, that his near-death experience as a young man, and most recently Chris's fatal one in the clutches of nihilistic resentment, may have shaped his thoughts.

In the opening of this final chapter Jordan wrote,

> One of these "hostile brothers" or "eternal sons of God" is the mythological hero. He faces the unknown with the presumption of its benevolence—with the (unprovable) attitude that confrontation with the unknown will bring renewal and redemption. He enters, voluntarily, into creative "union with the Great Mother," builds or regenerates society, and brings peace to a warring world. The other "son of God" is the eternal adversary. This "spirit of unbridled rationality," horrified by his limited apprehension of the conditions of existence, shrinks from contact with everything he does not understand. This shrinking weakens his personality, no longer nourished by the "water of life," and makes him rigid and authoritarian, as he clings desperately to the familiar, "rational," and stable. Every deceitful retreat increases his fear; every new "protective law" increases his frustration, boredom and contempt for life. His weakness, in combination with his neurotic suffering, engenders resentment and hatred for existence itself.[21]

Acknowledging the inexhaustible potential for evil in the world, Jordan began to fear for his own very young children. With the birth of Julian, he held in his hands the tiniest living representation of human fragility. Almost anything, the slightest noxious breeze, an innocuous insect bite, or any number of unknown reasons could end the youngster's life in an instant, taking part of him, Tammy, and older sister, Mikhaila, with him. Wasn't everyone in the world, in their own way, just as vulnerable? Perhaps it was his ever-present depression speaking, a postpartum reaction to the awesome responsibility he now added to his load, but it wasn't wrong. Perhaps he was overly sensitive because they had also noticed something was wrong with Mikhaila.

Tammy saw that something was off about Mikhaila's gait, the way she walked. She attributed it to the rides on Jordan's shoulders that seemed to cause the child pain when they were over. He stopped giving his daughter the rides that they both enjoyed so much. This was the feather's edge of a painful and prolonged battle with childhood rheumatoid arthritis that would afflict Mikhaila for years to come.

He would later write of this moment in *12 Rules for Life*,

> What sort of God would make a world where such a thing could happen, at all?—much less to an innocent and happy little girl? It's a question of absolutely fundamental import, for believer and non-believer alike.[22]

And if that was the actual state of the world, he wondered, how could a normal human being, even a political zealot, willingly promote even more tragedy and malevolence than already existed? Hadn't every legend, fairy tale, and religious story warned them for millennia that they would get caught in their own web of evil? Did they even know what evil was, or had it died a hundred years ago and been forgotten along with God?

In all his work and years of deep contemplation on this, it seemed as if there were very few even talking about such things beyond immediate outrage. Hideous new levels of malevolence were blooming with every mass shooting, every violent riot, and every new, hateful demonization of a social or political group. It was springtime in hell.

Whatever was operating now in the Western mind, after the collapse of the old world order, was something deeper than surface consciousness. It was deeper than biology because it overrode even the instinct to survive. It was at the very core of being.

Would the Petersons' tender-aged children even survive? And what was his part going to be in all of this? Would he stay safe behind the ivy-covered walls of academia? Would he say *yes* to the comfortable life he was promised and join the long, gray line of tenured professors? Or would he pitch everyone he loved back into the depths with him for another round with the Prince of Darkness?

CHAPTER SEVEN

A COMFY NEST OF VIPERS

The devil is the spirit who underlies the development of totalitarianism; the spirit who is characterized by rigid ideological belief (by the "predominance of the rational mind"), by reliance on the lie as a model of adaptation (by refusal to admit to the existence of error, or to appreciate the necessity of deviance), and by the inevitable development of hatred for the self and world.

—JORDAN PETERSON, *MAPS OF MEANING: THE ARCHITECTURE OF BELIEF*

The year 1993 marked the culmination of Jordan's postgraduate work at McGill University's Douglas Hospital, his most prolific period of academic publication including 9 papers such as "Social Variability, Alcohol Consumption, and the Inherited Predisposition to Alcoholism" with his longtime mentor Dr. Robert Pihl and others, published that year. Eventually Jordan would contribute to over 140 papers in his career, many in the early years focusing on alcohol and drug use, then skewing toward his interests in Jungian archetypes and mythology in "Neuropsychology and Mythology of Motivation for Group Aggression" in 1999, his integration of psychology and Western religious traditions in "A Psycho-ontological Analysis of Genesis 2–6" in 2006, and on toward practical and political integration of his research in "Spiritual Liberals and Religious Conservatives" in 2013.

The language of science being necessarily precise, unemotional, and exhaustive had wreaked havoc on Jordan's writing style as he attempted to make his insights more palatable to general readers in *Gods of War*. For instance, the typical abstract (edited for brevity) of "Social Variability, Alcohol Consumption, and the Inherited Predisposition to Alcoholism" reads,

> This study examines psychological and demographic differences between (other) drug-using and non-drug-using alcoholic women and two contrast groups of controls in a population-based nonclinical sample of women.

The first chapter of *Gods of War*, a book that was in Jordan's own words "quite dense," begins with,

> The world can be validly construed as forum for action, or as place of things. The former manner of interpretation—more primordial, and less clearly understood—finds its expression in the arts or humanities, in ritual, drama, literature and mythology. The world as forum for action is a place of value, a place where all things have meaning. This meaning, which is shaped as a consequence of social interaction, is implication for action, or, at a higher level of analysis simplification for the configuration of the interpretive schema that produces or guides action.[1]

Not quite Shakespeare, but a useful starting place for his students of Introduction to Personality at Harvard University where he was recently accepted as an assistant professor. *Gods of War* was their textbook.

In July 1994, the Petersons moved from their cramped, ghetto-adjacent apartment in Montreal to a small row home on a leafy, quiet street in Amherst, Massachusetts. With two-year-old Mikhaila and infant Julian, Tammy found herself fully occupied with making adjustments to suburban American life in support of Jordan who had leaped several rungs up the academic ladder from McGill postgraduate fellow to assistant professor at prestigious Harvard. Tammy was further restricted to homebound concerns by the fact that she had not been given a work visa for the United States as Jordan had. For now, she was fully and happily engaged with the care of her family and would soon become a magnet for the care of other neighborhood children as well.

At Harvard, Jordan quickly developed a reputation as an engaging and enthusiastic teacher. His students found his style of wide-ranging, on-the-fly discussion more like improvisational performance than rote lecture and responded strongly to him. Student Hassan Lopez said in the journal of Harvard student life *The Crimson*, "Anyone who's taking his class can immediately recognize that he's teaching beyond the level of anyone else."[2] Jordan's initial Introduction to Personality course was unique in a number of ways. First, he was teaching from his own unpublished book *Gods of War* rather than a standard introductory textbook on elemental psychology. Students were instantly freed from an uninspiring, expensive, and heavy standard textbook, and instead gifted with a personal work of art in progress. Jordan summarized his book at that time saying, "It describes what I think myth means and what I think about how our brains work."[3]

His students were also among the first to enjoy the convenience of the digital age when Jordan transferred his fragile, spiral-bound manuscript to a digital version on Harvard's new internet servers. He also was among the first to consistently record his classroom lectures on videotape for later access and review. These digital assets were the first green shoots of what would become distance learning and Jordan's online presence.

Students immediately recognized they were co-voyagers on an authentic journey into psychology and flocked to his classes. Jordan's innovative, free, and shareable online textbook also encouraged his students' enthusiasm and set a trend that would expand years later for a Harvard psychology and computer science undergraduate named Mark Zuckerberg who would launch www.thefacebook.com at Harvard to help students also share personal details like class years, mutual friends, and telephone numbers.

Second, students were getting firsthand, curated results of current psychological research on topics as wide-ranging as Jordan's interests in psychology, literature, art, politics, and human potential along with the practical implications of each of these.

Student Alisa N. Kendrick said Jordan's,

> wide breadth of knowledge allows him to create beautiful theories linking together ideas from mythology, religion, philosophy and psychology. He just seems to be much more knowledgeable and on the cutting edge of where psychology is going.[4]

Student Naomi Reid said,

> The way he synthesized information, he didn't just talk about the theories but he talked about some of his own ideas and different sources of information.[5]

And third, the excitement of all this intellectual tumult triggered an explosion of the students' own ideas for research that Jordan encouraged no matter how unconventional the topic, such as studies on body piercing and the suicidal pathology of singer Kurt Cobain of the rock band Nirvana. They included studies on pain sensitivity, loneliness, and aggression among adolescents.

Student Hassan Lopez commented on Jordan's growing reputation as an eccentric saying, "If you have a strange project, [the psychology department] will immediately send you to [Peterson] because they know he'll take them." Lopez commented on Jordan's reach outside of the psychology department, saying, "Philosophy students even go to him for advice on these."[6]

Jordan's approach garnered him attention from ardent students and pleased administrators, but his disdain for radical leftist politics turned heads among some administrators, alumni, and faculty. Harvard remained largely dormant after the volcanic explosion of the 1960s and resurgence of the 1980s. Professor Richard Lewontin, a prominent molecular biologist and self-proclaimed Marxist, said of the role of Harvard in the ongoing struggle for social justice,

> What does Marxism have to offer the bourgeois university? Preferably nothing. That is, Marxism can do nothing for the university; the real question is what can Marxists do *to* and *in* the university?[7]

Reportedly at this time there were about a dozen neo-Marxists in Harvard Law School alone. Of the over two thousand professors then at the school, a conservative estimate of those who thought like Lewontin in the other departments might easily be in the hundreds. Among the relatively few who may have thought like Jordan was Harvard professor Harvey Mansfield. Mansfield had been a professor at Harvard for seven years when the communists of Students for a Democratic Society raided and took over Harvard's main administrative offices in University Hall in April 1969. Two hundred and fifty students packed into the President's and Fellows' Rooms spouting revolutionary slogans and threatening violence. They threw "establishment lackeys out of the building, rifled through their files, and announced to humanity the dawning of a revolution."[8] Of course, the police were called and dragged the pampered revolutionaries out, effectively sunsetting the brave, new revolution after a few hours.

When Jordan began teaching at Harvard, Mansfield had been there for thirty years and would soon receive the National Humanities Award for his decades of work as a political philosopher. In that time, he apparently had developed a dim view of the '60s radicals who had once taken over Harvard and had returned there and elsewhere in academia as professors. He said of their political philosophy and them, that they were "neither so outrageous nor so violent as at first. The poison has worked its way into our soul, the effects becoming less visible to us as they become more ordinary."[9]

Unfortunately for Jordan and his welcome to his new American home, these "poisonous" influences weren't restricted to Harvard. At nearby Massachusetts Institute of Technology, linguistics professor Noam Chomsky, also a recognized scholar in Harvard's Society of Fellows, had said of America's struggle with the postwar Soviet Union,

> The United States was picking up where the Nazis had left off, *and had engaged* . . . a "secret army" under U.S.-Nazi auspices that sought to provide agents and military supplies to armies that had been established by Hitler and which were still operating inside the Soviet Union and Eastern Europe through the early 1950s.[10]

This might have been brushed off as an arcane conspiracy theory by an embittered '60s radical, but Chomsky was a Harvard Fellow, a lifetime appointment that recognized extraordinary academic potential. Never rebuked or censured by his esteemed senior Harvard Fellows, Chomsky appeared to be speaking largely for the sentiments of the Harvard establishment even as his venom toward the United States became unusually poisonous. According to him, during the Cold War, the United States also wiped out communist uprisings in Latin America with "the methods of Heinrich Himmler's extermination squads," adding, "a close correlation [exists] worldwide between torture and U.S. aid."

In regard to the Vietnam War, "the major policy goal of the U.S. has been to maximize repression and suffering in the countries that were devastated by our violence. The degree of the cruelty is quite astonishing."[11]

And so consequently, "legally speaking, there's a very solid case for impeaching every American president since the Second World War. They've all been either outright war criminals or involved in serious war crimes."[12]

And then there was the kindly, avuncular Howard Zinn self-described as, "something of an anarchist, something of a socialist. Maybe a democratic socialist," just over the Charles River at Boston University who would lecture students,

> I think it's very important to bring back the idea of socialism into the national discussion to where it was. . . . before the Soviet Union gave it a bad name . . . Socialism basically said, hey, let's have a kinder, gentler society. Let's share things. Let's have an economic system that produces things not because they're profitable for some corporation, but produces things that people need. People should not be retreating from the word socialism because you have to go beyond capitalism.[13]

In spite of these surrounding storms, Jordan set sail again in his pursuit of good and evil. But unnoticed in the dark hold of his ship was a nest of vipers.

As an introduction to his course Introduction to Personality, Jordan's preface in *Gods of War* revealed his own torment and brush with madness as a young undergraduate. He described a time when he was approximately the same age as the students he now intended to teach, sitting in the same type of rows as his students were now sitting, and taking a similar introductory psychology course.

> Some of the courses I was attending at this time were taught in large lecture theaters, where the students were seated in descending rows, row after row. In one of these courses—Introduction to Clinical Psychology, appropriately enough—I experienced a recurrent compulsion. I would take my seat

> behind some unwitting individual and listen to the professor speak. At some point during the lecture, I would unfailingly feel the urge to stab the point of my pen into the neck of the person in front of me. This impulse was not overwhelming—luckily—but it was powerful enough to disturb me.[14]

Although written matter-of-factly, such a personal confession was no doubt disturbing to several of his new students as well. And that was just the early part of his introduction. Along with his unsettling emotional honesty came his more brutal intellectual honesty about his politics, socialism in particular.

> Orwell described the great flaw of socialism, and the reason for its frequent failure to attract and maintain democratic power (at least in Britain). Orwell said, essentially, that socialists "did not really like the poor. They merely hated the rich." His idea struck home instantly. Socialist ideology served to mask resentment and hatred, bred by failure. Many of the party activists I had encountered were using the ideals of social justice to rationalize their pursuit of personal revenge.[15]

And there it was—in black and white—a declaration of war against socialism and socialists in Jordan's own words. The word went out among the Harvard neo-Marxists, including economics professor Stephen Marglin, law professor Duncan Kennedy, and critical race theorists like Noel Ignatiev, publisher of *Race Traitor*—Peterson was the enemy.

As the course progressed and he became more comfortable illustrating concepts in his book with his personal experiences, Jordan would motor along through the assigned reading from his book grabbing memories from his childhood, a quote from Jung, a fragment from Dostoevsky or Orwell, a study he'd come across on bio-mechanics; but sometimes he'd get stopped in midsentence. A long-ago personal moment or an account he had read of Solzhenitsyn's gulags would slowly overwhelm him. There was no hurry or attempt to quash the rising emotions. His eyes filled with tears as they had all his life since early childhood, and as he was able to, he struggled on with a cracked, wavering voice to convey the depths of some human depravity he saw in his mind. The horror and pain of human existence was unavoidable for anyone taking Jordan's class. It was an emotional tour de force. His popularity among students soared, even as the whisper campaign against him among Harvard's radical faculty, students, and administrators grew.

At home, Tammy adjusted to the domestic life she had once scoffed at as a young girl. Unable to legally apply for work, she found that she was happy to care for the children of working mothers in the neighborhood. The Peterson house was soon full of preschool children for Mikhaila to play with and baby Julian to watch in wonder. Tammy apparently enjoyed the work, feeling a natural empathy for the challenges of children. Jordan was often home when the children were in the house and also enjoyed their antics as a break from the intense focus needed for his classes and research projects.

Tammy and Jordan had been able to see and feel the emotional landscape between and around themselves since childhood. It seemed certainly part of the dynamic that almost instantly bonded them together as children and likely prompted Tammy's choices as an adult to become a healer, parent, day-care provider, and eventually a serial foster parent.

To the Petersons, a house full of children, their own and other people's, was enjoyable. Jordan could easily spend hours drawing them pictures of monsters and letting them test their strength against him in roughhouse play. But keen empathy and several years of honing his sensitivity to human cruelty could also detect even slight evidence of problems in a child's behavior.

Jordan came home one day to find a four-year-old boy standing alone on the Petersons' enclosed porch, head down, not playing among the riot of other preschoolers surrounding Tammy in the living room. He didn't recognize the boy, but said hello. The boy did not respond. He asked if the boy wanted to come in and play with the others, but again, no response. Recognizing something significant was up, Jordan squatted down to eye level and tried to break through the boy's protective stance that seemed more typical of a one-year-old than a four-year-old. He smiled and gently invited the boy to come and play as he wriggled a finger into the boy's armpit, tickling him. The boy wriggled away, tightening his protective stance. Jordan tried again and again. Nothing; a complete refusal to engage. He stopped and understood why Tammy had let the boy stay by himself on the porch.

Jordan went in and asked Tammy what the situation was. She said the boy's mother, apparently a psychologist as well, had dropped the boy off in desperation because the boy's regular nanny had been in some kind of accident and couldn't care for him. The woman had said, "He probably won't eat all day, but that's okay."

As Jordan would later retell the story in one of his classroom lectures, the mother's statement was not okay. Jordan told this story as a long, personal digression, apparently one of several that preceded it, in his increasingly improvisational style. It was recorded in an undated video running nearly twenty minutes as he stands at an overhead projector attempting at several moments to return to the primary subject of the class. He is drawn away from his prepared lecture, back to the story again and again as he becomes more emotionally caught up in it. The video doesn't extend beyond this digression. The original subject of the class is only indicated by his reference to an image on the projector of "this dragon," the mythological representation of destruction and chaos.[16]

As Jordan told his class, the mother's statement about her son not eating was not okay. First, because she so glibly admitted her inability to properly care for her son, and second, because the child would soon become distraught and disruptive if he didn't eat, and third, and most concerning to Jordan, was because the boy had obviously learned to ignore adults. As he then emphasized to his class, ignoring adults was not a good psychological strategy.

> You don't want your four-year-old to have learned that it's okay to ignore adults or that you *should* ignore adults or that you *can* ignore adults. . . . If they don't respect adults then of course they don't have any respect for what they're going to be. . . . Why the hell grow up? You end up like Peter Pan because that's what Peter Pan is about, right? Peter Pan wants to stay in Neverland with the Lost Boys where there's no responsibility because, you know, he looks at the future and all he sees is Captain Hook, a tyrant who's afraid of death.
>
> That's the crocodile, right, that's chasing him with the clock in his stomach, that's the same thing as this dragon.[17]

In the Petersons' kitchen, the children were seated around the table for lunch. Tammy had gone to the porch and retrieved the boy who still refused to raise his head, look her in the eye, or respond to her invitations. She led him by the hand to the table and sat him next to her where she could focus all her attention on him. As the other children made their messy ways through the meal, Tammy used the tried-and-true method of a gentle, tickling poke in the ribs to get the boy's attention.

In his classroom, Jordan digressed further from the main topic of the class, beyond the four-year-old boy's story to what in scientific terms might be called a lower level of analysis. He analyzed the poking technique of child feeding that Tammy was using.

At about nine months old, his son Julian also would not eat and would only play with his food. A broad smile and a little laugh brightened Jordan's face as he recalled his son's tricks to avoid eating. These included smearing food in his mother's hair.

But whenever a spoonful of food was presented, Julian shut his mouth and eyes tightly. Eventually, repeated gentle pokes in the ribs got Julian to open his mouth in annoyance, *Aaa!* With a quick swipe of the poised spoon, food went into Julian's mouth and if necessary, his mouth was held closed until the food went down. This took many hours of trial and error to discover and exhaustive patience to execute.

At this lower level of analysis, the problem of the four-year-old boy who wouldn't eat was revealed. The poke-feeding technique required more time and attention than the four-year-old boy's mother was capable of, or willing to invest in her son. It also revealed that the boy had probably been like this since he was approximately nine months old. He'd been neglected for almost three years.

Returning to the first level of analysis, Jordan went on to explain that the poke-feeding technique worked exactly the same way on the four-year-old boy as it had on Julian, and added that every time the dreaded spoon went into the four-year-old's mouth, Tammy rewarded the boy with a pat on the head and told him he was a good boy.

Jordan paused in his retelling of the story at the point where the boy had finished his entire meal with a big show of praise and caresses from Tammy. His voice cracked with emotion as he seemed to see the boy's face in front of him.

> And Jesus, you should have seen what happened to that kid. Man, it just about broke my heart. . . . his eyes got big and he smiled and he was just, like, he was super thrilled because he'd finally accomplished this absolute basic necessity that he hadn't mastered in four years! He finally got it right![18]

Then another pause as his emotions turned even more tender, his voice halting and straining as he fought to maintain composure,

> You think of all the meals that he went through either being ignored or failing three times a day for, like, three years! Nothing but failure and bad responses. And you know he'd internalized all that, he thought he was a bad kid and then all of a sudden, poof, he figured this out! . . . He just lit up and that whole shell that he had on, that he was, like, using to protect himself when he was in the porch, that just melted

> away! It was horrifying and amazing at the same time. . . . And he followed my wife around after that in the house just like a puppy dog, like, he wouldn't get more than one foot away from her. It was unbelievable! . . . And then we went downstairs to watch a movie with the kids and she sat on a rocking chair, he climbed right up on her lap and grabbed her just like that Harlow monkey grabbed the, you know, the little soft mother instead of the wiry mother. Boop! He was like this [clutching to his chest tightly] and he was like that for, like, two hours! He wouldn't let her go![19]

The mood turned gray, then black, as Jordan recounted the boy's mother returning to pick up her son.

> So then his mother came home and she came downstairs and she looked at what was going on, you know, and this kid was, like, glommed on to my wife and she looked at her and she said, "Oh, super mom."
>
> And, you know, took her kid and went home. . . . Jesus, if you don't think there's a dragon in that story, man, you're not listening to it! . . . Because the dragon in that story was her. And it was something she did not want to admit. And she was willing, perfectly willing, to sacrifice her child to [her] failure to realize that she could be a dragon, so that meant that the *child* was the problem. And that's a hell of a thing to do to a four-year-old.[20]

And then the final, angry turn of mind,

> So it was not pleasant, it was really not pleasant. In fact, we probably did damage to the child by actually getting [him] to do something good because we opened him up to the possibility that he could behave properly and be rewarded for that and that

> gave him hope. And so you can bloody well be sure that that hope was dispensed with the next day.[21]

This was Jordan's irrepressible illustration of the random malevolence of existence, the mindless evil inflicted even on innocent children by well-meaning parents. The only thing that made life bearable, in his view, was the reduction of human suffering, even if temporary. That was the meaning of Jordan's life. It was the one message behind all his efforts.

Trouble was brewing in the administrative offices of Harvard. Faculty members were finally rebelling against a decades-long power grab by administrators who were overwhelming the faculty. Harvard professor of economics David S. Landes said,

> There has been a major change in the governance of the University and the balance of resources. A silent shift has occurred in the past 25 years, resulting in the proliferation of University administration. . . . There are two parts of the central administration which I'm told would be most unhappy that we might want to know more about how things work. . . . The function [of legal counsel] has changed from advice to governance. The givers of counsel have turned into givers of law.[22]

The second part of the out-of-control administration was a bloated public relations department according to Landes. "In the past, Harvard officials spoke out as called for," Landes said. "Now the masters of spin want to create work for themselves."[23]

This was not a reassuring environment for untenured Professor Peterson. The split between Harvard's aggressive administrative bureaucracy and its faculty reminded him of the power struggle that Solzhenitsyn had written about between the Soviet politburo and Russian intellectuals, particularly since Harvard's new ruling politburo seemed to favor, or at least tacitly ignore, the disruptive and vocal socialists on their campus. For someone as sensitive as Jordan to neo-Marxist aggression and prone to anger when encountering it, this growing menace must have been more than just aggravating. He had lived in the midst of its resurgence since his days at McGill over ten years earlier. Now it literally surrounded him, invaded his classroom, threatened his career and the future stability of his family.

Professor Landes had been referring, in part, to Harvard's energetic support of the new wave of "political correctness" that had been sweeping through college campuses since the late 1980s. It was reaching fever pitch during Jordan's first years at Harvard after the publications of Roger Kimball's *Tenured Radicals* in 1990 and Dinesh D'Souza's *Illiberal Education* in 1991. These books condemned the "liberal" promotion of self-victimization, multiculturalism, affirmative action, and postmodernist changes to university curricula.

Shocking new evidence of socialism's encroachment at Harvard came in the public turn of mind of its "star" economist Stephen Marglin in *Z Papers,* an anti-capitalist publication. In his article "Why Is So Little Left of the Left?" he openly disparages capitalism and implies that urgent radical action was needed beyond just "liberating" oppressed workers to revitalize socialism.

> The obstacles to liberating the workplace lie not only in the dominance of classes in whose interest it is to perpetuate the authoritarian workplace, but also in the dominance of the knowledge system that legitimizes the authority of the boss. In this perspective, to liberate the workplace it is hardly sufficient to overthrow capitalism.[24]

Harvard undergraduate G. Brent McGuire fired back, calling out the stealthy approach of activists like Marglin who were cloaking themselves with obscuring labels such as *liberal* and *progressive* instead of using the correct but alarming term of *socialist.* McGuire said,

> Socialist ideas are very pervasive at Harvard, but they're not called that by the socialist. It's a play on words, but the ideas are as socialist as ever. [These ideas] are very dangerous because Harvard is so respected.[25]

Jordan was now center stage in a philosophical crossfire. Like the multi-headed Hydra that he used to illustrate the proliferation of psychological impulses when they are forcibly repressed, the proliferation of social identities took the place of the beheaded dragon of Marxism in Western society. Reformed Marxist David Horowitz explains these emerging social identities at Harvard and elsewhere,

> As an expression of its nihilism, the contemporary left defines and organizes itself as a movement against rather than for. Its components may claim to be creating egalitarian futures in which racism, "sexism" and corporate dominance no longer exist and in which "social justice" prevails . . . and makes it possible for . . . anarchists, eco-radicals, radical feminists, "queer" revolutionaries, Maoists, Stalinists, and vaguely defined "progressives" to operate side by side. . . . The continuity between the generations of the Communist and neocommunist left is, in fact, seamless. It is the product of a leftist culture that openly embraces the intellectual forerunners, political traditions and anti-capitalist perspectives of the Communist past.[26]

By far the most bitterly divisive social identities emerging at this time were the particularly American ones of black and white. This racial wound was still fresh in the minds of most Americans, and so was easily exploitable by neo-Marxists desperate for a new class war. They attacked America's historic and assumed systemic racism with revolutionary zeal and quickly overran Harvard. Jordan was forced to retreat from this particular attack. As a Canadian, he had no authority in America's ongoing war with itself. But there were many other fronts opening in the left's multipronged campaign. When "whiteness" itself was attacked, clearly a racist move, Jordan's internal alarm must have sounded and may have even disturbed his sleep. This was a subject, identifying oppressor and oppressed classes, in which he had significant authority.

White Marxist Harvard graduate student Noel Ignatiev took direct aim at whiteness as the cofounder and coeditor of the magazine *Race Traitor*, published just prior to Jordan's arrival at Harvard. He responded to a reader who objected to the magazine's obvious racial animus:

> We'll keep bashing the dead White males, and the live ones, and the females too, until the social construct known as the White race is destroyed. Not deconstructed, but destroyed.[27]

Ignatiev's use of "deconstructed" referred to the philosophers Jacques Derrida and Michel Foucault, two of Jordan's intellectual nemeses after Karl Marx, who were then riding the French New Wave of postmodern deconstructionism into the hearts and minds of Harvard students and faculty. Jordan reentered the fight, summarizing postmodernism this way,

> You can think about it as an attitude of skepticism and irony towards and rejection of grand narratives, ideologies and universalism including the idea of the objective notions of reason, that's a big one, human nature, that's a big one. Social progress, absolute truth and objective reality, all those things being questioned.
>
> The head Joker at the top of the postmodern hierarchy is Derrida. Foucault is often mentioned as are a number of other people. Here's some other attributes of postmodern thinking; there's a recognition of the existence of hierarchy, that's for sure. And there's an echo of that idea, the recognition of hierarchy, in the term patriarchy because of course patriarchy is a recognition of hierarchy. Now it's a very particular kind

> of recognition because the postmodernists also tend to define hierarchy as a consequence of power differential. And so the world they envision, as far as I can tell, is something like a sociological Hobbesian nightmare . . . every individual in some sense at the throat of every other individual.[28]

It must have been maddening for Jordan to debate postmodern neo-Marxists.

Their reasoning was so convoluted by Derrida's deconstructionism, their language so obscure as a result, their scholarship in departments such as Women's Studies so atrocious as seen in Peggy McIntosh's seminal paper in the discipline "White Privilege and Male Privilege," that people like Jordan must have just thrown up their hands in frustration. But to his credit, he never quit. He constantly rearmed himself with fresh perspectives and new information from others inside and outside of academia.

Another witness to the quackery of Women's Studies was professor Camille Paglia, a noted feminist writer at the University of the Arts in Philadelphia. Jordan interviewed her on this subject in October 2017.

> These departmental models, okay, were to me totalitarian to begin with . . . separating the language into fiefdoms and to create the Women's Studies department absolutely out of the air, just snap your fingers . . . The English department had taken a century to develop. And all of a sudden to create a department where they politicize agenda from the start and by people without any training whatever in that field? . . . The administrators wanted to solve a public relations problem. They had a situation with very few women faculty nationwide, at the time when the women's movement had just started up. The spotlight of tension was on them. They needed women faculty fast. They needed the women's subject on the agenda fast. So they just like, poof! "Let there be Women's Studies."[29]

Paglia elaborated on the other associated "frauds" of postmodernism,

> This postmodernist thing, this thrashing of the text, this encouragement of a superior and destructive attitude toward the work of art we're going through with red pen in hand finding all the evidence of sexism, check, racism, check, homophobia, check. I am sick and tired of these people . . . they're frauds.[30]

Attesting to the fraudulent nature of postmodernism, its leading proponent intellectual Jacques Derrida was accorded the same degree of fame in France as a movie star would be in America. And accordingly, his fame rested on public performance such as his refusal to attempt explanations of a foundational theory of postmodernism, an "intellectual sleight of hand" according to Jordan, called deconstructionism. Instead of defending deconstructionism, Derrida offered only partial answers as to what deconstructionism *wasn't* or largely indecipherable blather, "thrashing of the text," as Paglia insisted, that maintained his aura of intellectual superiority.

An interviewer asked Derrida, "You're very well known in the States for deconstruction. Can you talk a little bit about the origin of that idea?"

The philosopher responded,

> Before responding to this question, I want to make a preliminary remark on the completely artificial nature of this situation. . . . I want to underline rather than efface our surrounding technical conditions, and not feign a "naturality" that doesn't exist.
>
> I've already, in a way, started to respond to your question about deconstruction because one of the gestures of deconstruction is to not naturalize what isn't natural—to not assume that what has been conditioned by history, institutions or society is natural. The very condition of the deconstruction may be at work in the work

> within the system to be deconstructed. It may already be located there already at work, not at the center but in an eccentric center, in a corner whose eccentricity assures the solid concentration of the system participating in the construction of what it, at the same time, threatens to deconstruct.
>
> One might then be inclined to reach this conclusion; deconstruction is not an operation that supervenes afterwards from the outside one fine day. It is always already at work in the work since the disruptive force of deconstruction is always already contained within the very architecture of the work. All what [one] would finally have to do to be able to deconstruct, given this [is] always already, is to do memory work yet since I want neither to accept nor to reject a conclusion formulated in precisely these terms. Let us leave this question suspended for the moment.[31]

Obscurantist postmodern leaders aside, Jordan was particularly incensed by the lack of scholarship that accompanied the establishment of postmodern university programs such as Women's Studies and derivatives such as Gender Studies, LGBTQ Studies and Critical Race Theory. They all seemed to spring from one essay written in 1988 by Peggy McIntosh, a Harvard graduate and senior research associate at the Wellesley Centers for Women entitled "White Privilege and Male Privilege: A Personal Account of Coming to See Correspondences Through Work in Women's Studies."[32] A personal account? Not a peer-reviewed, deeply researched work of impeccable scholarship? No.

Jordan's reaction to this founding document of the postmodern feminist movement reveals his frustration with the deconstructed intelligence of his new colleagues in academia.

> The original paper on white privilege wouldn't have received a passing grade for the hypothesis part of an undergraduate

> honors thesis. Not even close. There's no methodology at all. It was called "White Privilege and Male Privilege: A Personal Account of Coming to See Correspondences Through Work in Women's Studies."
>
> Well, first of all, personal account is, like, sorry, no. She [the author] says these are personal examples of her unearned privilege or unearned privilege that she saw, as she experienced in the 1970s, 1980s. This idea is the opinion of one person who wrote one paper that has absolutely no empirical backing whatsoever, which is a set of hypotheses which has never been subject to any statistical analysis.[33]

Yet, onward the postmodernists and their politically correct multitudes marched until they were literally coming through Jordan's classroom door. In one heated exchange witnessed by undergraduate Gregg Hurwitz, another student challenged the theories of mankind's psychological development as posed in Erich Neumann's book *The Great Mother*, a classic text in the canon of psychology that was being discussed in Jordan's class. The challenge apparently followed a deconstructionist argument that the ideas of "mother" and the feminine goddesses of the past were simply social constructs of the male patriarchy. To which Jordan shot back something remembered as, "If you can posit a better alternative theoretical framework then please do. But tearing down scientific progress without offering a superior solution doesn't get us anywhere."[34]

It seems that Jordan may have been reacting to increasing political heat on Harvard's campus. Harvard history professor Stephan Thernstrom had already been taken down for his similar politically incorrect view of American history.

> I was subject to trial by a newspaper. The PC thought police [were the] editors at The Crimson. During McCarthyism, I didn't see any case of a professor being called before a committee

> because of what he said in class. People got in trouble because of their political involvement in private life . . . It did not affect the daily life of the university.[35]

In reaction to the growing mob mentality, Thernstrom and a few other Harvard professors formed the National Association of Scholars in 1987 that was "devoted to preserving the traditional western curriculum."

Within the association's charter documents they commented on the postmodern programs being rapidly adopted in academia:

> An examination of many women's studies and minority studies courses and programs disclose little study of other cultures, but maintains that too often these fields are put into the curriculum for political, not academic reasons.[36]

The battle lines of the coming Culture War were drawn. But it was more like a culture riot since there was no clear strategy involved on the postmodern side, only an idea—the old Marxist chestnut of oppressors and the oppressed—dusted off for a new generation. But this time instead of abused workers, senior research associate Peggy McIntosh was as certain as a senior research associate could be that it was women, all women, who were and had always been oppressed.

Then in 1989, the year after McIntosh's eureka moment, UCLA professor Kimberlé Crenshaw discovered that not only women, but women and black people were, and had always been, oppressed. Crenshaw discovered intersectionality in her academic paper "Demarginalizing the Intersection of Race and Sex: A Black Feminist Critique of Antidiscrimination Doctrine, Feminist Theory and Antiracist Politics"[37] that claimed black women, as part of two distinct oppressed groups—blacks and women—were doubly oppressed.

Unifying all the new radical theories facing Jordan and traditionalists like him, the following year University of California, Berkeley professor Judith Butler published her book *Gender Trouble: Feminism and the Subversion of Identity*. It became the founding document of the emerging area of scholarship called Queer Theory.

Butler's thesis expanded on the unfounded assumptions of Peggy McIntosh's "White Privilege and Male Privilege," Derrida's nonsensical deconstructionism, and Crenshaw's intersectionality to suggest, against the interests of traditional feminists, that the term *woman* was now simply a subcategory like class, ethnicity, and sexual proclivity. She wrote,

> Further, it is no longer clear that feminist theory ought to try to settle the questions of primary identity in order to get on with the task of politics. Instead, we ought to ask, what political possibilities are the consequence of a radical critique of the categories of identity?[38]

So, the old-fashioned, single identity of "woman" was out, and multiple intersectional identities were in. Butler, a self-identified lesbian, went on to make sure that the connection between sex and gender was completely deconstructed, claiming it was a false distinction under the same theory of intersectionality.

> If one "is" a woman, that is surely not all one is; the term fails to be exhaustive . . . because gender intersects with racial, class, ethnic, sexual, and regional modalities. . . . As a result, it becomes impossible to separate out "gender" from the political and cultural intersections in which it is invariably produced and maintained.[39]

While the motives behind this third-wave feminism were clearly political by the same "peevish and resentful" Marxist types Jordan had identified as a teenager in the NDP, the threat that this sweeping revival posed was as real and as clearly motivated by resentment as any totalitarian movement of the past. He stated his concern with academic dispassion in his nearly completed manuscript of *Gods of War*,

> Degeneration into chaos—decadence—might be considered the constant threat of innovation undertaken in the absence of comprehension and respect for tradition. Such decadence is precisely as dangerous to the stability and adaptability of the community and the individual and as purely motivated by underground wishes and desires (resentment) as is totalitarianism or desire for absolute order.[40]

He would eventually come to refer to this junta of the oppressed in less scholarly terms as an "ill-informed, ignorant and ideologically-addled mob."[41]

That kind of statement would come to be known as a *microaggression* in the thrashed new language of Jordan's multiplying enemies. Among his first skirmishes was one fought in defense of student Gregg Hurwitz's thesis "A Tempest, a Birth, and Death: Freud, Jung, and Shakespeare's *Pericles*" before the assembled Harvard psychology department. The opening salvo was fired by a psychology professor, presumably probing for latent Nazism, who claimed, both off-topic and personally directed at Jordan, "I believe Jung chose the wrong side in World War II." Jordan fired a personal shot right back, "That's an incredibly ignorant statement."

Hurwitz describes what happened next, "And we were off to the races. Then I had to defend my thesis to an angry room!"[42]

No doubt the angry exchange brought Assistant Professor Peterson to the attention of other, more senior antagonists in and around Harvard Yard. Along with his combative stance toward ignorant academics, Jordan was stained with the whiteness of an obvious oppressor, and so became a straight, white, male sitting duck. He arrived at the front lines with only his experience and years of study of Marxist thought that told him these new advocates for oppressed women, blacks, and gay people weren't really interested in the liberation of any of these; they were really only interested in power. And, they didn't really even like women, blacks, or gay people, they just resented straight, white men.

So Jordan, with few colleagues, manned the lonely ramparts of academia. His straight, white, male lectures and microaggressions would not escape collective vengeance for long. The postmodern neo-Marxists were inside the gates, and it was only a matter of time until they came for him.

CHAPTER EIGHT

CHILD'S PLAY

> **Gradually it was disclosed to me that the line separating good and evil passes not through states, nor between classes, nor between political parties either—but right through every human heart—and through all human hearts. This line shifts. Inside us, it oscillates with the years. And even within hearts overwhelmed by evil, one small bridgehead of good is retained. And even in the best of all hearts, there remains . . . an un-uprooted small corner of evil. Since then I have come to understand the truth of all the religions of the world: They struggle with the evil inside a human being. It is impossible to expel evil from the world in its entirety, but it is possible to constrict it within each person.**
>
> **—ALEKSANDR SOLZHENITSYN, *THE GULAG ARCHIPELAGO, VOL. 2***

The Petersons had two couches in their living room that faced each other and formed a kind of gladiator's arena where Jordan would rough-and-tumble play for hours with Mikhaila, three, and Julian, one. It may have been the most fun he would ever have in his four years of teaching at Harvard. It was certainly among the children's favorite activities, of which they never seemed to tire.

Of course, this consuming fun for the children drew their father's tireless curiosity. He saw in their play-fighting a testing of each other's strength, their strategy, and their tolerance for fear and pain. When he played the monster, their delighted shrieks filled the house. When he let them win and defeat him, their confidence skyrocketed, it reset the game to start and renewed their interest. He saw the game as providing important instruction, and he remembered the thrill of discovering Jean Piaget's work on child's play.

Developmental psychologist Piaget discovered in child's play a natural development of morality. From two-year-olds' rough-and-tumble wrestling and tag through seven- and eight-year-olds' playing "house," children learned the rules of society including fair play. They explored levels of the social hierarchy and set the baseline of their morality. Here Jordan had discovered the missing link in his own work. Piaget had uncovered the foundation of human good and evil.

In Piaget's analysis, he identified four stages of childhood development; one, children first discover the world through actions like rough-and-tumble play; two, they then describe things they've discovered with words; three, they begin to think logically about the qualities of these discovered things; and four, they then start using reason to sort out the value of what they logically understand.

Jordan saw the reflection of these four stages of human development in mythological and religious world origination stories such as the Christian story of Genesis. In Genesis, God first acts: "In the beginning God created the heavens and the earth." He then uses words that describe his action, "And God said, 'Let there be light,' and there was light." God then logically recognizes what he's done and assigns it a value: "God saw that the light was good."

This moral progression was also evident in the work of one of Jordan's earliest influences, Carl Jung. Jung had identified archetypal characters who represented facets of morality throughout ancient mythologies. In his book *The Archetypes and The Collective Unconscious,* Jung categorized the basic "personalities" of mythology that populated the human psyche including the great mother, father, child, devil, god, wise old man, wise old woman, the trickster, and the hero. Jung's theory of mankind's basic moral structure was convincing but wasn't scientific proof that a prevalent moral structure actually existed. Piaget then provided the proof that human morality could be observed, measured, and repeatedly generated in child's play. It was Jordan's first glimpse of a solid connection between mythological/religious belief and scientific method. Piaget's work was not only the foundation of good and evil, but also Jordan's missing link.

Decades of investigation into the basis of good and evil had been rewarded. By the time his manuscript called *Gods of War* had developed into the completed book called *Maps of Meaning* toward the end of his time at Harvard, Jordan had fully integrated the works of Jung, Piaget, Freud, Nietzsche, Solzhenitsyn, Dostoevsky, Orwell, Dante, Goethe, Stephen Hawking, Lao Tzu, Konrad Lorenz, brain scientist Alexander Luria, Milton, Voltaire, Wittgenstein, and the Christian Bible into a comprehensive examination of good and evil and the pivotal role that meaning played between them.

Maps of Meaning was meant to be the Rosetta Stone, the Grand Unified Theory, an explanation of how and why evil existed and persisted in the world. Even an indicator toward an antidote to the sense of meaninglessness, or nihilism; his work accounted for the source of so much evil. A boon to mankind, the Golden Fleece was what Jordan had won through horrifying trials, brought back from his hero's journey through hell. He wrote in his conclusion to *Maps of Meaning* entitled "The Divinity of Interest,"

> Who can believe that it is the little choices we make, every day, between good and evil, that turn the world to waste and hope to despair? But it is the case. We see our immense capacity for evil, constantly realized before us, in great things and in small, but can never seem to realize our infinite capacity for good.[1]

She was such a happy little girl. "Happy, happy, happy," she sang to herself while sitting in her safety seat in the car. Jordan was over the moon in love with his daughter Mikhaila, his firstborn, as he watched one of the tenderest moments of his fatherhood bloom and quickly fade forever into memory. Too soon, her quiet little song ended and she looked at him with her devastating half smile that told him she felt safe with him. It was an inexpressible moment of joy that a lucky parent enjoys from time to time while watching the face of their growing child. Then, as the upturned corners of her tiny rosebud lips flattened, the unspoken question intruded, "What's next?" And the moment was gone. Jordan put the key in the ignition and started the engine.

Tammy had been the first to notice the hitch in two-year-old Mikhaila's step that told her something was wrong. Then, when Mikhaila began to cry and sit down after a gentle ride on Jordan or Tammy's shoulders, they realized her hips, along with her ankles, were bothering her. For a time they hoped it was just normal growing pains, but the time for that hope soon passed.

Jordan became extra gentle during their wrestling matches in the gladiator's arena between the two couches, but his concern deepened as Tammy's healing massages failed to relieve any of Mikhaila's increasing pain. Jordan's concern occasionally spiraled down into depression as Mikhaila's symptoms worsened and no cause was found. When this burden was added to his yearly seasonal depression as the days darkened toward December, he sank even further beyond depression into torment.

By 1996, when Mikhaila had turned four, the wear on Jordan's mind was obvious. He knew that both he and Tammy had passed on certain genes that had caused various inflammatory diseases in their daughter. Now inflammation seemed to be taking over her body. She suffered fevers and rashes that came on and disappeared. She was diagnosed with juvenile idiopathic arthritis—idiopathic meaning no one had any idea what was causing it. On certain days her energy flagged until the happy little girl was reduced to a silent, suffering rag doll. The only relief for the Petersons was that two-year-old Julian showed no signs of the illness.

Jordan's pace didn't slacken but his energy was draining faster than he could regenerate it. He was losing sleep, often lying awake most of the night listening for the slightest whimper of pain from Mikhaila's room or scouring his memory for any scrap of Western medical information, Canadian native Cree Indian herbal remedies, or old wives' tales about arthritis. He was overworking late into the night preparing for his daytime courses, rewriting and polishing his manuscript, compiling research with Pihl and new collaborators at Harvard, and reviewing case files of his clinical patients. It was beginning to show. Particularly in midwinter when his depression was at its most ferocious.

> There were times when I was in Boston when I was lecturing especially around January where there were years when I wasn't sure I'd be able to do it because I lecture spontaneously and when my mood goes down I can go way out on an idea limb but I have a hard time coming back. And it takes a lot of confidence to lecture spontaneously as well, and a lot of presence and a lot of energy and all those things would go.[2]

His only defense against depression at this time was watching an electric light that emitted the full spectrum of natural sunlight. He was self-medicating against a recently recognized condition called seasonal affective disorder (SAD) by attempting to replace waning natural sunlight.

In his popular classroom, Jordan read from his spiral-bound manuscript in the last of thirteen lectures based on the work. He read a passage about what one could say to a dying child. His voice wavered from strong to almost inaudible. He stopped occasionally as if to catch his breath. Knowing his readiness with tears, an experienced observer might conclude he was taking a moment to maintain his composure. Only thirty-four years old, he looked young and fit, with long, curly brown hair falling past his collar nearly to his back, but he seemed frail as he frequently rested his head in his hands and read unevenly, perhaps of his waking nightmare at home.

> We blame God, and God's creation, for twisting and perverting our souls, and claim, all the time, to be innocent victims of circumstance. What do you say to a dying child? You say, "You can do it; there is something in you that is strong enough to do it." And you don't use the terrible vulnerability of children as an excuse for the rejection of existence, and the perpetration of conscious evil.[3]

Jordan's research work clearly began to suffer. In an informal survey of research scientists, it is suggested that one to three scientific papers published per year is an acceptable average.[4] The year Jordan arrived at Harvard, 1993, he and Pihl published nine papers together, mostly related to aggression and alcohol with titles including "Alcohol, Serotonin, and Aggression," "Alcohol, Drug Use and Aggressive Behavior," and "Heart-rate Reactivity and Alcohol Consumption among Sons of Male Alcoholics and Sons of Nonalcoholics." The following year, 1994, he produced one. The year he left Harvard in 1998, he produced none.

Among his peak output in 1993 was one paper that broke the trend of his almost exclusively male-oriented research; it was about women. The title was "Anxiety Sensitivity and Risk for Alcohol Abuse in Young Adult Females." It stated an interesting observation in its conclusion: "High anxiety sensitive women show a sober attentional bias favoring the processing of physically threatening information."[5]

This snippet about "anxiety sensitive" women noticing "physically threatening information" was the first faint hint about the motivation of his most aggressive political foes in the emerging culture war. Many politically liberal women would come to see Jordan and his work with traditional religious and mythological archetypes as physically and socially threatening because of its seeming misogynistic and racist implications. This was particularly disheartening because he considered himself the opposite of these opinions. He adored all the women in his life, his mother in particular, including his students who were 80 percent women, his sister, sister-in-law, mother-in-law, wife, and daughter. He had always maintained an "old world" cowboy ethic around women, a genteel deference and respect for them. His growing realization that women, particularly female university professors, were becoming radicalized, postmodern leftists, and therefore ideological enemies, was a heartache and no doubt added to his depression.

He seemed to be entering hell for the second time but instead of descending into the underworld to fight his own few demons, thousands were being ideologically possessed in the daylight world to surround and overwhelm him. In princely revenge, they were going to make an example of him after a slow, fiery siege against his precious Mikhaila weakened him for the final blow.

In 1995, even as the first small cadres of university women were being spun up into a radical movement, Jordan unknowingly was preparing his fortress against the coming slings and arrows. With longtime research partner Robert Pihl, Jordan established Examcorp, a psychological testing company to help employers evaluate and select the best employees.

He'd been working with Pihl on Examcorp's primary tool called Self-Authoring since their earliest research work together at McGill. Self-Authoring was designed to help people improve themselves by identifying a small number of their virtues or faults so they could focus on improving the virtues and correcting the faults. Early tests on eighty-five McGill undergraduates who were struggling academically found that after completing Self-Authoring the students' collective grade point average rose by 29 percent in a single semester. Jordan and Pihl also developed the Understand Myself report, a survey of personality traits designed to help people understand the general structure of their personality and precisely how they compared to others. Again, this was a diagnostic tool to help people decrease their suffering and improve their lives. Both tools were adapted to the internet very early in the web's development and were priced under twenty dollars each for wide usage among everyday people.

Both tools were developed from a fundamental research standard called The Big Five that categorizes five broad personality traits that each have two aspects. It is also called the Five-Factor Model, or FFM, in professional circles and includes the five traits of Openness to Experience, made up of the aspects Openness/Creativity and Intellect; Conscientiousness, made up of the aspects Orderliness and Industriousness; Extraversion and Introversion, made up of the aspects Enthusiasm and Assertiveness; Agreeableness, made up of the aspects Politeness and Compassion; and Neuroticism, made up of the aspects Withdrawal and Volatility.

Around the time Examcorp was established, an unexpected ally appeared named Xiaowen Xu, a female graduate student in psychology at the University of Toronto.

Xiaowen contacted Jordan and proposed a research project to determine the personality traits that might predict whether a person would be a political liberal or conservative. Xiaowen's project would eventually involve five authors, including Jordan, and be titled "Compassionate Liberals and Polite Conservatives: Associations of Agreeableness with Political Ideology and Moral Values." The summary or *abstract* of this research would include the statement,

> In two studies, using a personality model that divides each of the Big Five [personality traits] into two aspects, the present research found that one aspect of Agreeableness (Compassion) was associated with liberalism and egalitarianism, whereas the other (Politeness) was associated with conservatism and traditionalism. In addition, conservatism and moral traditionalism were positively associated with the Orderliness aspect of Conscientiousness and negatively with Openness-Intellect. These findings contribute to a more nuanced understanding of personality's relation to political attitudes and values.[6]

This study revealed that a dominant personality trait of agreeableness was most likely to predict a political liberal. Coincidentally, the dominance of agreeableness in a person was also most likely to predict that that person was female. And so another outline was being added to the sketch of who would soon be attacking Jordan as a dangerous conservative, misogynist, transphobe, homophobe, and white supremacist.

Jordan and Xiaowen would go on to put a finer point on political orientation with their paper "Does Cultural Exposure Partially Explain the Association Between Personality and Political Orientation?" that concluded in its summary, "Exposure to culture, and a corollary of this exposure in the form of acquiring knowledge, can therefore partially explain the associations between personality and political orientation."[7]

In layman's terms, culture, including movies, newspapers, television, and the internet all influence a person's political views. Jordan seemed to be well ahead of this particular research. He had been video recording his lectures since 1992 at McGill and was among the first to begin posting his work on the internet. He had already seen the world far beyond the confines of academia and imagined the influence the internet would have on it. The growing legions of his enemies were also coming online.

His work at Harvard, particularly his classroom lectures, were gaining wide popularity. His manuscript, *Gods of War*, the textbook for the lectures, was going to be published under the title *Maps of Meaning* by Routledge, the publisher of Albert Einstein, Bertrand Russell, and Carl Jung. This was the pinnacle of achievement in many academic circles. He was now in the company of the immortals of his field. His elevation from assistant professor to a full professor with tenure at Harvard seemed assured.

But his internal battle with depression had steadily chipped away at his self-confidence until recently and unknown to the outside world, the despair had fractured his will entirely. From the outside, it was hard to imagine a more deserving candidate for tenure, but something, or someone, if you believe in such things, had a psychic stranglehold on him. In the dark recesses of his mind, a vengeful hand was suffocating him. He was panicking. When it came time to apply for tenure, he had no strength left. He later spoke of this time,

> I have periods of depression and unfortunately at the time when I should have been prepared to engage in that battle, I didn't have the presence of mind, let's say, and the clarity of mind necessary to make the case properly, and I've regretted that.[8]

And so it appeared that the first battle of Jordan's part of the culture war was a defeat. He would not ascend to the heights of academia as a tenured professor at Harvard. He would not join Harvard's professors in the National Association of Scholars. He would not man his position on the front line. Depression had gotten the better of him. He would instead retreat to Canada behind the fortress walls of the University of Toronto and move his family farther away from the increasing incoming fire.

By the time he and Tammy had decided to pack up the family for the move to Toronto in 1998, Jordan had been awarded the prestigious Joseph R. Levenson Teaching Prize by Harvard. This prize for excellence in undergraduate teaching was awarded annually to one senior faculty member, one junior faculty member (that would be Jordan), and one teaching fellow. Harvard undergraduates nominated their choices to the undergraduate council. Finalists were selected in each category and the winner was announced at a dinner attended by the finalists, nominators, undergraduate council members, and representatives of the Levenson family.

Perhaps this, rather than full professorship and tenure, was the most fitting achievement for Jordan at Harvard. The honor tacitly acknowledged his years of extraordinary work exploring the human mind and the implications for society, and explicitly confirmed his extraordinary veneration among students, mostly young women, who had taken his classes.

Female graduate student Shelley Carson recalled that Jordan had, "something akin to a cult following. Taking a course from him was like taking psychedelic drugs without the drugs. I remember students crying on the last day of class because they wouldn't get to hear him anymore."

Months earlier, Jordan had applied to the University of Toronto for the position of assistant professor of psychology. In the early spring of 1998, he arrived on campus for his interview and luckily first met with professor Bernard Schiff, a member of the department of psychology's search committee. Schiff was instantly impressed with Jordan's energy and quick mind. They fell into a spirited conversation that wandered into areas of research they were interested in pursuing. Unfortunately, none were of mutual interest. This was very likely because Jordan had clearly deviated from his early work with Pihl on alcohol and aggression. Although still a practicing psychologist, his research was now generally concerned with psychometrics, measurements of the human psyche. Even with this difference of interests, a fast friendship was formed, and Jordan gained a powerful ally.

Schiff ushered him before the committee who reviewed Jordan's outstanding experience including stellar references, his PhD from McGill, and five-year spotless record at Harvard including his Levenson Teaching Award. But in private review, the committee was skeptical and felt Jordan was too "eccentric." Obviously he had spun off onto tangents from psychology into social science and philosophy. In his *Maps of Meaning* manuscript, he even seemed to be favoring the tenets of Christianity that were sure to be controversial. Schiff defended Jordan in spite of the committee's objections:

> I pushed for him because he was a divergent thinker, self-educated in the humanities, intellectually flamboyant, bold, energetic and confident, bordering on arrogant. I thought he would bring a new excitement, along with new ideas, to our department.[9]

Schiff prevailed and Jordan was hired. The two men developed a closer friendship, Schiff assuming the role of protective mentor.

Shortly after the family arrived in Toronto, Mikhaila was diagnosed with juvenile rheumatoid (rather than idiopathic) arthritis. Internally, her entire body seemed to be in flames. She was put under general anesthesia to avoid the excruciating pain of injecting forty joint sites with anti-inflammatory cortisone. This was only a temporary measure; soon her internal fires returned and spread.

In a desperate effort, she became the first child in Canada to take the biological drug Enbrel and then the combination of Enbrel and methotrexate naproxen. The actual common side effects included, ironically, joint pain. Other common side effects included bloody vomit, diarrhea, reddening of the skin, sores in the mouth or lips, stomach pain, and swelling of the feet or lower legs.

Also, after four years of increasing torment, her mind began to stagger under the weight of undeserved punishments. She developed a fear of the dark and would hallucinate terrifying faces staring at her from the darkness of her room. She began to fear that people would break in at night and kill her entire family, leaving her alone.

The Peterson family curse of depression was now added to the once happy little girl's misery. She was now fully submerged in one of the deepest parts of her father's personal hell.

As Jordan frantically attended to Mikhaila, prepared for the fall semester, and also attempted to rehabilitate an older house that they had bought, he began to neglect his own mental health, recalling, "We also bought a wreck of a house . . . the day before she was diagnosed and I spent six months running around trying to get Mikhaila sorted out and fixing up this house *and* not watching my [therapeutic] light."[10]

Schiff came to the family's rescue, offering to take them in while Jordan sweated through heat and dust of late summer making his dilapidated house livable.

> For five months, they occupied the third floor of our large house. We had meals together in the evening and long, colourful conversations. There, away from campus, I saw a man who was devoted to his wife and his children, who were lovely and gentle and for whom I still feel affection. He was attentive and thoughtful, stern and kind, playful and warm. His wife, Tammy, appeared to be the keel, the ballast and the rudder, and Jordan ran the ship. I could not imagine him without her.[11]

In spite of Schiff's support, it seems that this particular Christmas of 1998 was a time of impending chaos.

> And that Christmas I was . . . it was not good. I thought that I was . . . it was unlikely that I would be able to go back and lecture. So that's when I first tried antidepressants.[12]

Jordan teetered at the edge of the abyss. He nearly succumbed to the seasonal depression that had ended his father's career as a teacher almost twenty years earlier. A later student gives an approximate idea of what sitting through a Jordan Peterson lecture at this time might have been like:

> If he sticks to the subject matter he seems to know his stuff but then he enters into flights of weird speculation that he is passionate about but doesn't seem to be course relevant. Imagine a hyperactive teen who just got a library card and needs to share some random thought about each book he has read in an angst ridden stream of consciousness.[13]

A trace of light broke through the Peterson home that year, just after the sun began to go south for the winter. An advance publication review in *Harvard Magazine* indicated *Maps of Meaning* might be successful, writing, "*Maps of Meaning,* which took 13 years to write and which

Routledge will publish next spring, is a grand, sprawling, ambitious undertaking, an intellectual adventure that aims to synthesize disparate knowledge in the classic, old-fashioned tradition of social science."[14]

With medication lifting his depression enough to allow his teaching to continue, he also published three scientific papers that year, and for the first time, he was the only author. One was called "Neuropsychology and Mythology of Motivation for Group Aggression" which began with a disturbing passage from Solzhenitsyn's *The Gulag Archipelago*,

> A. B v has told how executions were carried out at Adak—a camp on the Pechora River. They would take the opposition members "with their things" out of the camp compound on a prisoner transport at night. And outside the compound stood the small house of the Third Section. The condemned men were taken into a room one at a time, and there the camp guards sprang on them. Their mouths were stuffed with something soft and their arms were bound with cords behind their backs.
>
> Then they were led out into the courtyard, where harnessed carts were waiting. The bound prisoners were piled on the carts, from five to seven at a time, and driven off to the "Gorka"—the camp cemetery. On arrival they were tipped into big pits that had already been prepared and buried alive. Not out of brutality, no. It had been ascertained that when dragging and lifting them, it was much easier to cope with living people than with corpses.[15]

Jordan described the thesis of his paper with this opening sentence,

> The individual is fundamentally territorial and, furthermore, is a creature capable of endless abstraction. Deep understanding of these two characteristics immensely furthers comprehension of the human capacity for the commission of atrocity in the service of belief.[16]

Still in the healing process, he continued to relentlessly pursue the answers to the problem of evil. He seemed more committed than ever to exposing every dark corner of the human mind and soul—eerily like he was waging a personal vendetta. At some level he must have known he was playing with fire.

In his own life, he had faced the abyss and once again fought the chaos that threatened to consume him and his family to a draw. Mikhaila was stabilized but still a very sick little girl, his modest row house in Toronto was a habitable wreck, and his career was again tolerable as his wounded mind limped back toward composure.

Maps of Meaning: The Architecture of Belief was published on March 26, 1999, weighing in at 564 pages. Jordan had poured his heart and everything he had learned in his scientific research for the past fifteen years into the book. So, like the author himself, it was an eclectic mixture of soaring, empathetic philosophy grounded in concrete science. *The Chronicle of Higher Education* described the book in a later interview with Jordan as,

> It was not the sort of book that a psychological researcher following the well-trod path to academic success would take on. It does not zero in on a phenomenon or stake out unclaimed ground in a subfield. Instead the book is a sweeping attempt at making sense of man's inhumanity to man, the purpose of existence, and the significance of the divine.[17]

The chairman of the psychology department at Harvard at the time, Sheldon White, was impressed, calling it a " brilliant enlargement of our understanding of human motivation."

In the *Montreal Gazette,* religion columnist Harvey Shepherd wrote,

> To me, the book reflects its author's profound moral sense and vast erudition in areas ranging from clinical psychology to scripture and a good deal of personal soul searching. . . .

> Peterson's vision is both fully informed by current scientific and pragmatic methods, and in important ways deeply conservative and traditional.[18]

Yet financially, the book was a flop, selling less than five hundred hardcover copies. It could not be easily categorized as either philosophy or social science and so failed as both. Jordan later commented, "I don't think people had any idea what to make of the book, and I still think they don't. No one has attempted to critique it seriously."[19]

He entered the imposing gothic towers of the University of Toronto with his masterwork a failure, his home a barely habitable construction site, and his Mikhaila seriously ill and now showing signs of obsessive compulsive disorder as well as depression. His guardian across the threshold of the university, Professor Bernard Schiff, his mentor, host, and close friend, would eventually betray him in the battles to come saying,

> He has played havoc with the truth. He has studied demagogues and authoritarians and understands the power of their methods. Fear and danger were their fertile soil. He frightens by invoking murderous bogeymen on the left and warning they are out to destroy the social order, which will bring chaos and destruction. . . . In retrospect, I might have seen this coming. I didn't.[20]

CHAPTER NINE

ORDER AND CHAOS

The pale-fac'd moon looks bloody on the earth,
And lean-look'd prophets whisper fearful change:
Rich men look sad, and ruffians dance and leap,
The one in fear to lose what they enjoy,
The other to enjoy by rage and war.

—WILLIAM SHAKESPEARE, *RICHARD II*

It was obvious by now that Jordan was being surrounded by a hostile collection of postmodern neo-Marxists, each advancing a specific ideology with a specific line of attack. In a nod to his growing use of Christian ideas such as demonic possession to describe the world, he devised the catch-all term *ideological possession* to describe the mental state of many of his multiplying antagonists. He saw ideological possession in the fierce and often illogical arguments that had begun to be lobbed at him both inside and outside his classrooms. In the emotional pleadings for their rights to a sustainable environment, organic food, the rights of animals, or aggrieved people, these advocates for the oppressed seemed somewhat impervious to logic and resistant to reason. All that apparently mattered were their emotions often stoked by prevalent disinformation, paid instigators, or flash mobs, both online and offline. Some sacrificed their individual ability to think critically and instead embraced the historical, collective ideology of Marxism. They indicated this often consuming collective identity by adopting the title of social justice warrior, or SJW.

Jordan had spent his life studying the causes and results of ideological possession, starting with the ideological possession that brought the world to the brink of nuclear war. He suffered its effects firsthand in witnessing the slow mental unraveling and eventual suicide of his early childhood friend Chris, ideologically possessed by his own brand of nihilism, and by the suffering of his landlord Denis, ideologically possessed by the violent code of the Hell's Angels.

In *Maps of Meaning*, Jordan wrote extensively on what he had learned about ideological possession, its representation in world mythologies and its concrete effects throughout recorded history.

> The individual who denies his individual identification with the heroic (the striving toward a deep, personal meaning in life as a flawed individual in an unjust world) will come to identify with and serve the tyrannical force of the past—and to suffer the consequences. This principle is aptly illustrated by the mythic story of Judas. Judas sacrifices Christ, the hero, to the authorities of tradition—for all the best reasons—and is then driven to destroy himself in despair:
>
> "Then Judas, which had betrayed him, when he saw that he was condemned, repented himself, and brought again the thirty pieces of silver to the chief priests and elders, saying, I have sinned in that I have betrayed the innocent blood. And they said, What is that to us? See thou to that. And he cast down the pieces of silver in the temple, and departed, and went and hanged himself." (Matthew 27:3–5)[1]

Over the weekend of April 7–9, 2000, Common Struggle, an anarchist communist organization was officially convened in Boston, Massachusetts. At this meeting were anarchist and communist individuals including former Atlantic Anarchist Circle affiliates and organizations including Love and Rage, a federation of anarchist groups promoting the popular new white privilege doctrine and *Demanarchie,* an anarchist newspaper collective from Quebec City, Quebec. They agreed to coordinate efforts in support of Common Struggle.

With their new collective of supporters, Common Struggle quickly established branches internationally including one in Toronto. They further coordinated with the local TAO Collective (The Anarchy Organization), founded in Toronto, that had been actively opposing the ruling classes and their hierarchical society since 1994. TAO Communications provided communication and logistics during anarchist demonstrations and reported on police activities. Jordan's home was now on the front line of the coming progressive assaults and maneuvers.

Exactly one month after the Marxist/anarchist Common Struggle meeting in Toronto, Vladimir Putin was inaugurated as president of Russia. Putin embodied the totalitarian impulses refined by eighty-two years of Russian Marxist dictatorship. He was the progressive movement's largest sponsor, proudly leading the way for thousands of Common Struggles, Occupy Wall Streets, and other anti-Western movements around the world. With Putin's election, the era of Soviet Marxist propaganda officially ended, and modern Russia's global information war for power began.

Jordan and others who were paying attention recognized Putin's new propaganda as just shined-up old hammers and resharpened sickles. Jordan heard the totalitarian's creed coming from the mouths of his students in phrases like *social justice.* He noted it in university administrative meetings calling for *collective action.*

True to form, Putin's first act was to seize NTV, an independent news channel. He discarded its investigative reporting in favor of news promoting Russian interests. Jill Dougherty, former Moscow Bureau Chief for CNN, would write, "Moscow's mission, as he [Putin] told journalists from RT, Russia's global broadcasting arm, is to break the 'Anglo-Saxon monopoly on global information streams.'"[2]

Clearly, ex-KGB officer Putin intended to pursue the old Soviet "disinformation" or "direct action" psychological warfare campaigns with new tools including the internet. He had an entirely new generation of "useful idiots" online, literally at his fingertips. His purpose in this new information war was the same as the old Marxist Cold War—the corruption and eventual domination of the West. With new energy and abundant cash, Putin was updating aggressive totalitarian techniques for a new, morally weakened Western generation, such as Jordan's students.

But the Russian leader was suddenly besieged. The Americans had mastered the technique of horizontal drilling. When combined with the well-established technique of hydraulic fracturing, or *fracking,* that had been used safely for both oil and water wells for over 130 years, it became a direct threat to Russia's main source of cash: petroleum production. Here was the first test of Putin's new propaganda machine.

With a war chest close to $1 billion a year,[3] Russia's information war against fracking was launched with the help of generational connections in the Democratic Party, dimly lit Hollywood luminaries, Western academia, and legions of usefully idiotic grandchildren of the Woodstock generation.

Thousands of articles, videos, and several full-length documentary films were produced showing the devastating health and environment effects of fracking. The campaign spurred a wide-ranging coalition of anarchists, eco-radicals, radical feminists, "queer" revolutionaries, Maoists, Stalinists, and progressives, similar to the 1960s communist-encouraged antiwar movement. These neo-Marxists, as Jordan called them, or neocommunists, as 1960s radical-to-conservative convert David Horowitz called them, were ideologically identical to the 1960s radical activists throughout the West. Horowitz describes the connection between the two:

> [Neocommunists] may or may not reject the Leninist idea of a vanguard party; they may depart from particular aspects of the Communist future like the "dictatorship of the proletariat" or

> the "central plan." But they are inspired by the same hostility to private property and the market economy, and to the corporate structures that produce society's wealth. It is this common enemy, capitalism, which unites them in the battles they join whether against the structures of "globalization" or the war on terror.[4]

Unfortunately for this fractious anti-fracking coalition, their laudable efforts for the environment and human health were doomed by their Marxist anti-capitalism and the provably false propaganda of their Russian patrons who were now, ironically, the most aggressive capitalists in the world.

Jordan published four scientific papers in 2000 that indicated his move from the study of alcohol and aggression into the more primal aspects of existence. The first part of his abstract on his solo authored paper *Maps of Meaning: The Architecture of Belief* (précis) for the journal *Psycoloquy* reflects this new direction,

> It is not clear either that the categories "given" to us by our senses, or those abstracted out for us by the processes of scientific investigation, constitute the most "real" or even the most "useful" modes of apprehending the fundamental nature of being or experience. It appears, instead, that the categories offered by traditional myths and religious systems might play that role, despite the initial unpalatability of such a suggestion.
>
> Such systems of apprehension present the world as a place of constant moral striving, conducted against a background of interplay between the "divine forces" of order and chaos (Peterson, 1999a).[5]

There was certainly interplay between order and chaos in his own life and in the world at large that he doubtless reflected on. The recent chaotic rise of neo-Marxism in the West and the maintenance of iron-fisted order by communists in the East showed this yin and yang interplay in geopolitics, an area of lifelong interest to Jordan.

The previous year in May 1999, just after Jordan's *Maps of Meaning* was published, the Chinese communists celebrated the fiftieth anniversary of the establishment of the People's Republic of China with the traditional, precision-orderly military parade in Tiananmen Square. They were demonstrating their orderly control of the country to the world and to the one million Chinese who had disrupted the previous fortieth anniversary by gathering in the square and erecting a papier-mâché statue they called Goddess of Democracy. The chaos of that moment was short-lived. Roughly a thousand people were shot and killed, their statue was torn apart, and order was reestablished. According to Jordan's thesis, the only reality that remained was the mythic reality of a lone individual standing defiantly in front of an advancing tank, offering his life to the mythic Goddess of Democracy.

Five months later, the new order of democracy was welcomed in the West after the chaotic collapse of the Berlin Wall. In regard to this, the recent chancellor of West Germany, Willy Brandt, also attested to Jordan's idea of a more durable mythic reality, saying, "Walls in people's heads are sometimes more durable than walls made of concrete blocks."

Continuing his investigation into the "most real" realities, Jordan followed Jung's trail into the reality of dreams and metaphor as compared to waking life with his next paper, "Metaphoric Threat is More Real than Real Threat." The abstract begins,

> Dreams represent threat, but appear to do so metaphorically more often than realistically. The metaphoric representation of threat allows it to be conceptualized in a manner that is constant across situations (as what is common to all threats begins to be understood and portrayed).[6]

He goes even further into the nature of reality and existence with his paper published by *Behavioral and Brain Science* called "Awareness May Be Existence as Well as (Higher-order) Thought" that might be summarized in a portion of the abstract that reads, "Consciousness plays a fundamental unrecognized ontological (the metaphysics of being) role, as well, conferring the status of 'discriminable object' on select aspects of otherwise indeterminate 'being.'"[7]

To paraphrase, consciousness is a fundamental but not completely understood part of existence. It is the part of existence that recognizes things that are outside of a person and things that are inside or part of a person. It is part of being self-aware, but is more than just being self-aware. What else consciousness contains, we're not completely sure about.

Unhappily, this research received about the same reception as his book, gathering a total of 10 citations between all three papers, as compared to his fourth paper that year with one of his graduate students from Harvard, Shelly Carson, that addressed the more orderly scientific subject of "Latent Inhibition and Openness to Experience in a High-Achieving Student Population." That paper got 151 citations, i.e., mentions in other publications.

Clearly, he was now committed to an area of study that had widespread "initial unpalatability" as he acknowledged in his abstract of *Maps of Meaning: The Architecture of Belief* (précis), but that didn't seem to slow him down or diminish his enthusiasm. His lectures on the subject continued to enthrall students and attract friends such as television producer Wodek Szemberg of Ontario educational television, TVOntario, or TVO.

Szemberg contacted Jordan and after reviewing his presciently videotaped classroom lectures, agreed to produce thirteen *Maps of Meaning* lectures for Canadian audiences. The two-hour lectures were edited down to thirty minutes each. Szemberg's series attracted the attention of other TVO producers including producers of *The Agenda,* an interview show exploring current world affairs.

Because of his verbal skills, his grasp of twentieth-century political history, and unique perspective on current affairs, Jordan was soon a frequent guest on this show. On one show or another, he was suddenly a rising television star speaking primarily to Canadians, but also to scattered audiences in Europe and America, often appearing several times a week. He was quickly becoming a telegenic and admired public figure outside of the University of Toronto as well as an admired professor on the university campus.

This was not a happy occurrence for some people. Jordan was also being watched with growing jealousy and alarm by those outraged by his open hostility to Marxism, and others outraged about his frequent references to Christianity that seemed to disparage feminism, gay rights, and the entire University of Toronto humanities department in general. He was drawing unhelpful attention from fellow professors, radical students, and administrators who saw him as a threat in their midst. Even his most ardent supporter at the time, Bernard Schiff, who made sure Jordan received his promotion to associate professor and then went on to make sure he got a raise after the psychology department chairperson refused to consider it, eventually denounced Jordan's "murderous" view of Marxism writing,

> Calling Marxism, a respectable political and philosophical tradition, "murderous" conflates it with the perversion of those ideas in Stalinist Russia and elsewhere where they were. That is like calling Christianity a murderous ideology because of the blood that was shed in its name during the Inquisition, the Crusades and the great wars of Europe. That is ridiculous.[8]

Schiff's worldview of Christianity and Marxism as roughly equivalent (two hundred thousand deaths during the Crusades versus two hundred million under Marxist regimes, and zero Christian genocides versus ten Marxist genocides)[9] was revealing of how intimately surrounded Jordan was by opposing worldviews that eventually turned into antagonism.

It seems certain that Jordan would have sensed his environment becoming more hostile by the day as he became more publicly prominent. And with the winter of 2001 now whistling around his front door, his depression was becoming unbearable. Apparently staring at his full spectrum light was no longer as effective, perhaps adding a ripple of panic to his depression. At thirty-nine, Jordan was nearly the same age as his father when depression suddenly spiked and caused Wally Peterson to end his own teaching career and resign his position as chief of the local fire company. It had been a devastating blow to young Jordan and now, over twenty-five years later, he no doubt recognized history repeating itself.

He sought medical help and was prescribed selective serotonin reuptake inhibitors (SSRIs). Jordan described the profound effect this had on him:

> [Before medication] it was hard to move so it'd be like moving through molasses. That's annoying, that's called psychomotor slowing. . . . if that goes [on] for a couple of days I'm in real trouble.
>
> When I took this antidepressant first it was . . . it was . . . it was an indescribable relief. I mean, what happened was, it kind of knocked me onto the couch for about three days and I could feel muscles in my body relax. . . . It was such a relief. I could feel muscles in my body relax that probably hadn't relaxed for fifteen years . . . when your serotonin levels go up then your musculature can relax. You know, they'll [be] tensed up and ready for the worst and being like that, for like ten years, is no joke. So when I took the serotonin reuptake inhibitor, I thought I will never stop taking this, ever.[10]

He would certainly need it. Nine-year-old Mikhaila's physical and mental conditions continued to deteriorate all through that winter. Within months, her obsessive compulsive behavior and depression became so severe that the as-yet-untested use of SSRIs on children was recommended. Antidepressants were added to her medication list that also included Enbrel, naproxen, and pain medications. Soon after she began taking this new configuration of powerful medications, her energy almost completely drained away. She became so physically tired, unlike her young classmates who were bouncing with energy, that she wouldn't be able to get out of bed in the morning. This trend continued until she was sleeping up to seventeen hours a day. At that point, she was diagnosed with chronic fatigue, and stimulants were added to her growing list of medications.

She accepted at this point that her depression would be a life sentence considering the history of it on her father's side of the family going back to her great-grandfather. She suggested in a later television interview the severity of her family's type of depression, "Yeah, I really don't know how . . . I'm on antidepressants now and I don't know how anybody in my family would have really survived without them."

At that same later television interview, Jordan echoed her concerns and described his own increased medication for depression,

> The depression in our family happens to be extremely severe and sometimes that requires the use of more than one medication, and so I take serotonin reuptake inhibitor which is SSRIs . . . and I also take a drug called Wellbutrin . . . its primary purpose is to increase positive emotion rather than decreasing negative emotion.[11]

He certainly needed a boost back in 2002 when Mikhaila began taking experimental SSRIs for the first time. It must have been particularly worrying since they were combined with Mikhaila's powerful anti-inflammatory drug. It is hard to imagine that anyone was sleeping well in the Peterson house as little Mikhaila appeared to be inexorably spiraling down.

When studies of SSRIs on children were completed two years later, they only increased the stress in the Peterson home. The US Food and Drug Administration report said,

> On children with major depressive disorder [the study] found statistically significant increases of the risks of "possible suicidal ideation and suicidal behavior" by about 80%, and of agitation and hostility by about 130%.[12]

So even as Jordan's career was diversifying and steadily becoming more stable and orderly with his proficiency on television, the growth of Examcorp, increasing recognition in publishing, and success in academia, his home life was descending into a terrifying medical chaos.

CHAPTER TEN

THE DEVOURING MOTHER

For Neumann, and for Jung, consciousness—always symbolically masculine, even in women—struggles upwards toward the light. Its development is painful and anxiety-provoking, as it carries with it the realization of vulnerability and death. It is constantly tempted to sink back down into dependency and unconsciousness, and to shed its existential burden. It is aided in that pathological desire by anything that opposes enlightenment, articulation, rationality, self-determination, strength and competence—by anything that shelters too much, and therefore smothers and devours. Such overprotection is Freud's Oedipal familial nightmare, which we are rapidly transforming into social policy.

—JORDAN PETERSON, *12 RULES FOR LIFE: AN ANTIDOTE TO CHAOS*

Radical feminists had been teaching Women's Studies at the University of Toronto since 1971. At that time, Jill Ker Conway and Natalie Zemon Davis offered the first class in Women's Studies called HIS 348H: The History of Women. Conway, a Harvard graduate, in 1969 said about herself, "I was a good historian, but I couldn't pretend I was going to be Marx or Hegel, someone whose interpretation of history changed the way the world thought."[1]

Appropriately then for Conway, she became part of a teaching collective on the UT campus concerned with the postmodernist perspective that saw the world as divided between oppressed women and oppressive men. Other factions such as race, culture, gender identity, and disability would soon be discovered and added to the curricula of social division.

Apparently radicals of the 1960s, like Conway, had decided to take control of the children, particularly the girls, and lead them into the ahistorical, classless future of equality. This became the stated mission, supplanting traditional, biological motherhood, of many radical feminists throughout secondary and higher education. They would tear down the old, oppressive patriarchy for the new world of equal opportunity, employment, speech, dress, and eventually even biology. To scholars of this phenomena, like Jordan, this was a historical nightmare repeating itself. The posters of Soviet inspirational art he'd begun to collect were full of muscular, working-class women standing shoulder to shoulder with muscular working-class men depicted as nearly sexless comrades staring separately and triumphantly toward the future, fists raised in solidarity. As in all Marxist cultures, the children, the young pioneers of a new age, needed to be closely controlled and properly educated. And starting in the 1970s in the Western world, they were.

Conway elaborated on her personal perspective in educating young women but avoided using any recognizable Marxist or postmodern terms. This obscuring "thrashing of the language," as feminist Camille Paglia suggested, was the same linguistic dodge used since the 1960s to make radical concepts seem more acceptable.

Conway intended to teach young women, dismissing young men almost entirely. She wanted young woman to avoid falling into the social norm of marriage (*paired couples*) and instead to pursue social justice (*the civic virtues*) in capitalist (*commercial*) societies:

> It seemed to me that the cozily domestic, introduced too early in youthful development, had the effect of obliterating or muting civic and social responsibility. My nineteenth-century feminist theorists about social evolution had all worried about where and how commercial societies could instill social val-

> ues that went beyond personal satisfaction and self-interest. I agreed with them that the development of the civic virtues tended to be slighted in exclusively commercial societies, and that leadership and the talent for action came from an education which did not take the paired couple as its social norm.[2]

But when professor Jordan Peterson arrived at the University of Toronto, thirty years into the reign of the postmodernists, he was one of the few people to openly oppose what he considered to be Conway's unfounded curriculum and dangerous worldview. Conway had by then moved on to become president of Smith College in Massachusetts, but the concept she shared with other radicals of an overwhelming, oppressive patriarchy was well established. It was only a matter of time before his outspoken criticisms of Women's, Gender, and Race Studies and his increasing public profile touched off an intramural war at UT and brought the global culture war home. It didn't help his case that he often ridiculed his antagonists:

> It's so comical watching the feminist postmodernists, in particular, rattle on about the absence of gender reality and act out the archetypal devouring mother at exactly the same time. For them the world is divided into predators and infants and the predators are evil and need to be stopped, and the infants need to be cared for.[3]

To Jordan, postmodern radical feminism was not only an attack on him, it was an attack on vital concepts like capitalism, marriage, and the remarkable advances of civil rights underlying Western civilization. It was particularly poisonous to the fundamental Western concept of the sovereign individual that always drew Jordan's ire:

> In the postmodernist world there are no sovereign individuals. That's a Judeo-Christian, oppressive, Western, patriarchal, arbitrary presupposition. It's your group identity that's primary

> and paramount. You don't have ideas and thoughts, you have what you've been socially conditioned to believe, and the exchange of ideas is nothing but a power game that's played between groups of people who are opposing each other for predominance on the world stage. That's it.[4]

Rejection of individual sovereignty was really the end of the world as Jordan knew it. Because it was the foundation of all Western law; the entire canon of Western civilization would collapse if it was dismissed. But that was exactly what was happening.

Mythologically, these overbearing postmodern educators were also a twentieth-century reincarnation of Jung's archetypal Devouring Mother, represented in the East by the fearsome Hindu goddess Kali, and in the West by Freud's Oedipal Mother.

According to Jung, this is an all-powerful dominating mother who clings desperately to her children during childhood, controls them completely through adulthood, and insists on defending them, even against their wishes, as adults. In the process, she devours every scrap of personal strength and individual initiative, and prevents her children from developing the ability to even defend themselves. She ends up killing them, either by making them too weak to survive, or by devouring them herself if they disobey. It is the witch in Hansel and Gretel who invites the infantile children into her safe gingerbread house to fatten them up for the oven. It is the quite grim fairy tale of the goddess Kali in the East as told by Paramahansa Yogananda, a respected teacher of Western audiences:

> Kali stands naked. Her right foot is placed on the chest of her prostrate husband. Her hair streams out, disheveled, behind Her. A garland of human heads adorns her neck. In one of four hands she brandishes a [bloody] sword; in another, a severed head. Her tongue, usually painted a bright red, lolls out as though in blood-lust.[5]

Challengers in the modern world, like Jordan, who could see Conway's obscured motives clearly, were destined to become another severed head on Kali's necklace. He was the snake in Conway's walled garden of Eden for young women. This archetypal behavior was likely not intentional or even conscious to Conway. Like all Devouring Mothers she was doing everything for the children. That was the authentic impulse, certainly. But her conscious goal was to destroy the oppressive patriarchy and so, she must have known her efforts were all about power.

Jordan clarified how Devouring Mothers actually operated in current Western society,

> The devouring mother archetype is one that can be described as a woman who selfishly loves her children, "protecting" them from the real world to such an extent that they become permanent infants—incompetent wards of the mother for life. She is only loving when her children do what she wants, and she is hateful, cruel, and even homicidal when they don't.
>
> She is the various so-called civil rights movements that seek to suppress free speech in the name of political correctness. And she is the unacknowledged social policy that implores parents to lie to their children in an effort to "keep them safe" all while robbing them of the very life experience they need to face the world with wisdom.[6]

Modern Devouring Mothers, such as university professors and administrators acting in loco parentis, would soon provide safe spaces, trigger warnings, speech codes, banishment of controversial speakers, and free coloring books, milk, and cookies for young adults who had been offended or might feel unsafe with opposing points of view or microaggressions on campus. These same young adults would also be encouraged to skip classes and engage in emotional direct action demonstrations for the rights of the oppressed.

Of course, if they challenged the wisdom or motives involved, they were punished with lesser grades, possibly even banishment, forfeiting tens or hundreds of thousands of dollars paid toward a degree that was promised to provide them with the key to wealth for life.

This was a complete and convincing fairy tale, often lived inside the ivy-covered walls of replicas of medieval castles. They, the *children,* were fed, attentively cared for, and adopted into an academic family that stretched back generations. They were clothed with the venerable family crests of the University of Toronto, Yale, Dartmouth, and Harvard. They were given champions, warriors in shining helmets, to cheer for on fields of contest. But, like all fairy tales, a dark secret lie in wait, hidden by an enchanting dream.

The promised power to control their lives was being drained day by day. They were being educated with a road map to a life that in no way matched the world outside the fortified walls. Some realized this and rebelled. They were punished. But for most who continued to believe, they were inescapably trapped inside the castle walls, eventually isolated on their cell phones, and the tragic results soon became obvious.

The bloody goddess Kali began calling on families around the world. In the years between 2000 and 2017, she delivered tens of thousands of corpses to parents. The suicide rate had increased 43 percent among those aged twenty to thirty-five. By 2015, suicide became the second leading cause of death for college students. Ironically for radical feminists and tragically for all, in the later years of this trend, the rate of suicide among young women increased by 70 percent.[7]

The Family Policy Institute of Washington, a pro-family, pro-religion organization published "4 Reasons Suicide Is Increasing Among Young Adults." The four reasons were,

1. Delayed Marriage: These unmarried (unpaired) millennials sacrifice the benefits that come with being united to a committed partner in marriage. A survey of scientific literature

conducted by the Marriage and Religion Research Institute found that married individuals are healthier, happier, and more financially secure than their unmarried peers. They experience greater emotional and psychological well-being than those who are unmarried. Notably, married individuals are less likely to commit suicide.

2. Increased Worker Mobility: Researchers have discovered a link between residential mobility and suicide. "Indeed, residential mobility can be associated with higher levels of stress, crime, poor health, and what sociologists call 'social disorganization,'" writes Ryan McMaken for the Mises Institute.
3. Decreased Religiosity: A Pew Research Center study published two years ago found that only 28 percent of millennials born between 1981 and 1996 attend religious services weekly, significantly less than 51 percent of the Silent Generation (those born between 1928 and 1945). Younger millennials are also less likely to believe in God (80 percent) or consider religion to be an important part of their lives (38 percent).

Unsurprisingly, religiously unaffiliated individuals had "significantly more lifetime suicide attempts" than their religiously affiliated peers, according to a study published in the *American Journal of Psychiatry*. The study's authors also concluded that "subjects with no religious affiliation perceived fewer reasons for living, particularly fewer moral objections to suicide."

4. Postmodernism: Millennials attain higher levels of education than previous generations. This makes them more susceptible to postmodernism, the prevailing worldview taught in higher education. Postmodernism posits that reality is unknowable and meaningless. In attempting to overthrow traditional values, postmodernism dispenses with objective and transcendent truths that provide individuals with a realistic framework through which to perceive the world.

> Postmodernists sort everyone into one of two groups: the oppressors and the victims, the latter of which suffer from systemic societal and cultural oppression at the hands of the former.

> Survey data indicate a considerable number of millennials have bought into the postmodern worldview propagated by their colleges and universities. Only 40% of those under age 35 believe "right and wrong never change," and just 4% of millennials hold to a biblical worldview.
>
> Philosopher Richard M. Weaver observed decades ago that "ideas have consequences." Teaching the next generation that life is meaningless, truth is unknowable, and that tradition and conventional wisdom must be discarded yields predictable results. Such a corrosive worldview will only produce rotting fruit.[8]

In 2004, as tensions on campus and online escalated around Jordan, Tammy convinced him to attend a craft fair in Comox, British Columbia, on Vancouver Island. She hoped to distract him for an afternoon and help him relax. Jordan wasn't anxious to see old hippies scratching out a living selling dreamcatchers and perfumed candles, but it was a beautiful, sunny day, so for a moment he put down his endless labors and let Tammy have her wish.

As they wandered around the festival, listening to live music, they came upon an open-air display of striking carved images—eagles, ravens, crooked beak masks, sun masks, a wild woman. Jordan was struck by the craftsmanship and the dreamlike quality of these images. They were in fact the dream images of tribal chief Charles Joseph of the Canadian Pacific coast Kwakwaka'wakw tribe. Charles's wife had also dragged him to the festival but to display his carvings, hopefully speak to a few interesting people, and enjoy himself for a little while. Not totally cooperating, Charles sat inside a dark tent nearby letting his carvings speak for themselves.

Outside, Jordan saw Charles sitting in his tent and, excited to meet the artist, walked in and struck up a conversation. It was clear Jordan was a genuine fan of Charles's work and had admired other Pacific coast tribal art for a very long time. Charles caught some of Jordan's enthusiasm and guided him through a thick photo album of his other carvings for close to an hour.

The two bonded over their mutual fascination with archetypal characters revealed through dreams and visions—the source of Charles's art. Eventually, Charles recounted his horrifying Canadian residential school past. The brutality inflicted upon Charles and other young wards at St. Michael's shocked Jordan in spite of his decades of work with psychologically traumatized people.

Jordan bought a few small pieces, cementing their friendship, and then made a long-term deal with Charles. The artist could send Jordan a major piece every three to six months at whatever price Charles thought it was worth, and they would see how that went. The deal continued for close to ten years and included several extra pieces Jordan bought for his family. It was all added to the Soviet-era propaganda art also in a growing collection in Jordan's house. Perhaps unconsciously, his collection was of his personal images of heaven and hell. It was a collection of the powerful, unadorned archetypes of the feared Russian Marxist and beloved native Canadian cultures.

Charles shared more intimate details about his terrifying experiences at St. Michael's, and how his dreams were filled with the characters he carved. Jordan listened to the story of each dream character, comparing them to Jungian archetypes and trying to piece together their psychological meaning. They talked about Christianity, its helpful and destructive influence on the Kwakwaka'wakw people, including many of Charles's own relatives. They spoke for hours about art and how it had at least partially redeemed Charles. They became active in promoting Canadian/First Nations interests, traveling together to Ottawa to attend peace and reconciliation ceremonies.

Eventually, Jordan was invited into Charles's family. They held a traditional adoption ceremony where Jordan was required to perform the ancient dance of the tribe to show his commitment to tribal tradition. Over time, he transformed the third floor of his Toronto home into a tribal Big House. He filled it with traditional carvings and totem poles. Big Houses were used to gather together and celebrate potlatches where gifts and offerings were exchanged between and among tribes. He was given the Kwakwaka'wakw name *Alestalegie,* or "Great Seeker," and Tammy was given the tribal name *Ekielagas,* or "Kindhearted Woman" in two extensive ceremonies.

Yet much of this goodwill, friendship, and love would come to a bitter end by poison-tongued enemies now whispering against Jordan. This was the hidden price of his outspoken loathing for the Devouring Mothers and their Oedipal obsessions. It was the price he reluctantly paid to raise his voice against those purveyors of suicidal nihilism who were usurping his students' freedom of speech, individual autonomy, and more often now, their lives.

At fourteen, Mikhaila was still sleeping much of the day even with stimulants to keep her awake during school. Now to add even more misery, she was beginning to itch all over. As the winter of 2006 rolled along, the itching increased until "it was like mosquitoes everywhere." A more hellish existence was hard to imagine for Mikhaila and her parents.

A saving grace was the brave, tireless support everyone received from twelve-year-old Julian, truly a champion-hearted brother and son. Julian dedicated himself to Mikhaila's care and faultlessly did his part in every emergency. Especially during the longest, darkest nights of the winter, his strength of character held the line against the freezing winds of chaos whistling in the cracks around his family's front door.

In June 2007, Jordan's detractors were dismayed to review the just published book *Better Together* by Harvard political scientist Robert Putnam. The book, six years in the making, was an unsuccessful attempt to shoehorn the discrediting facts from Putnam's original 2000 study into a support of postmodern concepts of inclusion and diversity. A summary of the original study by Michael Jonas of *The Boston Globe* includes,

> The greater the diversity in a community, the fewer people vote and the less they volunteer, the less they give to charity and work on community projects. In the most diverse communities, neighbors trust one another about half as much as they do in the most homogenous settings. The study, the largest ever on civic engagement in America, found that virtually all measures of civic health are lower in more diverse settings.[9]

Putnam was a liberal academic at Harvard, a contemporary of Jordan's when he discovered the bad news in his data in 2000. He spent several months attempting to disprove his facts. He was unsuccessful at this, so published the results of the study in a brief press release in 2001. No doubt as he expected, howls of scorn descended on him from his fellow postmodernist diversity fans. He then spent several years testing other possible explanations hoping to find errors in his work. The facts stubbornly remained the same. After this final attempt to find an alternative explanation for his facts, he spent the last years of his seven-year odyssey to prove himself wrong by writing a scholarly analysis to theorize some redeeming value in diversity. Unfortunately for his reputation as a topflight scientist, he was unable to restrain his compassion for the oppressed and attempted to create value where there was none. His final, editorialized version of the study done in 2000 was published in the journal *Scandinavian Political Studies* and as a book in 2007. He faced even more heated criticism from social scientists and academics for attempting to skew the implications of his data to suit his personal politics. He hypothesized that the negative effects of diversity could be remedied and that eventually it might fade in importance—two untested assumptions that did little to bolster his credibility.

Columnist Ilana Mercer in her opinion article "Greater Diversity Equals Greater Misery" in *The Orange County Register* wrote of Putnam,

> Like many social scientists living in symbiosis with statists, Putnam doesn't confine himself to observations; he offers recommendations. Having aligned himself with central planners intent on sustaining such social engineering, Putnam concludes the gloomy facts with a stern pep talk. Take the lumps of diversity without complaining! Mass immigration and the attendant diversity are, overall, good for the collective. (Didn't he just spend five years demonstrating the opposite?)[10]

This bitter diversity pill for the postmodern Marxists, like the collapse of the Marxist Soviet Union itself, did nothing to slow them down. This is little wonder considering the extraordinary efforts and risks a brilliant, highly regarded professional like Putnam was willing to undertake. It seems to give greater credence to Jordan's concept of ideological possession. How else could the unshakable commitment to obviously false and destructive ideas of postmodern neo-Marxism be explained?

This degradation of consciousness accelerated throughout Western universities, large and small. They had been offering courses in subjects like Women's and Gender Studies for years. Now preeminent schools were offering courses in the original class consciousness philosophy of Marxism itself. The 2003 annual report Comedy & Tragedy published by Young America's Foundation said,

> Amherst College offers Taking Marx Seriously. The University of California at Santa Barbara offers Black Marxism. Rutgers University offers Marxist Literary Theory. University of California at Riverside offers a Marxist Studies minor.[11]

The other leading universities offering Marxist courses included Brown University, Columbia University, Cornell University, Dartmouth College, Harvard University, Princeton University, University of Pennsylvania, Yale University, Bucknell University, Carnegie

Mellon University, Duke University, Emory University, New York University, Stanford University, Syracuse University, University of Chicago, Amherst College, Carleton College, Oberlin College, Reed College, Vassar College, Wellesley College, University of Arizona, University of Colorado, University of Florida, University of Iowa, University of Kentucky, University of Massachusetts, University of Michigan, University of Minnesota, University of Missouri, University of North Carolina at Chapel Hill, Pennsylvania State University, Rutgers University, University of Texas, University of Virginia, University of Washington, University of Wisconsin, and virtually the entire University of California system.[12]

Jordan's concern was now bordering on alarm. The intellectual roots of the hideous, human catastrophes of the twentieth century were spreading at lightning speed throughout academia. The obsolete missiles of Armageddon were replaced by universities promoting Marxist lesson plans to once again elevate the proletariat. As always, their primary targets were impressionable and easily impassioned young people.

The Millennial generation, deprived at an early age of much of Western history, were now condemned to repeat it. As in generations past, they were entranced by the tens of thousands by the old sirens' song of justice for the oppressed, updated to the irresistible tune of compassion for the less fortunate. As before, at the heart of this new compassion was the highly motivating resentment for the rich and powerful.

With the explosive reach of the internet, the immersive promotion within academia and hundreds of millions of dollars of intentionally divisive propaganda coming from Western enemies including Russian and China, postmodern neo-Marxism was once again chic and, au courant, and nearly universal.

One of several aggressive enemies at the University of Toronto, Dr. Nicholas Matte, was beginning to emerge with accusations directed at Jordan personally. Originally accused of misogyny, racism, and lack of compassion, Jordan was increasingly facing accusations from various sources of Nazism, white supremacism, fascism, and promoting hate speech.

Eventually face to face on the TVO program *The Agenda,* Dr. Matte said to Jordan in regard to Jordan's concern over the new radicals' attacks on free speech, "I don't care about your language use. I care about the safety of people being harmed."[13]

Clearly compassion for the less fortunate and the assumption of "harm" was overriding any concern for freedom of speech, a common and growing sentiment among Dr. Matte's colleagues on the political left. Free speech was the sacrifice necessary to protect vulnerable people, of which there were many and a growing number. Yet, Dr. Matte, as with white-privilege inventor Peggy McIntosh and other fringe academics, had no evidence and almost no expertise, other than as an activist, to justify his attack. The University of Toronto's Centre for Sexual Diversity Studies' introduction of Nicholas Matte describes him primarily as the curator of a museum collection: "Nicholas Matte is a politically-conscious interdisciplinary historian who curates the Sexual Representation Collection and teaches in the Sexual Diversity Studies program."

The first descriptive term of Dr. Matte is *politically-conscious.* That seems unusual, unless that was his primary job. Curator of the Sexual Representation Collection is quite clear, but "teaches in the Sexual Diversity Studies program" apparently means that he taught as a curator and not as a professor. The description of *historian* seems a bit *thrashed* or obscure in the postmodern tradition since he referred to himself as a *medical historian,* but the collection he curated was primarily of pornography of the twentieth century.

As a teacher of Sexual Diversity Studies, Dr. Matte seems to be in the postmodern school of thought on diversity and also to have extended the theory on diverse sexual identities. He was indeed quite politically conscious to the point of being a busy activist. The university description continues,

> Dr. Matte has worked on and been involved with numerous community-based organizations, events, and research and education projects and teams, including feminist working group Emilia-Amalia, Transforming Justice, TransEd, LGBT Digital Archives and Oral History Collaboratory, and others. Matte also sits on the Advisory Board of Digital Transgender Archives.[14]

To get a better idea of the type of activism that appealed to Dr. Matte, the conclusion of his online biography seems to the point,

> Matte's teaching and research reflect longstanding interests in how sex, gender, sexuality, health, disability, race and capitalism inform individual desires, embodied social experiences, identities, relationships, community formations, and sociocultural advocacy.[15]

His longstanding interests in disability, race, and capitalism seem a bit remote for a sex historian, but are exactly aligned with postmodernist class distinctions. As far as a teacher, he seems to have been quite unsuccessful. On ratemyprofessor.com, Dr. Matte scores a disappointing 1.5 out of a possible 5 rating. Jordan is rated 4.3 by comparison.[16] The very few student comments on Dr. Matte's page are uniformly negative; in fact, they are uniformly *awful* in the classifications of the site, including this one that states,

> Awful professor. Was required to take this course by the administration and it was a miserable experience. Very slow in grading and handing back papers/disseminating information. I asked him to explain why there's no such thing as biological sex and he said he couldn't unpack it for me in the interest of time, and then proceeded to never do so.[17]

In spite of Dr. Matte's obvious unpopularity as a teacher, the UT administration apparently made his course a requirement in certain cases. Another student comment with the rank of *awful* seems to clearly indicate Dr. Matte was aggressively promoting his personal political views in class as an activist, writing, "Forces politics and his ideals onto others in class. Bad ideology in my honest opinion and he is not willing to accept the opinion of others and only views people with different opinions as enemies."[18]

By the administration's slanted description of Dr. Matte and their active promotion of his course, it appears that they supported his political activism and even favored it over his value as an educator. This seems undeniable when realizing that the administrator over Dr. Matte was David Rayside, the founding director of Matte's employer, the Mark S. Bonham Centre for Sexual Diversity Studies.

Rayside created the center as society was being carved up into new social classes by Kimberlé Crenshaw's theory of intersectionality. It opened just after Jill Ker Conway created her courses in Women's Studies at the university. Like Matte, Rayside was a committed activist. He belonged to the Right to Privacy Committee, a response to police raids on gay bathhouses; contributed to *The Body Politic,* one of Canada's first LGBT magazines, the Citizens Independent Review of Police Activities, and the campaign to add sexual orientation to the Ontario Human Rights Code as a special protected class. He also cofounded the Canadian Lesbian and Gay Studies Association and the Positive Space Campaign at the University of Toronto.

The Positive Space Campaign seems to have been the forerunner of the now ubiquitous *safe spaces* on many college campuses. The Conference Board of Canada, an independent, evidence-based applied research organization describes it this way, "A Positive Space is a designated area with an indicator showing that the space is one with a trained Positive Space champion who is sensitive to LGBT concerns."[19]

Rayside served on the boards of the Canadian Political Science Association and the American Political Science Association promoting *equity* in academic life. To demonstrate Rayside's postmodern neo-Marxist bona fides, consider the definition of equity by Independent Sector, a collective of community and charity organizations:

> Equity is the fair treatment, access, opportunity, and advancement for all people, while at the same time striving to identify and eliminate barriers that have prevented the full participation of some groups. Improving equity involves *increasing justice* [emphasis added including below] and fairness within the procedures and processes of institutions or systems, as well as in their *distribution of resources*. Tackling equity issues requires an understanding of the *root causes of outcome disparities* within our society.[20]

Clearly, Professor Rayside was a postmodern neo-Marxist collaborating with Dr. Matte who, like Matte, focused primarily on political advocacy over education.

But by far, the most disturbing element of their popular concept of equity for Jordan was the focus on "outcome disparities." They did not want equal opportunities for people, they wanted equal outcomes. This was the intellectual red line for Jordan. There could be no quarter given to people who insisted, like nearly a dozen murderous Marxist regimes around the world before them, on equality of outcome. Jordan addressed the issue this way on Joe Rogan's popular podcast, *The Joe Rogan Experience* (episode #1070), to over five million listeners and viewers,

> Thomas Sowell (American philosopher) has talked about this a little bit too he said, ". . . what the people who are agitating for equality of outcome don't understand is that you have to cede so much power to the authorities, to the government, in order to ensure equality of outcome, that a tyranny is inevitable."
> And that's right.[21]

Unlike Matte and Rayside's dedication to advocacy over education, the same cannot be said for Harvard professor Putnam, who unwittingly exposed the disastrous outcomes of diversity. Putnam clearly dedicated his life to science and education. Yet all three men were, by Jordan's definition, ideologically possessed.

Tellingly, they all used the same postmodern term of *diversity* as the focus of their work. It seems they were all possessed by the old Marxist ideology of oppressed classes of people in a neo-Marxist diversity package. As Jordan often paraphrased Jung, "People don't have ideas, ideas have people."

In direct opposition, Jordan was committed to the idea of the *sovereign individual* rather than social classes. One could argue that he was also ideologically possessed, except that he was not in lockstep with anyone of any political or social movement. He was not advocating for protective laws or attempting to justify contradictory data. He was instead in constant open inquiry about the concept of individual sovereignty. He welcomed contradictory data and viewpoints. He was educating himself and his students, using his own evolving, unique arguments. And, unlike Dr. Matte and Professor Rayside, he was committed to education over advocacy.

In one of his earliest online videos, he lectured about the transcendental and unifying power of music on individuals, the opposite of the rational and divisive power of diverse classes, genders, and races. In the video, Jordan appears deeply tired, this being a sleepless time at a new crisis point for Mikhaila, but his energy rallied as he delved into the subject:

> The reason music plays such a powerful, such a popular role in our culture is because the meaning that music speaks of is beyond rational critique. And we're very rational and very intelligent, so we've been able to make intellectual hash out of most of the things that had traditionally offered people a grounded sense of meaning (i.e., postmodernism). . . . It [music] seems to have been able to maintain its experiential connection with transcendental meaning despite the fact that our rational mind seems to have destroyed everything else that is transcendental.[22]

He goes on for nearly an hour, as usual without notes, on how an individual perceives meaning in faces, images, and life experiences. It was typical of his convoluted, interconnected lectures. And in spite of the fierce antagonism now being directed at him and his supporters, certain brave students wrote of him,

> He was one of the most intelligent and eloquent people I have ever had the chance to meet. Provides space for discussion, deliberation, and disagreement, and respects differing points of view. Fantastic person and profound speaker.[23]

Jordan's research output was a prolific seven academic papers in 2007. One in particular marked a significant new direction in his search for the healing qualities of personal meaning. It was entitled "A Psycho-ontological Analysis of Genesis 2–6." The edited abstract reads,

> Individuals operating within the scientific paradigm presume that the world is made of matter. . . . Individuals within the religious paradigm, by contrast, presume that the world is made out of what matters. From such a perspective, the phenomenon of meaning is the primary reality. This meaning is revealed both subjectively and objectively, and serves—under the appropriate conditions—as an unerring guide to ethical action. . . . Genesis describes the primary categories of the world of meaning, as well as the eternal interactions of those categories. . . . Eden is a place where order and chaos, nature and culture, find their optimal state of balance.
>
> Because Eden is a walled garden, however—a bounded state of being—something is inevitably excluded. Unfortunately, what is excluded does not simply cease to exist. Every bounded paradise thus contains something forbidden and unknown. Man's curiosity inevitably drives him to investigate what has been excluded. The knowledge thus generated perpetually destroys

> the presuppositions and boundaries that allow his temporary Edens to exist. Thus, man is eternally fallen. The existential pain generated by this endlessly fallen state can undermine man's belief in the moral justifiability of being—and may turn him, like Cain, against brother and God.[24]

His immersion into Christian thought brought him full circle, thirty-two years later, back to his mother's faith. He was still not a believer in her God as were his heroes Carl Jung and Aleksandr Solzhenitsyn, but he'd found the source material for many of their ideas and a path toward deeper meaning in life.

Exactly six months after "A Psycho-ontological Analysis of Genesis 2–6" appeared, Jordan's next paper "The Meaning of Meaning" was published with the abstract (edited for brevity):

> The world is too complex to manage without radical functional simplification. Meaning appears to exist as the basis for such simplification . . . consisting of three classes. The first class . . . are meanings based in motivation, emotion, and personal and social identity . . . grounded in instinct and tend, at their most abstract, towards the dogmatic or ideological. The second class . . . are meanings based on the emergence of anomaly, or ignored complexity . . . also instinctively grounded, but tend towards the revolutionary. The third class . . . are meanings that emerge first as a consequence of voluntary engagement in exploratory activity and second as a consequence of identifying with the process of voluntary exploration. Third class meanings find their abstracted representation in ritual and myth, and tend towards the spiritual or religious.[25]

Jordan identified meanings that tend toward the dogmatic or order, toward the revolutionary or chaos, and toward the mediation between order and chaos provided by religion. This is the dance of the yin and yang and the *divine path* of the individual at the borderline of order and chaos that provides a harmonious life. From this abstract idea Jordan found the concrete value for an individual in his conclusion to "The Meaning of Meaning,"

> Our greatest stories therefore portray the admirable individual, engaged in voluntary, creative, communicative endeavor; they portray that individual generating a personality capable of withstanding the fragility of being, from such endeavor. We are thus prepared to find sufficient sustenance in stories portraying the eternal confrontation with the terrible unknown, and its transformation into the tools and skills we need to survive. If we act out such stories, within the confines of our own lives, then the significance of our being may come to overshadow our weakness. It is in the hope that such a statement might be true that we find the most profound of the many meanings of meaning.[26]

At sixteen Mikhaila was told she would need a hip replacement by the age of thirty. The Enbrel and methotrexate were giving relief, with the side effects of endless itching all over her body, the risk of fatal infection, and exhaustion, but they were not stopping the progression of arthritis in her right hip. Within months of her prognosis, her hip locked in place while shopping at a market, paralyzing her in agony. Her hip was not going to make it to thirty; a replacement surgery was scheduled.

The surgery, although "intense" and terrifying, went well. Oxycontin was added to her medications for pain while recovering. As recovery progressed and the pain in her hip began to subside, the cartilage in her left ankle "just disappeared." This too became a crippling bone-on-bone agony. A second replacement surgery was scheduled.

By this time Mikhaila had missed a full year of school. As the list of medications and their side effects mounted, the progression of her disease accelerated and her energy waned, depression began creeping back into her thoughts despite the Cipralex (SSRI) medication for it. The emotional strain on her immediate and extended family was taking a steady toll on everyone. Her ankle replacement was done. She faced several months, possibly another year, of hobbling on essentially two broken legs before she would have complete recovery.

Jordan did not publish anything on his own in 2008. He was second or third author on four academic papers that weren't published until the last quarter of the year. The papers were incremental technical achievements with titles including "Cognitive Abilities Involved in Insight Problem Solving: An Individual Differences Model." They lacked Jordan's soaring ambition to explore the core of existence like the previous year's "The Meaning of Meaning."

At this time, in September, he was interviewed again on TVO's *The Agenda* program concerning the recent financial crisis in the United States and the possible collapse of the global banking system. The subject was trust. He was asked by host Steve Paikin, "A rapid movement on this issue seems to be impossible. How important would you gauge trust to the smooth operation of a modern Western society?"

Jordan replied, "All the abstractions that we use to keep track of what constitutes value . . . are all based on interpersonal trust, so I think it's the most fundamental of natural resources. It's a psychological resource but it's the most fundamental thing."

Paikin summarized, "I think that answer goes a long way to explaining why the Washington bailout package failed because apparently there is *zero* trust between Republicans and Democrats."[27]

The world, by most accounts, seemed to have slipped into another Cold War of ideologies complete with intractable and blind adherents on both sides. A bitter resentment had again seeped into conversations turning vitally important discussions into arguments that led nowhere. People were again left waiting for Godot, as in Samuel Beckett's absurdist play representing mankind's inability to resolve the original Soviet-American Cold War, with many again steeped in nihilistic nausea as a result. For the second time in Jordan's life, the world faced mutual assured destruction, this time financial destruction.

It may have seemed to Jordan at this point that nihilism and resentment had once again overwhelmed mankind's weakness in resolving its own problems. The universities were breaking into warring factions, the media and popular culture had largely fractured into opposing points of view, and the government was now reflecting this disunity. The Devouring Mother was descending on her weak and wayward children.

CHAPTER ELEVEN

REALITY AND THE SACRED

I want to talk to you today about what I think is a relatively new way of looking at your experience but maybe even more broadly than that, a new way of looking at reality itself.

—JORDAN PETERSON, UNIVERSITY OF TORONTO LECTURE REALITY AND THE SACRED

Over thirty years of ceaseless study, research, and meditation had transported Jordan into a new reality. It was a fantastic world of monsters and heroes who were motivated by recognizable psychological complexes. Monstrous Jungian archetypes seethed with Freudian complexes. Heroes fought and struggled through Herculean challenges and if they were strong enough and lucky enough, they won the day.

This world was described in ancient stories, myths, and in sacred literature as a place of moral (or immoral) action. It was not a place of things and ever smaller parts of those things as science now describes the world. This was a world of psychological, not scientific reality, one that many modern people now dismiss as outdated and useless. But millennia before science was invented, this world of stories was the only reality.

It was a place where characters both good and bad, divine and mortal, acted out our ancestors' deepest fears and prayers in an endless battle for dominance. People preserved hard-won life lessons in these stories, and following generations mapped their lives to these stories accordingly. By following the worn paths of their heroes, ancient peoples were able to ethically cooperate and build towering cultures of art and science.

Culture itself was then mythologized and usually represented as paternal, as in Atlas holding up the world. Nature was generally mythologized as maternal, as in Mother Nature. The individual, male and female, was mythologized as both a hero and villain. Each had a lighted or conscious side and a hidden or shadow side.

Culture offered people security and prosperity, but held the threat of tyranny. Nature brought renewal and solace, but also death. The individual as hero offered freedom and the strength to overcome even the gods, but as a villain also embodied evil.

The path that Jordan had been clearing through this fantastic world for decades showed that it was possible for an ordinary, modern person to make the catastrophe of human life significantly more bearable by aligning their lives properly with these sacred stories.

> Over the last twenty years I would say there's been a revolution in psychology and the revolution has involved the transformation in the way that we look at the world and that's what I want to talk to you about today.
>
> I entitled this talk Reality and the Sacred. It's a strange title for a talk to modern people because we don't really understand what the sacred means unless we live within a worldview that's essentially, I wouldn't say archaic, but at least traditional for modern, free-thinking, fundamentally liberal people. The idea of the sacred is anachronistic or if not anachronistic, incomprehensible, so I want to start with a story from the Old Testament.[1]

Jordan had cleared the weeds from the oldest Christian stories and would now begin to analyze them as a modern clinical and research psychologist. His lectures were enlivened by his evident commitment to combatting evil and to healing.

Healing was still his second full-time job as a psychologist with about twenty current patients, and so, human suffering was never far from his mind. He wanted his students to also bear this suffering in mind as they wrestled with the preserved wisdom of the elders of Western civilization.

> There's a scene in the Old Testament when the ancient Hebrews are moving the Ark of the Covenant . . . a device manufactured to contain the Word of God . . . the bearers of the Ark of the Covenant trip and a man reaches out to steady it and when he touches it, God strikes him dead. . . . Modern people look at a story like that and the first thing they think is, that seems a little bit harsh on the part of God given that the man was attempting to do something that he believed was good. But what the story is designed to indicate, in my opinion, is that there are certain things that you touch at your peril regardless of your intentions, and those things that you touch at your peril regardless of your intentions most cultures regard as sacred, as untouchable. I want to make a case for you today that those things exist and also why they exist and why it's necessary for you to know that they exist.[2]

Before attempting to reveal the sacred in everyday reality, he spoke of the difficulties students faced in even comprehending the concept of sacred,

> If you're properly educated in the university especially with regards to the humanities, which are in some conceptual trouble at the moment, what essentially happens to you is that you're introduced in a relatively secular way to the concept of the sacred. You're here in the university to learn about the eternal values of humankind, and I think that people who tell you that

> those values do not exist or that they're endlessly debatable do you an unbelievable disservice. Now I'm gonna tell you first how you think about the world. I think.[3]

This was among Jordan's first condemnations in an official university lecture of the postmodernists, primarily in the humanities, who claimed that eternal values did not exist or were endlessly debatable. Apparently he felt the danger to his students was now too great, and possibly the attacks against him were becoming too treacherous to remain silent. He continued into the nature of God and why God cannot be conceived by most scientifically minded people.

> It appears classically that people have regarded their encounters with the absolute, which is all those multiple levels of being that are beyond your perceptual capacity, as equivalent to an encounter with God. . . . And what all that means is that the absolute is always something that transcends the finite frame that you place around your perceptions. So as soon as you start talking about it, representing it, making statues of it or idolizing it, you lose your connection with the absolute because you've turned it into something that's understandable in concrete.[4]

Jordan gives a number of examples of the finite frame that people use to simplify and make the world understandable. One example is the lecture theater where he stood before his students. He explained the thousands of levels of reality, such as the electrical system, that were hidden, the complexities of which were at that moment incomprehensible to every student in the theatre. He emphasized that the room is orderly and the hidden electrical system is quite likely to be chaotic and beyond the finite frame that students perceive as the room.

In fact, the frame of the room is so well known that it is unconscious to the students and automatically controls their actions:

> When you walk in here the room tells you what to do. The reason it tells you what to do is because all the seats are pointed in the same direction . . . the theory behind the room is that the thing that's interesting in the room is happening at the front, it's a theater. . . . The room tells you what to do so you don't have to think about what to do. . . . You can just do it.[5]

On a projection screen at the front, he showed the simplest representation of the orderly known and the chaotic unknown. It was the Taoist symbol of yin and yang—a circle divided in half by a black paisley with a white dot in it and an opposite white paisley with a black dot in it. The circle formed by the two halves signified the absolute or all the known and unknown. The black and white dots represented the potential of the known within chaos and the unknown within order. The *S* curve between black and white halves depicted the ever-changing sacred path between the known and the unknown. In the Taoist tradition, an individual must walk this path, one foot in order, one in chaos to successfully navigate life.

He changed the image on the screen to a medieval Christian statue of the Virgin Mary. Below Mary's head and neck was a display of all the primary elements of Christian reality. It was splayed out as if all of reality was within the body of Mary. Jordan pointed out the images in the display.

> A medieval Christian representation of the nature of reality. On the outside you have the Virgin Mary, inside the Virgin Mary you have God the Father, and God the Father is supporting a crucifix with an individual on it. The individual is Christ. What does this image mean? . . . The Virgin Mary is standing for Mother Nature. Out of Mother Nature arises order and tradition. . . . So in the state of untrammeled nature as Hobbes pointed out, it's every man for himself, and without the order that tradition brings there's nothing but chaos, and chaos is murderous and unproductive.

> Well, there's a problem with order. If you look at the history of the twentieth century, it's a toss-up whether Mother Nature is being harder on us or whether our governmental traditions have been harder on us. You know of course that the dictatorship of Hitler killed six million Jews, 120 million people in the Second World War. You may not know that the Stalinist dictatorships in the Soviet Union killed an estimated sixty million people in internal repression, not counting those people who died in the Second World War. And the internal repression that characterized Mao's communist China killed a hundred million people.[6]

He changed the image to a side-by-side medieval depiction of a king on his throne, a crucifix at his left hand, and the same king without crucifix, mouth wide open, and about to eat a prince, his own son.

> And so the problem with tradition is that sometimes it's a wise king and sometimes it's a king that eats his own sons, which means that although we need tradition to guide us and to structure even the manner in which we perceive the world, our traditions can become archaic and outdated and cruel and inhuman and as a consequence they can pose a worse threat to us than chaos itself.[7]

Jordan switched back to the image of the Virgin Mary.

> And finally in this representation you have a representation of the individual . . . and that's Christ. And it's a terrifying representation, it's a remarkable representation because it's not a representation of transcendence, it's a representation of suffering. . . . The manner in which the story unfolds is that Christ as the archetypal individual, the model for individuals

> from a psychological or mythological perspective, knows that he's limited and knows that he's doomed to both suffering and death. In the garden of Gethsemane, the night before his crucifixion, he has an argument with God and the argument basically is, "Do I actually have to do this?" and the answer is twofold: "Well, no, actually you don't have to . . . voluntarily accept your suffering, but there are consequences if you don't."[8]

Jordan leaned in, over the podium, and directed his comments at randomly selected but specific students. His intensity and focus were both ratcheted up. He seemed more intent, even slightly dangerous and definitely not someone to be ignored.

> Now the Christian story is predicated on the idea that if you voluntarily accept your suffering you can simultaneously transcend it. It's a remarkable philosophy and it's also something that we have very good support for from a psychological perspective. So for example if I'm treating someone (as a psychologist) who has an anxiety disorder, panic disorder, who can't go out of their house without their heart rate elevating . . . the way you cure that person is by getting them to voluntarily approach the things that they're afraid of and it turns out that physiologically, if I force you to accept a certain kind of challenge, your body will go into emergency preparation mode and you'll become stressed and that stress will cause you physiological damage including brain damage if it's sustained for long enough. But if I present you with the same challenge and you accept it voluntarily, your brain doesn't produce stress hormones and completely different physiological systems kick in. And what that means is people have evolved two modes for dealing with the unknown, one is voluntary approach and the other is panic-stricken paralysis and flight.[9]

Having made the concept of chaos into a concrete reality, he moved on to explain the development of the sacred as a concrete reality and its phenomenal impact on the world.

> The late Renaissance was the first time in human history where human beings dared to presume that sacred images could be given an individual human face. And that idea was actually what launched the Enlightenment and launched the development of modern culture. The late Renaissance thinkers, the artists in particular, were the first people to posit that there was some direct relationship between these sacred images and actual people.[10]

In the video recording of this lecture, it briefly cut away to two young female students in obviously rapt attention. The video cut back to Jordan and then to a new projected image of a medieval drawing of St. George and the Dragon.

> The oldest story we know, which is a Mesopotamian creation myth, features a God who confronts a reptilian monster. . . . He faces her, she's terrifying, he cuts her up into pieces, and out of the pieces he makes the world. Now the Mesopotamians five thousand years ago were trying to figure out what the nature of individuality was and what the nature of consciousness was. They didn't think the way we think in . . . philosophical processes. They thought in stories . . . They came to the conclusion that the object of their ultimate worship was the god who confronted the dragon of chaos, cut it into pieces, and made the world. And that idea has echoed down through the ages.[11]

Referring to the projected image of St. George and the Dragon, the Christian reiteration of the Mesopotamian idea four thousand years later in medieval Europe, he continued, "So you see the castle in the background. The castle stands for order and it's a multi-walled castle. . . . But those walls are constantly breached."[12]

He digressed to offer another cautionary remark to his students, a warning about the invading barbarians of postmodernism who were attempting to knock down the walls of tradition,

> Now young people, especially modern young people are often very cynical about the traditions that they inhabit. They're cynical about them because they see the fact that the world is theoretically devolving into some kind of environmental catastrophe and they're cynical because there's still war, because there's still hunger. They're cynical because often the people who are teaching them the traditions don't seem to believe in them themselves. It's very easy for young people to look at the traditions that were and notice the breaks. But the truth of the matter is that throughout human history tradition has always been anachronistic and out of date.[13]

He turned back to the image of St. George and the Dragon and continued with a final warning against the murderous nihilism that resulted from Marxist oppression consciousness that surrounded them.

> And what you see in images of St. George and the Dragon is that the dragons always breach the walls which means that tradition is always under attack from chaos.
>
> Well, of course it is, because the future is different than the past, but that doesn't mean that the past should be abandoned. Because if you abandon the past and you knock down all your walls, you fall into a pit of chaos and that, classically speaking, is indistinguishable from hell. And I can tell you that if you spend long enough in that state you'll become bitter and cruel because that's what happens to people who suffer endlessly.[14]

Jordan goes on to cite another biblical story of Jonah and the whale, also illustrating that the terrifying, powerful monsters that lurk in the dark, underneath the world, like the dragon in his cave and the whale at the bottom of the sea, can be defeated by a brave individual hero who voluntarily faces terror. The hero is then rewarded with precious treasures that were guarded by the monster, and returns to the world with those treasures to benefit all. It is the story of Hercules, Jason and the Argonauts, Ulysses, Jesus Christ, Shane, Luke Skywalker, and hundreds of others throughout history. It is the classic hero's journey as described by Joseph Campbell in his book *The Hero with a Thousand Faces.*

Jordan then brought these ancient, sacred stories into a common reality for his young students. His intensity increased as he conveyed this familiar, deeply personal situation in a human life. His rate of speech increased slightly to 226 words per minute, close to the edge of comprehension and almost double the pace of an average speaker at 100 to 120 words per minute. The students were forced to pay attention. They didn't even have time to make notes.

> Imagine that you were in a bad relationship and maybe you weren't that happy about it but you know it was better than no relationship at all. And then the person that you're in the relationship [with] betrayed you and they did that because you actually weren't that happy with the relationship anyways. Maybe they did that because you're a little bit naive or maybe they did that because you're a little bit too easy to get along with and as a consequence a little bit on the boring side.
>
> So when they first leave you it's a catastrophe because your world falls apart. But when your world falls apart you're somewhere new and it's possible to learn something new in that place. So you might learn, for example, that you should be a little sharper the next time that you go out with someone. Or you should be a little bit more careful about picking up on

> clues that your partner is bored with you. Or that maybe you should stop associating with lying psychopaths [*the students laugh*] and your life would be a lot more positive. And stop thinking that you have the capacity to redeem somebody that is not after redemption in the least.[15]

Jordan then relieved the gloomy, personal realizations in the room by showing the benefit of students voluntarily facing their monsters lurking in the chaotic, shadowed unknown.

> People have an unbelievable capacity to face and overcome things they don't understand and not only that, that's essentially what gives life its meaning. . . . And what that means now and then, is that when you fall into the belly of a whale and you're swallowed up by something that lurks underneath . . . that exposes you to the part of the world that you don't understand. Every time you're exposed to a part of the world that you don't understand you have the possibility of rebuilding the structures that you use to interpret the world.[16]

He then revealed the opposite, the cost of not facing one's monsters. Referencing Buddhist dogma that asserted life is suffering, he warned that nihilistic people could assume from Buddhism that life was not worth living. He referred to twentieth-century history and the political leaders who were so nihilistic, so disgusted with human limitation, that they became genocidal, driving home his point,

> Suffering is real and it's inescapable, so the question is what do you do about it. . . . The purpose of life as far as I can tell from studying mythology and from studying psychology for decades, is to find a mode of being that's so meaningful that the fact that life is suffering is no longer relevant, or maybe it's even acceptable.[17]

He concluded the largest part of his lecture asserting the personal reward, in reality, for the sacred act of bravely facing suffering, defeat, and malevolence,

> You know when you're doing that, in part because you're no longer resentful. You think, geez, I could do this forever, right? There's a timelessness that's associated with that state of being. From a mythological perspective, that's equivalent to a brief habitation of the kingdom of God. That's the place where you are that's so meaningful it enables you to bear the harsh preconditions of life without becoming resentful, bitter, or cruel. And there's nothing that you can pursue in your life that will be half as useful as that.[18]

He began the final third of his lecture by revealing the permanent, unavoidable emergence of both order and chaos in life, both of which lead to suffering if left unchallenged. He recalled instantly the obscure example of how a traditional Taoist Chinese doctor might diagnose a suffering patient by first visiting the patient's home. The doctor would walk in and notice, perhaps, an extremely tidy and orderly home and diagnose that the patient was suffering from too much order. The doctor would prescribe treatment accordingly. Jordan brings this remote example closer to his students' world with the staccato cadence of a prosecuting attorney layering evidence upon evidence,

> I've been in houses like that. That's a house where all the furniture is covered with plastic. That's a house where if you put a glass on a wooden table the mistress of the house runs over with a coaster, slips it under immediately, and gives you a dirty look. That's a place where the children never play in the living room. That's a place where the lines in the carpet are vacuumed so precisely that they're actually parallel. That's a place where

> there's so much order that no one can survive because the person who runs the house is a tyrant. And that anyone who's sick in that house is sick because they're suffering from an excess of order.[19]

Knowing college students as he did, he then took the opposite tack and prosecuted the case of too much chaos with an unexpected bit of comic relief,

> You can even see this in your own room if you want. *Everything's in complete disarray.* You can't even look at that place. You're sick the moment you cross the threshold, because everywhere you look there's parts of untransformed chaos yelling to you, *Do something about this, loser!*[20]

Jordan and his audience break up laughing as he nails them using their own slang. He continued, again intent on making his finer, highly personal points, leaning over his podium, confronting individuals around the room,

> If you walk into your study and you have a stack of papers in the midst of which is buried your homework, you'll notice that you have a very tough time looking at that stack of papers. And the reason for that is that the stack of papers that you're ignoring, that's aging and causing you more trouble with each passing day, is a portal into order through which chaos is flowing. And if you ignore that long enough, the chaos will flow through that portal and take over your room and then take over your life. And you might think, well, that's a very strange way of looking at things and I suppose it is.[21]

He delved into more "weird" ideas, as he called them, such as deep and rewarding meaning in life is only found by taking on massive responsibility. The image of Atlas carrying the world on his shoulders appeared on the screen. He seemed to lose a bit of his intensity. His language became more everyday conversational, less precise.

> This is an old representation, right? Atlas with the world. Well it's a representation that says that that's the proper way to live, right? . . . [It] is to pick up a load that's heavy enough so that if you carry it you have some self-respect. That's a very weird idea because it's frequently the case that people do everything they can to *lighten* their load. But the problem with carrying a light load is that then you have nothing that's useful to do. And if you have nothing useful to do all you have around you, unless you're extremely fortunate, and that will only be the case for a very short period of time, *is meaningless suffering*. And there's nothing worse for your soul than meaningless suffering.[22]

His energy rallied as he attempted to clarify the essence of being, on the face of it a daunting task, but Jordan didn't break stride. He rolled into another strange idea with ease, like he was talking about a favorite recipe,

> There's an old Jewish idea, and the idea is that man and God are in a sense twins. It's a very strange idea but it seems to hinge on something like this, that classic attributes of God, these are the attributes of the absolute, are omniscience, omnipotence, and omnipresence. . . . There's a question that goes along with that, What is a being that's characterized by the absolute attributes that God lacks? And the answer [to] that is limitation. And that's an unbelievably interesting idea.[23]

His rate of speech accelerated again as he galloped to convey a critical, new understanding of reality,

> And the reason it's so interesting is because one of the things that modern psychology is increasingly telling us, is that without the limitation that a creature like us, with the structure of our consciousness, brings to bear on the world, there's no reality. That what reality is, is an emergent consequence of the interaction between something that's painfully limited like us and whatever the absolute is, which is something that is completely without borders. And what that implies, in a sense, is that without limitation there's no being, with limitation there's suffering. Without suffering then there's no being![24]

He concluded with a call to action, affirming everyone's unlimited potential for salvation through a meaningful life. He was at maximum intensity, nearly savage in his emotional delivery,

> These archaic stories that I've been telling you about, they have something to say to you. They say life is uncertain, you'll never know enough and not only that, you *never can* know enough. And not only that, everything that you stand on is shaky. And then they say, *But you still have to stand on it, and while you're standing on it you have to improve it.*
>
> And that's how life goes on and that's how you live your life. And if you forget those things or if you undermine them, you're in the same situation that the unfortunate man was that I told you about in the Old Testament—who reached out to touch something he should have left alone.
>
> To the degree that you're human, you have to abide by a certain set of truths. The truths that I told you about today are, as far as I can tell, something that's close to a minimal set. There's chaos, there's order, you're stuck with both of them. And they both have a cost, and they both have advantages and your job is to figure out how to serve as the appropriate mediator between the two. And you can tell when you're doing that because when

> you're doing that the dismal circumstances of your life manifest themselves to you as eminently acceptable. And it's in that situation that you know that you've placed yourself in a position in nature where everything is in harmony and that's the place to aim for.
>
> Nice talking to you.[25]

Toronto exploded into the largest riots in Canadian history. The Royal Bank of Canada in downtown Toronto was firebombed. Ten thousand neo-Marxist protesters including violent anarchist and anti-capitalist insurgents disguised in black masks attacked police, sending over 100 police and protesters to hospitals and causing nearly $1 million in damage. Their aims ranged from elimination of global poverty to enhancement of indigenous people's rights. As in the recent past, they were spectacularly unsuccessful in achieving anything but local and very temporary anarchy. They seemed to have no power, no vision at all, like petulant, flailing children.

Nominally, they were protesting the 2010 G20 economic summit, targeting supposedly the pinnacle of global capitalism and foundation of the oppressive patriarchy. Over 100 international organizations, modern dragons of chaos, if you will, had been attempting to breach the walls of capitalism for years. This included the previous year's G20 summit in London where 35,000 demonstrators attacked the Royal Bank of Scotland and the British Parliament.

The romantic vision of violent revolution and fighting in the streets seemed to be the rioters' base motivation, but even Marxist researcher at the University of London Slavoj Žižek, who would face Jordan in a future critical debate and who believed deeply in Marxist revolution, was confused by the protesters' efforts:

> The protesters, though underprivileged and de facto socially excluded, weren't living on the edge of starvation. People in much worse material straits, let alone conditions of physical

> and ideological oppression, have been able to organize themselves into political forces with clear agendas. The fact that the rioters have no programme is therefore itself a fact to be interpreted: it tells us a great deal about our ideological-political predicament and about the kind of society we inhabit, a society which celebrates choice but in which the only available alternative to enforced democratic consensus is a blind acting out.[26]

The London rioting spread to other nearby districts and villages. In total, 186 police officers and 10 firefighters were injured. Eight fire engines had their windshields smashed. Over 100 homes were destroyed causing the irretrievable loss of heritage architecture. Losses to British insurers totaled approximately £100 million in London and £200 million overall.

The following year the Arab Spring, later dubbed the Islamic Spring as Islamists ascended to power in various governments, offered a bit more clarity as to common causes between the under-forty disaffected youth of Toronto, London, and Cairo who carried out the riots. Writing for *Le Monde* in Paris, Antoine Reverchon and Adrien de Tricornot said,

> Catalysts for the revolts in all Northern African and Persian Gulf countries included the concentration of wealth in the hands of monarchs in power for decades, insufficient transparency of its redistribution, corruption, and especially the refusal of the youth to accept the status quo.[27]

What the 2010 London G20 protests did signify clearly was the beginning of an explosive increase in revolutionary political demonstrations and rhetoric. In 2009, there were 13 significant riots worldwide; in 2010 there were 59; in 2011 there were 104.[28] In 2011, this revolutionary fervor flooded into Zuccotti Park in lower Manhattan, New York City, with the Occupy Wall Street movement. Suddenly, the actual walls of global capitalism were in sight.

Jordan was about to take on a burden close to that of Atlas's. He was about to carry the modern world on his shoulders as the fulcrum between traditional Western European Enlightenment values such as the sovereign individual, private property, and free speech, and youthful revolutionaries who were desperate to breach the walls of Western tradition with opposing, collectivist values.

The young revolutionaries, particularly in the West, acquired powerful allies in 2010 including Russian Television with a reported budget of over $150 million that year. The network opened its American bureau that year in Washington, DC. Margarita Simonyan, the channel's editor, put the Russian news effort in perspective saying, "Our budget is really small. There are Chinese projects that will get $7 billion this year but whose audience is significantly smaller."

Since Russia's propaganda budget was reportedly well over $1 billion at that time, it is conceivable that Simonyan's actual budget might be a bit closer to the Chinese figure. It also might be assumed by comparing the government funding to audience size, that both Russian and Chinese news organizations had a different goal than most profit-oriented broadcasters, and those goals were obviously government directed.

The other significant advantage to revolutionaries that year was the worldwide adoption of the internet. As the primary global and local communication channel for the Arab Spring, the internet demonstrated its awesome potential. Leading this internet-based cultural revolution in North America was the Canadian Adbusters Media Foundation, a self-described "global network of artists, activists, writers, pranksters, students, educators and entrepreneurs who want to advance the new social activist movement of the information age."[29]

Adbusters was not only an anti-capitalist, as in neo-Marxist, magazine, it was an advocacy organization called The Culture Jammers Network that updated the concept of radio *jamming,* or interference for the information age. Under Soviet-style artwork of young, white, male and female workers marching bravely together under a red flag, the woman carrying a red-covered book appearing to be Mao's little red book *Quotations of Chairman Mao Tse-tung*, they stated their aim:

> Our aim is to topple existing power structures and forge a major shift in the way we will live in the 21st century. We believe culture jamming can be to our era what civil rights was to the '60s, what feminism was to the '70s, what environmental activism was to the '80s. It will alter the way we live and think. It will change the way information flows, the way institutions wield power, the way TV stations are run, the way the food, fashion, automobile, sports, music and culture industries set their agendas. Above all, it will change the way meaning is produced in our society.[30]

The battle line was now clearly marked. The Adbusters wanted more than Soviet totalitarian rule, they wanted Maoist totalitarian thought. They wanted to "alter the way we live and think." They intended to completely overturn the foundations of Western civilization. In temperament and mission, they resembled Orwell's thought police. They resembled Stalin's politburo and Mao's Red Guards who collectively killed between 100 and 120 million people. They were the same sort of "peevish and resentful" people Jordan had recoiled from as a young man. Now they had graduated from mere annoyances to mortal enemies and had declared global war.

War it was, and Jordan was unprepared and overmatched in everything except commitment. He had no organization, no allies, no funding, and no strategy. He had no defining mission statement for publication. He was an obscure college professor with a tenuous presence primarily in regional media. He was the father of vulnerable children. Yet he was unwavering in his commitment to combat neo-Marxism and had been for decades. The price for his opposition was about to skyrocket.

The Canadian radicals attacked. In rapid sequence, Adbusters launched international campaigns such as Buy Nothing Day, TV

Turnoff Week, and in September 2011, their greatest achievement, Occupy Wall Street—the plot heard round the world.

Occupy Wall Street achieved overwhelming support and publicity for the revolutionary fervor boiling over in universities and among the youth of Western society. Within three weeks of its launch in September, the movement had spread to over 951 cities worldwide including Toronto, 82 countries, and 600 communities in America.[31]

Red flags, Soviet hammer and sickle emblems, clenched red fists of resistance, and the anarchist symbol of the hand-drawn letter *A* in a circle branded the movement as implicitly Marxist and revolutionary as Adbusters intended.

In opposition, the American grassroots movement the Tea Party had escalated tensions from the conservative side six months before the Adbusters' attack. In March 2011, former governor of Alaska and vice presidential candidate Sarah Palin reflected on the origins of the Tea Party movement and mocked President Barack Obama, the de facto leader of the left since his election in 2008. Obama had indicated his intellectual kinship with Adbusters in several speeches that included his radical intention for "the fundamental transformation of America," and in his selection of leftist cabinet and staff members like Van Jones and communications director Anita Dunn whose remarkable quote, "Two of my favorite political philosophers, Mao Tse-tung and Mother Teresa, not often coupled with each other, but the two people that I turn to most," set up her hasty departure from the administration.

Governor Palin, as an outspoken conservative, had been disgusting and enraging radical leftists like Adbusters for years. She taunted them further in her speech in Madison, Wisconsin, the heartland of American Marxism, with a direct attack on their leader,

> And speaking of President Obama, I think we ought to pay tribute to him today at this Tax Day Tea Party because really he's the inspiration for why we're here today. That's right. The Tea Party Movement wouldn't exist without Barack Obama.[32]

Like many in various, scattered Tea Party factions, Jordan recognized the election of Barack Obama and explosion of Occupy Wall Street as clear demonstrations that a radical Marxist storm had surged and was aiming to collapse Western traditions as it had before. Violence was in the air.

In *Antifa: The Anti-Fascist Handbook,* historian Mark Bray recounted the Battle of Cable Street in 1936 London that showed civil violence could defeat a political movement so badly that it could destroy it completely.[33]

On October 4, 1936, tens of thousands of Zionists, socialists, blue-collar workers, communists, anarchists, and outraged, working-class Londoners stopped Sir Oswald Mosley and his British Union of Fascists from marching through their East End neighborhood. The anti-fascist coalition fighters attacked and defeated over three thousand Fascist Black Shirts and six thousand police officers by throwing marbles under their feet, turning over a burning truck in their path, exploding homemade bombs, and throwing rocks, brickbats, and the contents of chamber pots. The police and fascists were stopped and the fascists than dwindled in number and disappeared.

According to Bray's research, the modern anti-fascist coalition began with the infiltration of Britain's punk music scene by white-power skinheads in the 1970s and 1980s.[34]

Then, neo-Nazis and nihilistic anarchist punks surfaced in Germany in the 1990s after the fall of the Berlin Wall.[35]

In the 1990s and 2000s in America and Canada, loose coalitions began to form. They were called Anti-Racist Action, or ARA, whose proclaimed original mission was fighting racism, racism being more recognizable to Canadians and Americans than fascism. But by ignoring the protections provided by the fourteenth and fifteenth amendments to the United States Constitution and the Civil Rights Acts of 1866, 1964, and 1968, it seemed that ARA was simply seeking a foothold in the Western tradition of civil disobedience. As it evolved and was celebrated by academics, intellectuals, and media stars, it became increasingly apparent that the actual mission of ARA was anti-capitalist Marxist revolution.

Coincidentally, Bray, like Dr. Nicholas Matte, was a lecturer at the Gender Research Institute at Dartmouth whose mission statement was strikingly similar to that of Dr. Matte's Mark S. Bonham Centre for Sexual Diversity Studies. GRID's mission statement read,

> In its four years the Gender Research Institute (GRID) encouraged, facilitated, and showcased gender-related research, teaching, and social engagement that addresses why the 21st century is still a time profoundly structured by gender, racial, ethnic, sexual, and economic inequality.[36]

The emphasis again is clearly on facilitating "social engagement" or political activity on behalf of gender diversity, the goal of which seemed to be gender equity. GRID had a large vision for the theory that included not only all the standard classes of oppression, but promotion of the twin foundational theories of intersectionality and white privilege:

> GRID conceives gender beyond the framework of parity and equity. We support projects that examine gender as a framework that posits that multiple social categories (race, ethnicity, gender, sexual orientation, class) intersect at the micro level of individual experience to reflect multiple interlocking systems of privilege and oppression at the macro social-structural level.

But, as Jordan would observe and radicals would continue to promote, an entirely genderless society was more accurately what was intended by this new, radical offshoot of postmodernism. Jordan said,

> It's linked to the idea that there's something wrong with masculinity and so that the expression of masculinity should be limited in all sorts of arbitrary ways. The fact that kids can't

> really play at schools anymore is a manifestation of that fact. That male behavior is often diagnosed as attention deficit disorder, for example, is a manifestation of that. The elimination of competition as a valid form of human interaction and the failure to recognize that competitive sports, for example, are deeply cooperative in their fundamental nature. . . . It's easy to mistake masculine competence for the tyranny that hypothetically drives the patriarchy. It is part of an ideological worldview that sees the entire history of mankind as the oppression of women by men which is a dreadful way of looking at the world, a very pathological way of looking at the world.[37]

For example, Bray's colleague in Gender Studies, Professor Brenda Silver, seemed to exhibit this radical feminist pathology early in the movement. In 2002, *The Dartmouth Review,* an independent student paper, described Silver as, "An avid feminist critic, Professor Silver reads literature with the firm belief that anything longer than it is round must be a phallus. Silver is a vehement addict to anything anti-male, and holds out androgyny as the human ideal."[38]

This vision of genderless androgyny would eventually spawn the theory of toxic masculinity. This theory appears to have contributed to the debilitation of young men in a number of ways including higher rates of depression, suicide, and violence—possibly including the violence of Antifa. The harm caused by this derivative theory of toxic masculinity has been researched and appears in the peer-reviewed scientific literature:

> Research shows that constraining aspects of male gender norms negatively influence both women's and men's health. . . . We draw on ethical paradigms in public health to challenge programs that reinforce harmful aspects of gender norms (i.e., toxic masculinity).[39]

Violence was now not only in the air, it was in the streets. Political violence was the preferred tactic of the ARA. They disguised their intended political violence with the euphemism of *direct action*. In 2002, they initiated direct action by physically attacking a white supremacist speaker at a public parade in Portland, Oregon. The attack started a brawl resulting in twenty-five arrests. The movement was now "blooded" as a new initiate would be at his or her first successful fox hunt and enthusiasm soared. Their activists, since they operated clandestinely and had no official membership, included anarchists, socialists, communists, liberals, and the emerging political movement called democratic socialist.[40] They began launching vicious, highly personal attacks online that they called *digital activism*.

Over the next ten years ARA factions began to adopt the name *Antifa*. The name was derived from Antifaschistische Aktion, a movement formed in Germany in 1932 with the help of the German Communist Party.[41]

Antifa in America expanded their target list to include not only racists but fascists, conservatives, reactionaries, homophobes, xenophobes, Islamophobes, populists, nationalists, Tea Party patriots, the Republican Party, and the alt-right, or far-right. Their numbers grew steadily as the destructiveness of their direct actions increased. Direct and digital actions soon included firebombing, assaults with deadly weapons, motor traffic blockading, random motorist harassment, denial of free speech, online annihilation, and intimidation of conservative and "reactionary" speakers like Jordan. Ironically, the anti-fascist Antifa fighters dressed in *black bloc,* black outfits with black cloth masks to hide their faces and appear indistinguishable. They were reminiscent of the violent Black Shirts, the voluntary, paramilitary wing of Benito Mussolini's Fascist Party of Italy and allies of Hitler's Nazis. They were the armed and motivated wing of the modern progressive movement and were eager to attack again.

On January 19, 2012, Jordan took advantage of his new media firepower at TVO to launch his counterattack. An experienced personal manager might have looked at Jordan's situation and wisely counseled him that, at this point, discretion was the better part of valor. But that person and their advice were years in the future. In spite of his dire disadvantages, many of which must have been obvious to Jordan, he did not back down. He had seen the devastation being wrought in his students' lives. It was undeniable and increasing, as was the devastation of young people in general. It had become obvious in his own research as well, and he would no longer tolerate it.

Despite his insignificant material resources and virtually nonexistent social support, he stepped directly into the line of fire from the left and attacked the foundations of postmodern thought in a self-scripted, solo appearance for TVO called "Agenda Insight: Gender Forever":

> During the 1960s everyone remotely progressive proclaimed that the personality differences between men and women, if they existed at all, were merely products of social conditioning. A recent major study concluded the opposite. Such differences are large and persistent. Similar results were already reported more than ten years ago in a cross-cultural study of twenty thousand participants.[42]

This statement, if true, was the beginning of the end of the oppression narrative against women. The science was conclusive; women were intrinsically different from men so, first of all, the gender pay gap would have to be recalculated for the different interests, values, and abilities of women versus men. And, as it turned out, when these differences were factored into the equation, the gender pay gap disappeared completely. This immutable male/female distinction was a memo that progressives had been ignoring or discounting for ten years since the first, large cross-cultural study had been concluded.

This new, confirming study also rendered the entire gender diversity idea moot since the term itself was then redundant. It also undermined the basic intersectionality argument because the unique qualities of women collectively and individually would have to be accounted for in calculating their degrees of oppression. For instance, if women were actually *not* oppressed by lower wages for the same work, how then were they oppressed? If they were biologically distinct with a unique ability to bear children and voluntarily accepted all the resulting risks and costs in time and missed opportunities, then how was the oppressive patriarchy detrimental in that process? If the dream of a genderless society was in fact a dream, then the entire mission of equity (equality of outcome) for the sexes was impossible. And finally, if the theory of intersectionality about women in particular was so wrong, for so long, wasn't the entire theory of oppression then disproved?

Progressives (the term Jordan first used publicly here and will remain in this writing as the general term for postmodern neo-Marxists) and particularly third-wave feminists, were publicly discredited and humiliated. To make things worse, he went on to quote precisely the research results on how much more sensitive to emotional pain women were than men. It made the entire radical feminist movement appear more like an emotional outburst than a reasonable alternative to the status quo. The effect of this on the progressive feminist community is hard to imagine, but Jordan went even further, adding injury to his insult. He pinpointed the cost of radical feminism to young women:

> These differences [in men and women] are significant and telling. They matter in part because they indicate that intimate caring relationships are more important to women. We teach girls that career trumps everything. At nineteen they believe this and express serious doubts about [having] children. This attitude starts to change as they approach their late twenties. By thirty the typical woman has inverted her priorities and is desperately planning for children with less and less cooperation from men her age.

His tone became quite stern, fatherly, as if he'd had enough dispassionate scientific palaver. For a committed feminist this may have seemed to be the ultimate patriarchal condescension, "Let's get something else straight. Most people do not have careers, they have jobs, and jobs are not more important than home and family, particularly not to women."

He concluded his attack with a final thrust, again at the foundations of progressivism, condemning radical feminism by name, example, and leaders. And even calling it possibly the most offensive insult of all, *old*:

> Simone de Beauvoir, Jean-Paul Sartre's feminist partner, insisted in 1975 that a woman should not be *allowed* to stay at home and raise her children because too many women would do just that. I don't agree.
>
> I want to make an observation that appears taboo among the educated. Speaking to younger women trying to make their way in a confusing world, the world of work is overrated. If you want children and a family, you're healthy, not brainwashed. And make your men pay attention. The sixties are over. It's high time everybody noticed.
>
> For *The Agenda* with Steve Paikin, I'm Jordan Peterson.[43]

CHAPTER TWELVE

THE INTELLECTUAL DARK WEB

There's a technological revolution, it's a deep one. The technological revolution is online video and audio immediately accessible to everyone all over the world. And so what that's done is . . . it's turned the spoken word into a tool that has the same reach as the printed word. So it's a Gutenberg revolution in the domain of video and audio and it might be even deeper than the original Gutenberg revolution because it isn't obvious how many people can read but lots of people can listen. . . . Now all of a sudden we have this forum for long-form discussion, real long-form discussion, and it turns out that everyone is way smarter than we thought, right? We can have these discussions publicly.

—JORDAN PETERSON ON *THE JOE ROGAN EXPERIENCE*, PODCAST EPISODE #1139

Jordan now faced hordes of red-faced, outraged enemies beyond his imagination.

Academia, popular culture in both Canada and America, and large swaths of public media had been swayed by the new revolutionaries. Democratic socialism, the new Marxism Lite, was now the official designation of his old crew in the New Democratic Party (NDP), and they had been working for decades writing socialist regulations and passing socialist laws.

In his own cerebral, some might say naive way, he had been

preparing for the conflicts ahead. He had researched the moral values that predicted political opinion in "Compassionate Liberals and Polite Conservatives: Associations of Agreeableness with Political Ideology and Moral Values" (2010). He examined the motivation for group aggression and the damage done under the stress of conflict in "Neuropsychology of Motivation for Group Aggression and Mythology" (2010). He examined the pathologies of creativity, including destabilizing, revolutionary ideas in "Creative Exploration and its Illnesses" (2011). He investigated the motivation of his enemies in "Extreme Liberalism and Reactivity to Arousing Stimuli: a Neurophysiological Investigation" (2012).

Naturally, he preferred studying his enemies to gambling with his career, his family, and possibly his life in fighting them, but the moment of decision had passed. Jordan was committed and the enemy was on the move. The NDP had recently seized power without winning an election. He now faced their rule as commissioners of "the most dangerous organization in Canada,"[1] the Ontario Human Rights Commission (OHRC).

The OHRC was established in 1961 to administer the Ontario Human Rights Code.

As a government agency, OHRC was unaccountable to the people, but empowered to investigate and indict citizens, violators of the code, through the attorney general of Ontario. It was as close as the Western world had ever come in real life to the fictitious, tyrannical Ministry of Truth that controlled information, news, entertainment, education, and the arts in George Orwell's novel *1984*.

In November 2005, longtime NDP member Barbara Hall was appointed chief commissioner of the OHRC. She set right to work on a report investigating the bullying of Canadian Asians fishing illegally on Lake Simcoe. True to form, Hall felt that racism must have caused the bullying, not the fishermen's illegal activity.

Logically, according to her statement below, she may have also felt that because the accused were from an oppressed class of Asians, that racism caused them to break the law in the first place. She noted the harassment of these unlawful fishermen aimed to "remind us that racism and racial discrimination exist in Ontario. We're looking for communities across Ontario to have an open dialogue and take action on racism. Although this is often hard to do, it is necessary to make communities welcoming and safe for all."[2]

Canada's Devouring Mother, the OHRC, was going to make Canada safe and welcoming for all her hapless children. In April 2008, Hall and NDP colleagues on the OHRC dismissed a complaint against *Maclean's* magazine alleging Islamophobia, but issued a chilling statement denouncing the magazine that read in part,

> This type of media coverage has been identified as contributing to Islamophobia and promoting societal intolerance towards Muslim, Arab and South Asian Canadians. The Commission recognizes and understands the serious harm that such writings cause, both to the targeted communities and society as a whole. And, while we all recognize and promote the inherent value of freedom of expression, it should also be possible to challenge any institution that contributes to the dissemination of destructive, xenophobic opinions.

And so the Overton window, the range of acceptable public thought and speech, shifted again further toward the radical left. The media was now on notice, publicly, that Devouring Mother had identified "destructive, xenophobic opinions," and was watching. In a later interview, Hall warned,

> When the media writes, it should exercise great caution that it's not promoting stereotypes that will adversely impact on identifiable groups. I think one needs to be very careful when one speaks in generalities, that in fact one is speaking factually about all the people in a particular group.[3]

Hall made her move for entry-level control of the press in February 2009. Canada's Devouring Mother wanted to keep her children safe by controlling the press, like Orwell's fictional Big Brother. In a report to the Canadian Human Rights Commission, Hall recommended the creation of a National Press Council that would be OHRC's media watchdog. Unlike past and existing press councils in Canada, membership would be compulsory for all media. Hall stated this was necessary to protect human rights. She promised that such a body would not result in censorship. It would, however, accept complaints of discrimination from "vulnerable groups" and have the power to force writers, editors, radio, and television producers to carry the council's decisions and counterarguments. Essentially the council would be an executive government editor at every newspaper, magazine, radio station, and television studio in Canada.

Blowback was immediate and intense; the conservative-leaning *National Post* howled that a mandatory national press council "is merely the first step toward letting the Barbara Halls of the world decide what you get to hear, see and read."

And continued, saying that Hall was a "pompous purveyor of social concern. [Who] . . . has the ability to judge which speech should be free and which not."[4]

With a wounded and beseiged OHRC watching, Jordan began to post his now-controversial lectures and television appearances on YouTube to global audiences. His lectures were an instant hit garnering hundreds, then thousands of views per week. Then, on March 30, 2013, he posted a previously recorded TVO solo interview called "What Matters." The video began with his captivating, entirely unique theory of existence:

> I'm not an atheist anymore because I don't look at the world that way anymore. I'm not a materialist anymore. I don't think the world's made out of matter. I think it's made out of what matters. It's made out of meaning.[5]

He then revealed the first layer of his decades of thinking on the subject:

> The problem with the standard view of matter is that it doesn't really deal with the fact that matter comes in arrays and in patterns. And the patterns and arrays, which is [*sic*] sort of lost when you think about atoms, that's where all the action is, that's where the reality is.[6]

He then argued for a foundational Judeo-Christian premise which refuted the progressive premise of gender as a social construct, continuing,

> There's a tradition in medieval Christianity and Judaism as well, that the first man was hermaphroditic, male and female together. And then separated into two separate entities which then were forever looking to be rejoined. And there's a very profound psychological idea there, which is that the union of masculine and feminine produces a kind of perfect wholeness. And you can think about that as being expressed biologically, given that males need females and masculine needs feminine. . . . So whatever consciousness is, it comes in masculine and feminine embodiments. The masculine and the feminine embodiment are equally representations of God. Which I think is quite remarkable because there's a whole line of feminist criticism of the Western tradition that makes the presumption that the whole structure is patriarchal. And I don't think that's true.
>
> If it was patriarchal, it would have been man that was created in the image of God. And it is explicitly not that.[7]

And so Jordan charged from his local and regional skirmishing over ideas into a rapidly escalating global war. His approach using Judeo-Christian Enlightenment values against progressives marked him for return fire. Comments in general to this post praised him, but several indicated he'd hit a deep nerve in certain communities. Someone calling themselves Con Gibbons commented,

> I do find it hard to credit when someone speaks of God this and God that, or that patriarchy is not a valid interpretation of male-dominated history because both Adam and Eve were made in God's image.(!!!) The notion of God as implied in Dr Peterson's discussion is unimaginable purely because "He" is presented as a Creator who has a direct say or organizational role in human life—if Dr Peterson could prove that, he's got me.[8]

A commenter calling him or herself informationwarfare pointed to time marker 1:43 on the video where Jordan references the Jewish idea about the original man being hermaphroditic with a subsequent separation by God into man and woman.

From the internet's anonymous darkness, he or she spit venom, "I was wondering where the origin of the phrase 'go fuck yourself' came from." This comment was removed by YouTube.

Someone calling themselves Rentaghost okish sneered, "I can see why the Alt-right love this guy."[9]

And so the long knives came out for Jordan Peterson in the war for Western civilization.

At the same time, the alarming phenomenon of intellectual fragility began appearing among college freshmen. Author, social scientist, and acquaintance of Jordan's from their Harvard days, Jonathan Haidt, noted this on a television appearance explaining the origins of his book *The Coddling of the American Mind,*

> The book has its origins in an observation from my co-author Greg Lukianoff. . . . in 2013 Greg began noticing that for the first time, it was the students who were asking for protections from words and books and ideas and speakers. Previously,

> students had protested speakers before, but they'd never before medicalized it.
>
> They acted as though if this person says something I will be harmed, damaged. People will be traumatized. And so this was something new and when they put [it] in terms of safety, well then administrators have to respond. . . . And it brought with it a whole package of innovations, you might say, microaggression training, safe spaces, trigger warnings, all this stuff appears from out of nowhere around 2013, 2014.[10]

What Jordan had forewarned as the devastation of the Devouring Mother in his decades of lectures, had obviously been too little and too late. New college students, seventeen and eighteen years old, had been undermined by technology and overparenting particularly since the appearance of Apple's iPhone in 2007 according to Haidt.

In Haidt's book they are referred to as the iGen, separate and distinct from the Millennial generation. They are fragile, easily terrified, and infantile in their reactions to threats. They are desperate for protection, particularly from the oppressive patriarchy and its racism, sexism, homophobia, and toxic masculinity. They arrived at universities ready to serve in the ranks of progressives.

Jordan had seen increasing intellectual fragility in his students and its early effects for years, but Dr. Haidt showed the true cost in devastating detail from updated research on youth suicide:

> So the boys are mostly doing video games which aren't so bad even if they're running around imaginary worlds killing people, as my son does with his friends. It's really cooperative, there's teamwork, they're talking. But what the girls are doing is putting something out [on social media] and then waiting anxiously while people comment on it. And so it's the social comparison. It's the fear of missing out.
>
> Also girls' bullying is relational, boys' bullying is physical, so social media, that doesn't really affect it. But girls can never

> get away if they're being bullied. So this is why we think that the suicide rate is up 25 percent for boys, but it's up 70 percent for girls.[11]

As a particularly active social scientist with nine published papers that year, Jordan was almost certainly aware of this research on youth suicide. As the parent of a young suffering daughter and as one who had personally been moved to tears by human suffering since childhood, it is hard to imagine he was not deeply affected by this new horror of surging suicide rates among girls. Late in the year, in October, he brought his overwhelmingly female class to an art exhibition at the Articsók Gallery in Toronto by artist Tadeusz Biernot called *Layers*. In theory, the trip was to examine the vital, psychological role of the artist in society.

Biernot's paintings, all faces of young Toronto women, softly obscured as if in a foggy dream, expressed a wide range of subtle emotions. They were quizzical, sad, hopeful, and determined. The paintings were huge. The girls' faces, just inches away, were seemingly hard to see.

To understand what the girls were communicating, one had to pierce the fog with imagination and look deep into the faces, piecing together each girl's subtle shading of expression. They appeared to be in a separate, untouchable reality, like new souls in the clouds of heaven still wrestling with emotions they'd not had enough lifetime to understand. Perhaps because no one had paid enough attention to them while they were alive.

Jordan introduced the paintings:

> What [artists] do is incredibly important. They civilize us, they teach us how to see . . . and what Tadeusz is doing with his paintings is . . . to make something, but then he takes away everything that makes it easy to see and that means you can't come in here and be perceptually lazy; you have to pay attention. . . . I'm going to tell you a little bit about what

> you've all seen artists do in cities. When a city is decaying . . . the artists [are the] first people to pick up on the possibilities . . . it could be beautiful again, if someone just paid enough attention to it.[12]

Mikhaila's suffering had advanced again to become nearly unbearable. She had entered university as the last of the Millennial generation, just before the iGens arrived, but she too suffered without the protection of her parents. Where Tammy had provided balanced, nutritious meals often using organic ingredients, Mikhaila now subsisted on instant noodles. Where she had been forced to rest and allow her body time to heal, she now forced herself to make up for the school time she'd lost. She later narrated a video about this time:

> God, things got really bad in university. I gained weight, my mood, my mood was just awful. I went completely nuts. I kept trying to fix my antidepressants and try . . . an SNRI which went really badly. I went up on Wellbutrin high enough that it gave me a seizure . . . then it started to hit my skin . . . doctors were telling me, "You know you're doing it yourself. Stop." . . . Because I kept going and saying my skin is like, dying, what's happening?
>
> And they're, "Well stop scratching." I was, you don't understand. So I'm in doctors' offices, crying, and they're like, "Well, you're crazy."[13]

Beyond Jordan and Tammy's protection now, all they could do was watch and worry. Jordan was now fifty-one years old, his hair turning gray. He had gained over fifty pounds, carried a large belly, and had rounded face cheeks. He had psoriasis and uveitis, an inflammation of the inner eyelid. His life-threatening depression that had been under control for years was beginning to cut away again at his peace of mind.

He intensified his study of the psychology in the rapidly unravelling political situation that wreaked increasingly deadly results. The universities themselves were committing suicide, not just the students. Universities in Europe and North America were being pressed to accommodate ever-increasing demands for progressive courses, and entire departments such as Women's, Race, Queer and Gender Studies. At Oberlin College in 2015, the Contemporary American Studies program offered How to Win a Beauty Pageant: Race, Gender, Culture, and U.S. National Identity with the course description, "This course examines US beauty pageants from the 1920s to the present. Our aim will be to analyze pageantry as a unique site for the interplay of race, gender, class, sexuality, and nation."[14]

The yearly cost to attend Oberlin in 2015 was $66,174. Occidental College's Critical Theory & Social Justice: Stupidity course received a remarkable postmodern thrashing of language in its description:

> Stupidity is neither ignorance nor organicity, but rather, a corollary of knowing and an element of normalcy, the double of intelligence rather than its opposite. It is an artifact of our nature as finite beings and one of the most powerful determinants of human destiny. Stupidity is always the name of the Other, and it is the sign of the feminine.[15]

A year at Occidental cost $63,194. The universities were abandoning traditional standards of achievement for the iGen "nobody loses, everybody gets a participation trophy" standard. On top of their difficulty with independent adulthood, they had now received monikers like *snowflakes* or *cupcakes* because of their extreme fragility.

Nearly every university was forced to dramatically increase the ranks of administrators and lawyers to fend off lawsuits from politically motivated professors and *triggered* students. They hiked tuition fees and reduced traditional course offerings such as American History. It was now possible to graduate from UCLA Berkeley with a PhD in history without ever studying American history. They built *safe spaces* manned by full-time counselors providing beds for naps, children's snacks for comfort, and coloring books.

Attempting to understand *snowflakism* and the associated phenomena driving his students and political opposition, Jordan contributed to several papers on the topic. One in particular, "Does Cultural Exposure Partially Explain the Association Between Personality and Political Orientation?," looked at cultural influences:

> Differences in political orientation are partly rooted in personality, with liberalism predicted by Openness to Experience and conservatism by Conscientiousness. Since Openness is positively associated with intellectual and creative activities, these may help shape political orientation. We examined whether exposure to cultural activities and historical knowledge mediates the relationship between personality and political orientation.[16]

One of the base notes in the death knell of Western universities was the shutting down of free speech, and with it, exposure to diverse viewpoints, the essential value of a traditional university education. Combined with the increasing corporate and political concerns of administrators, Jordan and many colleagues began to speak out that the university system itself, after 925 years, was doomed. For Jordan, his success as a television celebrity, entrepreneur, psychologist, and early success on the internet via YouTube presented possible future emergency exit strategies. But he remained deeply grateful for and committed to the university system where he had enjoyed his education and meaningful career. He was first, among his many pursuits, an educator. The damage being done to that special world and the students in it was a constant sorrow and source of rage to him now.

As Jordan had rightly observed, the disintegration of universities, and so the students attending them, was being led by the political left. This was primarily accomplished by disinviting controversial speakers, and if unsuccessful in that, disrupting their events, increasingly with violence. For the left in US universities, disinvitations began to climb in 2009 and spiked significantly higher beginning in 2013, while disinvitations from the right remained constant within a lower range. From 2015, the trend for the left went nearly vertical from twelve to thirty-eight successful disinvitations; for the right it declined from eight to five, making the difference 760 percent between left and right in 2016.[17]

In spite of Jordan's middling stature as a relatively unknown professor at a Canadian university far removed from the American Ivy League, his rapidly expanding YouTube exposure began to bring him to the attention of influential supporters and like-minded colleagues. Particularly important were the young early adopters of the internet who were leading the way in building large online audiences.

In 2012 at the age of eighteen, a young man named Charlie Kirk secured widespread support at the Republican National Convention in Tampa, Florida, to found his brainchild Turning Point USA (TPUSA). The mission of TPUSA was to reverse the advance of progressives on college campuses. This confirmed the opposing conservative political force implied in some of Jordan's research.

Kirk wisely employed tactics that appealed to iGen students to demonstrate the effectiveness of his proposed organization. He had gathered student volunteers to promote conservative ideas using pop culture themes that were attractive to iGens such as "The Healthcare Games," "Game of Loans," and "iCapitalism."[18] With the impressive results of this approach in hand, he secured support from a wide range of important Republican donors and sympathetic conservative organizations. With funding, he set the pace for each of TPUSA's now-paid workers to make at least 1,500 student contacts per semester.[19]

As a result, TPUSA's revenue exploded from inception in 2012 at $78,890 to $443,859 in 2013; $2,052,060 in 2014; $4,319,220 in 2015; and $8,248,059 in 2016.[20]

The internet in 2014 was awash with examples of its influence on Millennials and iGens in particular. Facebook had just exceeded one billion users. Jordan's own YouTube channel was approaching one million views.

Through his extensive research with Robert Pihl and others on motivation and personality, Jordan had developed tests for assessing potential employees and writing exercises for motivating existing employees. He saw the potential to adapt these tools to the people in his life who most needed it: his students. And beyond his students, to all young people whose personalities were left undeveloped and vulnerable to the stresses of popular culture and the disintegration of traditional Western culture.

Jordan, Pihl, and psychologist/software engineer Daniel Higgins adapted these tests and exercises for use on the internet. They created the online platform SelfAuthoring.com that had originated with Jordan and Pihl's research published as "Setting, Elaborating, and Reflecting on Personal Goals Improves Academic Performance" in 2010. Summarized, the findings of their research concluded,

> In the present study, we investigated whether an intensive, online, written, goal-setting program for struggling students would have positive effects on academic achievement. . . . After a 4-month period, students who completed the goal-setting intervention displayed significant improvements in academic performance compared with the control group. The goal-setting program thus appears to be a quick, effective, and inexpensive intervention for struggling undergraduate students.[21]

Multiyear testing of the platform at Rotterdam School of Management, Erasmus University, in the Netherlands concluded,

> The intervention boosted academic achievement and increased retention rates, particularly for ethnic minority and male students (who had underperformed in previous years). The gap in performance between men and women, and for ethnic minorities versus nationals, became considerably smaller within the intervention cohort.
>
> After Year 1, the gender gap closed by 98%, and the ethnicity gap by 38% (rising to 93% after the second year). All groups

> in the intervention cohort performed significantly better than control cohorts, but the effect was particularly large for males and ethnic minorities. The increase in performance was largest for ethnic minority males: they earned 44% more credits, and their retention rate increased 54%. Overall, the results indicate that a comprehensive goal-setting intervention implemented early in students' academic careers can significantly and substantially reduce gender and ethnic minority inequalities in achievement.

In a 2013 report, the US Department of Education praised SelfAuthoring.com as a promising tool for boosting perseverance and resilience, two critical strengths for Millennials and iGens coping with an increasingly high-tech but low-touch world. It was made available and remains available online for under thirty US dollars.

Next, the team adapted their personality assessment tools and called it UnderstandMyself.com. The mission statement appears on the website as:

> We believe that everyone's lives would be improved first by better understanding of the structure of personality, so that the similarities and differences between people are rendered more comprehensible and second by more precise knowledge of their own unique personality configuration (and the personality of those close to them). It's much easier to live, work and play with someone when you truly understand who they are.

The platform was built from research published in 2007, three years prior to the research for SelfAuthoring.com under the title "Between Facets and Domains: 10 Aspects of the Big Five" that concluded,

> The existence of 2 distinct (but correlated) aspects within each of the Big Five (major personality traits), representing an

> intermediate level of personality structure between facets and domains. . . . The correspondence was strong enough to suggest that the 10 aspects of the Big Five may have distinct biological substrates.[22]

Meaning they had sorted human personalities into ten reliable categories that could reveal an individual's strengths and weaknesses and, to some degree, was part of their biology. This was useful for employers who used it for screening potential employees but was potentially life-saving for university students under stress.

Jordan's team set about designing UnderstandMyself.com to measure anyone's Big Five traits and their ten subsidiary aspects. Those were then compared to the team's research database of ten thousand archived personality profiles using multiple variables to produce an accurate interior picture of a person's character. The goal was to help anyone understand their general psychological structure and how it precisely compared to others.

With these two online platforms, Jordan set the cornerstones of a solid psychological foundation for young people. He would help them build a tower, as he had done as a young man, out of their personal, suicidal hell. He knew what it was to be terrified to the point of madness and to build a way out. He remembered hearing two voices in his head, one telling him the truth and one urging him toward destruction. He recognized the same malevolence now in play among his students, a product of familiar resentments, bitter and cruel as ever.

But he also saw the young people in his classroom sit up straight and lean in when he spoke plainly of responsibility as the burden of Atlas, or commitment as the labors of Hercules. Or of voluntarily facing suffering as one of many meanings of the Christian cross. He'd seen them come alive when he told them to clean up their rooms. He heard them go completely silent and still when they began to see a more hopeful future. He was an educator and a healer. These weren't things he did, they were who he was. He knew his students' suffering intimately and took on the responsibility to reduce it as much as possible.

Jordan's young and powerful online colleagues continued to rise up and fight against progressive dominance. Even before iGen provocateur Charlie Kirk opened shop, Ben Shapiro had been a Millennial juggernaut against progressive influence since 2004 when he graduated summa cum laude and Phi Beta Kappa from the University of California, Los Angeles, at age twenty. That was the year his first book, *Brainwashed: How Universities Indoctrinate America's Youth,* first enflamed progressive sensibilities. It was exactly in line with Jordan's observations and confirmation that young people were waking up and fighting back to maintain the institutions and perspectives of the Enlightenment.

In the book, Shapiro argued that university students were not exposed to intellectually diverse viewpoints and so those who lacked strong opinions, or personalities, were being intellectually overwhelmed by the predominantly progressive atmosphere created by instructors, administrators, and fellow students. Shapiro started the first paragraph of the first chapter with an eyewitness account from the classroom, something that Jordan could not provide. He reported on his encounter with the pervasive postmodern nihilism that Jordan had been warning about and fighting against for years,

> "There is no such thing as a neutral or objective claim," said Professor Joshua Muldavin of UCLA. It was early in the quarter, and the professor was explaining to our class that there is no such thing as capital-T Truth. There is no right and wrong, no good and evil, he taught. We must always remember that we are subjective beings, and as such, all of our values are subjective.[23]

Tracing this belief back through the Marxist intellectuals in 1960s France, to the "active measures" of Russian intelligence that were designed to confuse and divide the youth of the West, it could be argued that this was confirmation of their success. This same nihilistic message had penetrated nearly every college in the West by this time and was partly responsible for turning the free world against itself. It took a phenomenally talented and perceptive young man, with firmly grounded Judeo-Christian ethics, to detect and expose this disorienting and divisive idea.

Ben Shapiro went on to earn a bachelor of arts degree in political science and graduate cum laude from Harvard Law School in 2007. By the time Jordan and Kirk were beginning to make inroads online in 2013, Shapiro's fifth book, *Bullies: How the Left's Culture of Fear and Intimidation Silences Americans* was published and provoked even more howls of progressive outrage. As with many of Jordan's efforts by this time, threats of physical violence found Shapiro. In fact, in a later study by the Anti-Defamation League, they found that Shapiro, a Jew, was the most frequent target of anti-Semitic tweets against journalists. To his credit, he remained resolute even when threatened by the tide of anonymous hatred online. He even escalated the fight by going online himself that year with the website Truth-Revolt, a media watchdog and activism effort, funded largely by the David Horowitz Freedom Center. On September 21, 2015, Shapiro escalated the brawl even further, by launching The Daily Wire with several million dollars of support. The site quickly became a leading internet broadcaster of conservative opinion and news.

The uprising against progressive influence was, in many cases, coming down to Millennials and iGens including Kirk, Shapiro, Joe Rogan, Bret and Eric Weinstein, Dave Rubin, Candace Owens, and Sam Harris with a few older Baby Boomers like Glenn Beck, Jordan Peterson, Dinesh D'Souza, and Dennis Prager thrown in who had mastered the new, online media. They began to form a fractious coalition of sometimes opposing voices that eventually became known as the Intellectual Dark Web for its unfettered, high-level discussions and debates on serious, challenging current topics.

Glenn Beck, in particular, who had high visibility on cable giant

Fox News, was the first to draw out the big guns of the opposing progressive view. RT (Russian Television) attacked him immediately. He was a prime target for what would become known as the resistance and emerging, progressive revolutionary leaders such as Linda Sarsour. Sarsour, an avowed Islamist and proponent of Sharia law, became the main spokesperson for the Women's March opposing Donald Trump's election and promoting the resistance movement.

Like some antiwar and environmental activists of the 1960s, Sarsour and her colleagues were amply supplied with outrage and revolutionary fervor by the Russian government through RT who fed inflammatory stories to friendly networks like CNN and MSNBC. The old reliable "active measures" of Russian intelligence were still very much alive, in fact, coming into full bloom.[24]

Alyona Minkovski, an attractive young woman, native Russian, and host of her own RT show, adopted the Millennial name-calling approach now common in chat rooms and on campuses in calling Beck,

> The doughboy nut job from Fox News . . . I get to ask all the questions that the American people want answered about their own country because I care about this country and I don't work for a corporate-owned media organization.
>
> Fox . . . you hate Americans. Glenn Beck, you hate Americans. Because you lie to them, you scare them, you try to warp their minds. You tell them that we're becoming some socialist country. . . . You're not on the side of America. And the fact that my channel is more honest with the American people is something you should be ashamed of.[25]

The irony of a government-controlled RT host accusing an American Fox News host of being corporately controlled was, one suspects, deliberately lost on Minkovski. The further irony of Minkovski being more honest and patriotic than Beck, a publicly recognized patriot, widely trusted, even though controversial public figure, might also be attributed to her overwrought emotional state.

As Jordan might have predicted, this was the emergence of the shadow side of the internet explosion. It was evolving in real time. He was fascinated by the hyper-mythologizing—gods being born overnight and exacting vengeance instantly—but was also keenly aware of the distant strains of totalitarian marching music hitting his ear.

Online character assassination, threats of violence, exposure of private information (doxing), and de-platforming were becoming powerful weapons on both sides of the progressive/conservative divide. Early internet provocateurs Milo Yiannopoulos and Alex Jones would fall to de-platforming as social media monopolies Facebook, Google, and Twitter revealed themselves to be in the progressive camp by using the new standard "hate speech is not free speech" to throttle conservative, or as Jordan described himself, traditionalist voices.

Jordan warned repeatedly against restricting any speech, particularly the hateful and vicious kind:

> It's extraordinarily dangerous to drive hate speech underground. There are a lot of terrible things that people shouldn't say, but that does not mean you should stop them from saying them, because you want to know who is saying them and you want to bring discourse to bear on their perspective.[26]

But underground is exactly where hate speech went as attacks and counterattacks multiplied geometrically. As Jordan had cautioned, extraordinarily dangerous, violent, partisan taunts and threats bloomed underground in unmodulated chat rooms like 4chan and the message board Voat, where Jordan's more vocal followers seemed to congregate. In this underground echo chamber, an odd, juvenile mythology sprang up using the Egyptian goddess of darkness and chaos called Kuk. Goddess Kuk had the face of a frog, a night creature of dark swamps. She was adopted as a *meme,* a symbol used to identify those interested in invoking her powers of chaos.

Somehow Kuk's name was transformed into *Kek,* some said from the frequently mistyped abbreviation LOL meaning laugh out loud, but the true origin of the name change was unclear. Soon, the image of Kek was transformed into the popular cartoon frog called *Pepe,* a more relatable, semi-ironic figure of playfulness to the increasingly angry young men who were rallying under Jordan's flag.

Fascinated by this dynamic god-making going on, Jordan began tweeting to his followers to get a grasp on what exactly was happening. Why did they invent a new god? And a cartoon frog at that? Were they serious or transient fun-seekers? Why were they so vicious? He tweeted for clues at the rate of about one hundred tweets per week. Incoming fire was hitting closer to home as threats escalated toward him personally. He saw *flame wars,* individuals and small groups locked in exchanges of bitter insults and hateful threats, things that would get them arrested or possibly physically attacked in the real world. Flame wars were erupting on every platform, as if the grievances of the world were being aired all at once. He gravitated toward Quora, a question and answer platform that minimized contention and focused on dialogue as he worked to quell some of the violent exchanges elsewhere:

> One of the things I've done is I've convinced many people on the right to moderate their viewpoints. They write and tell me that they were being pulled into radical nationalism of the more extreme and racist kind and as a result of listening to me they've moderated their views.[27]

The fog of war rose up around him and began to obscure friends and enemies. Yet he charged into the fray with thousands of tweets, hundreds of YouTube videos, and Quora questions. He witnessed the collective unconscious birthing its hideous nightmares in strange deities called Kek and Pepe. His insatiable hunger for answers to the many evils in a human heart drove him on. In hindsight, he might have proceeded more cautiously. The friendly cartoon frog Pepe, now a symbol of militant conservatives and disdained as the mocking face of the alt-right, would come back to bite him. An incautious photograph with the cartoon brought vicious accusations of white nationalism, homophobia, and transphobia against him.

Mikhaila had been suffering through college with bloating and itching sores all over her face, in addition to her depression and arthritis. The skin eruptions were new, but she'd felt itching all over her body since she was fourteen, for over eight years. By this time, she had accepted her fate that arthritis and particularly her depression were going to be with her forever, but she was determined to regain her beautiful skin. A new sequence of dermatologists had nothing for her. She kept insisting that her "skin was dying," but their only suggestion was that she stop scratching her sores. This dimwitted advice finally pushed her beyond her limits and she broke down into tears of frustration. The coup de grace, the last refuge of the truly clueless, was when her final dermatologist suggested it was a mental condition. That was it. Much like her father, when she'd reached the bottom of her personal hell, she was ready to fight:

> At 22 I was like, oh, this is actually killing me. So I started researching and I read. I started with the skin problem because I was like, okay, I'm gonna have depression for life, I'm gonna have arthritis for life but I really don't want my skin to look like that. So it was like a vanity thing.[28]

She focused on her skin and following her father's example, began to read. She read hundreds of papers on skin disorders. After what she described as "a very long time," she came upon information about celiac rash, an itching rash caused by gluten. She had found a key, a cornerstone to build her own tower out of hell.

Learning that gluten was bad for the gut, not just hers but everyone's, particularly those with the celiac gene, she underwent testing which confirmed she had the gene. Hence, she eliminated gluten from her diet. Her list of medications at this point was up to twenty, about half of them to counteract the side effects of the others.

Eliminating gluten had almost no effect. She began an elimination diet that excluded everything except meat, vegetables, and rice. Essentially the diet her mother, Tammy, had provided. After a week, she was getting cravings and made a batch of gluten-free, dairy-free, sugar-free, banana and almond flour muffins. She ate five of them immediately. The next morning she woke up and felt fine, except that her wrists were slightly sore. Whatever! The muffins were delicious—she ate four more.

Nothing happened; no bloating, no skin outbreaks, home free.

The following day her wrists were still a bit sore; no worries. She went shopping, probably for more almond flour, when suddenly both knees locked up. She was paralyzed and in agony, but with an important discovery even then filling her mind. The next two days were spent in bed. Experiment concluded.

Returning strictly to her elimination diet, the bloating disappeared. Losing three pant sizes and five pounds over the next month, she saw her abdominal muscles emerge for the first time. She'd been bloated her entire life. She patiently modified the amounts of each ingredient until she noticed that rice was affecting her. Rice was out, and eventually apples and root vegetables, excluding potatoes, were in. Months went by as symptoms slowly faded and medications began dropping off the list.

But she was not nearly out of danger. Bored with her diet, Mikhaila rashly decided to test "a pile of" untested foods including sugar. She was impatient and no longer meticulous in her food choices or portions. She reviewed this decision in a later presentation at the Boulder Carnivore Conference in 2019, but had no explanation for it. The results were, of course, predictable.

> I went to doctors and I was saying man I think I'm allergic to soy, I think I'm allergic to almonds, like I think I'm allergic

> to sugar. And they're going, "Well, it's not showing up on the skin test."
>
> Something's happening, did you look into other types of antibodies or inflammatory reactions? "No, those aren't real allergies."
>
> My arthritis is back, my skin is breaking out, I have body odor, my gums are bleeding, my face is puffy and I'm on the verge of hallucinating.

She stopped seeing her immunologist in February 2015, returning to a strict diet of meat, lettuce, salt, pepper, olive oil, and apple cider vinegar. It would be nearly a year before she achieved significant improvement.

CHAPTER THIRTEEN

THE MAELSTROM

Inside the collective is a beast and the beast uses its fists. If you wake up the beast then violence emerges. I'm afraid that this continual pushing by radical left wingers is going to wake up the beast.[1]

—JORDAN PETERSON, PROFESSOR OF PSYCHOLOGY, UNIVERSITY OF TORONTO

I think it's about abuse of power. Peterson is using his position as a university professor to build his revenue stream. . . . He took the life force from me and some of our students and dehumanized us for fun and profit and I'm still not ok with it.[2]

—A. W. PEET, PROFESSOR OF PHYSICS, UNIVERSITY OF TORONTO

He'd never been accused of stealing life force before, but then a lot of things were new in the language and the attitudes of former friendly colleagues. Jordan was beginning to take on a mythology of his own, growing horns, in the minds of some. According to naysayers, he was now actively harming people, particularly vulnerable students. Criminal prosecution was not out of the question if he could be tied to the actual harm, from the least harmful self-cutting to the most heinous acts of rape or suicide.

Campus rape was a new epidemic, likely the product of toxic masculinity and very likely a "crime by association" for those accused of promoting such acts. The OHRC and its reserve troops in the New Democratic Party were paying close attention after US president Obama sounded the alarm, followed by US senators Kirsten Gillibrand and Claire McCaskill who then campaigned for their Campus Accountability and Safety Act.[3] Senator Gillebrand said, "The price of a college education should never include a one in five chance of being sexually assaulted! . . . Women are at greater risk of sexual assault as soon as they step on a college campus."

Although Senator Gillibrand was doing her best to stem this tide of depravity, she was wrong about her statistics. But she wasn't completely to blame. Her "one in five chance of being sexually assaulted" for young women on campus had come directly from President Obama himself who stated it at a White House news briefing: "It is estimated that one in five women on college campuses has been sexually assaulted during their time there. One in five."

That was odd considering his own Department of Justice had just completed a six-year study on college rape concluding the ratio was in fact 6.1 in 1,000. This was 0.6 percent instead of the stated 20 percent. But it was Gillibrand's own mistake to say, "Women are at greater risk of sexual assault as soon as they step on a college campus," because the truth was they were safer. The government study also showed that compared to college students with a 0.6 percent risk, nonstudents had a risk of 0.78 percent. And unfortunately for the whole narrative, the study also showed that campus rape and sexual assaults had been decreasing steadily from 9.2 per 1,000 in 1997 to less than half that at 4.4 per 1,000 in 2013.[4]

Statistics aside, it appeared that the crisis was still a valid cause, and immediate legislation was needed to protect young women students. Particularly in Canada where Sara-Jane Finlay, associate vice president of Equity & Inclusion at the University of British Columbia insisted, "There has been a growing recognition across all campuses in North America that sexual assault really is a crime like no other. To deal with it in the best and most responsible way, it's important [for it to] have its own policy."[5]

Jordan's former comrades in the NDP were on it. Crises, particularly ones concerning crimes "like no other," made new legislation urgent and assured maximum media coverage. The rape crisis was perfect.

The NDP had tried for seven years to get an amendment inserted into Canada's criminal code that made it a criminal offense to "incite or promote hatred because of gender identity or gender expression."[6]

Presumably this also included the gender expressions *man* and *woman*, so in effect, everyone. Common sense definitions aside, the NDP bill precisely defined *gender identity* as "the individual's deeply felt internal and individual experience of gender, which may or may not correspond with the sex that the individual was assigned at birth."

Since gender identity was defined here by feelings rather than biology, it was akin to religious belief but without the traditional social proof of a consistent religious practice or canon of accepted documentation. It may be the first instance in English common law of a law based on deeply held feelings rather than deeply held beliefs. Citizens quickly labeled the law the Bathroom Bill since it protected men who felt they were women, if only for a moment, to enter and use a women's bathroom. This applied even if they'd just come off a construction site in hardhat and overalls, unshaven and without a stitch of makeup. And to be found guilty of this serious, discriminatory hate crime, one had only to create "evidence that the offence was motivated by bias, prejudice or hate based on race, national or ethnic origin, language, colour, religion, sex, age, mental or physical disability, gender identity, sexual orientation, or any other similar factor."

So, a woman who might feel threatened in a male-invaded bathroom could theoretically sue the lady in overalls, who in turn could countersue the threatened lady in lipstick for discrimination as well. As if the proposed law weren't vague enough, the end phrase "or any other similar factor" made certain that no one could possibly be left out of this legal carnival. Also, no one in the future who deeply felt they were a tortoise or field mouse, species being *similar* to, say, race, could be denied. Lawyer's groups must have found the legislation enchanting.

Conservative legislator Michelle Rempel, MP, admitted that she found the amendment vague to the point of being unpredictable in its effect:

> What constitutes the scope of discrimination against someone based on his or her gender identity in the eyes of my colleagues, as legislators, of members of the trans community and the courts? What kind of speech based on someone's gender identity could be considered hate propaganda? What does it mean in defined terms to have a bias based on a person's deeply held internal and individual experience of gender?[7]

Even NDP legislator Raymond Côté couldn't quite find the handle on the bill of his own party, saying, "First, it is important to point out that gender identity and gender expression are basically a state of being, or in other words, something that cannot be fully explained outside the personal experience of the individual in that state."[8]

Clearly, at least a few legislators in both camps were not sure of either the definitions or implications of the amendment. The plain reading of the amendment implies that anyone could be convicted for saying or doing almost anything that someone else felt was biased. Presumably, the OHRC would decide who was naughty.

Jordan was no doubt aware of his former comrades' efforts spanning many years. In 2005, the NDP first introduced their bill they called An Act to Amend the Canadian Human Rights Act and the Criminal Code (for gender identity). It failed. They reintroduced it in 2006; it failed again. In 2009, they attempted to add it to the hate crimes provisions of the criminal code. It failed. In 2011, it failed once more. In 2012, working with the Liberal Party, the NDP introduced essentially identical bills, C-276 and C-279, possibly to overwhelm or exhaust parliament. Both failed.

What passage of C-279 would have meant for Jordan was, if he had discriminated against women, or men who deeply felt they were women, or vice versa, by his aggressive encouragement of masculinity, he could have faced a tribunal of those "peevish and resentful" people he'd insulted nearly forty years ago. They were now administrators for the OHRC and officers for the prime minister and attorney general of Canada. In fact, with the rape crisis on campus spiraling into an epidemic, the time was rapidly approaching when the OHRC would ask to have a little chat with their disloyal comrade.

After the humiliating final defeat of C-279 in 2012, the NDP was in disarray. New blood was needed. Newly minted liberal politician Justin Trudeau, just forty-one years old, would do. He had a pedigree as the son of former prime minister Pierre Trudeau, a talent for debate, and two essential elements the NDP needed desperately: a devotion to progressive causes and ambition. Trudeau aspired to be "a positive influence in the world."[9]

He graduated from McGill University in 1994, then University of British Columbia in 1998 with a bachelor of arts degree in literature and a bachelor of education degree respectively. He went on to study engineering at Montreal's École Polytechnique in 2002 before dropping out in 2003. In 2004, he went back to McGill University to study environmental geography but again dropped out after one year. He had been a camp counselor, nightclub bouncer, and snowboard instructor, but eventually found steady work as a French and mathematics teacher at the private West Point Grey Academy. He then felt the urge to follow in his father's political footsteps and was ready to lead the country.

Arriving just in time, young Justin ascended quickly to the leadership of the NDP. Then riding the wave of progressive outrage over the repeated defeat of their agenda and the rise of traditionalist voices like Jordan Peterson, he led the Liberal Party to a sweeping national victory in 2015. The Liberal Party went from third place with 36 seats to a dominating 184 seats, the largest increase by a party ever in a federal election. He was sworn in as prime minister of Canada on November 4, 2015.

Jordan would come to have a few things to say about Prime Minister Justin Trudeau, including,

> I just shake my head . . . [a] man who capitalized without virtue on the name of his father . . . it's not excusable. You should move ahead on your own merits especially if you're daring to do something like run a country. You have a moral duty, if you have the advantage of a name, you have a moral duty to supersede the accomplishments of the person who bore that name and gave it its weight before you dare capitalize on it in the public sphere.
>
> Trudeau did none of that. . . . He knows how to behave, he knows how to act in public, he had the upbringing for it. Other than that there's nothing there. . . . He's not an impressive person in my estimation.
>
> He appointed females to 50 percent of his cabinet . . . he says well, because it's 2015. Your job was to pick the most qualified people period, regardless of their genitalia, because they're leading the country. [He] steadily abdicated his responsibility to make those difficult decisions and then wallpapered it over with this casual virtue of well, I'm going to promote women. It's like, no, you're going to promote competent people, you weasel.[10]

Once in office, Trudeau wasted no time. He issued a mandate letter to incoming liberal attorney general Jody Wilson-Raybould mandating that Wilson-Raybould avenge C-279 with stricter federal protections for gender identities. Wilson-Raybould set to work adding prohibited speech called *hate propaganda* to the proposed law.

In a liberal interpretation, for instance by the OHRC, this could create an entirely new set of values in English common law. Canadians who publicly "denied respect" to certain deeply felt gender identities by refusing to value them sufficiently in their choice of words, could wind up in federal prison for five years. Every bar and happy hour in Canada could become a breeding ground for disrespectful felons. Conservatives had to be stopped before someone got seriously disrespected.

Still apparently unaware of the rape and speech crime waves all around him, Jordan began 2015 by teaching Maps of Meaning: Object and Meaning (Part 2). In the video of the lecture, he appears energetic, physically well, and a bit thinner than before. Presciently perhaps, he begins the lecture by examining the psychological motives of political movements, saying, "Nietzsche said God is dead and he believed that things would fall apart as a consequence of that."[11] He continued,

> So Nietzsche's claim and Dostoevsky's claim were quite straightforward. They said that once you took the foundation out of something it would fall. . . . We should be very careful before we jump to the conclusion that values are, or even can be, something that people actually create. . . . One reason you might be hesitant to do that is that Hitler created his values, so to speak, and so did the Soviet communists and North Koreans. You know, they're trying to impose a rationalist value structure on a society. . . . As the Marxist revisionists rally back to the original beliefs, the estimate keeps going down but you know it was tens of millions of people, and in China, who knows, it was maybe a hundred million people [were killed] . . . so the act of attempting to rationally construct a value system and then impose it, that doesn't seem to work out very well.[12]

But constructing and imposing a rational value system was exactly what the NDP and Liberal Party were up to. Shutting down hateful speech against a proliferating number of genders was more valuable than defending freedom of speech for all. In his lecture, he delved into the origins of these human values:

> What Jung did . . . he said, well, maybe we have to go back down into the deep symbolic substrata of the human psyche to find the origin place of the ideas that we used to hold as religious. . . . the source of ritual, symbol and religious ideas . . . that strikes me as a wiser approach than the rational approach which says you can just create your values. It's like, we tried that. It didn't work, it *really* didn't work.[13]

It seemed clear that Jordan was on a collision course with the Canadian government. In April, Jordan's 104th academic paper, "Why Do Conservatives Report Being Happier than Liberals? The Contribution of Neuroticism," written with Caitlin Burton and Jason Plaks, shed some light on why Jordan and progressives like the NDP had such different values.

> Previous studies suggest that conservatives in the United States are happier than liberals. This difference has been attributed to factors including differences in socioeconomic status, group memberships, and system-justifying beliefs. We suggest that differences between liberals and conservatives in personality traits may provide an additional account for the "happiness gap." Specifically, we investigated the role of neuroticism (or conversely, emotional stability) in explaining the conservative-liberal happiness gap. . . . In both studies, neuroticism negatively correlated with conservatism. We suggest that individual differences in neuroticism represent a previously under-examined contributor to the SWL (Satisfaction with Life) disparity between conservatives and liberals.[14]

It made sense that progressive insurgents, like the NDP and the Liberal Party, might be unhappier than the people they were attempting to replace. It also made sense that unhappy people would be drawn into insurgent causes, reinforcing Jordan's earliest observations about the "peevish and resentful" people of the NDP.

It also might be guessed that irritable people would become more so in groups. How could they possibly not irritate each other? How could they possibly not become more peevish when sharing stories about the corruption and unfairness of the world? And how could all this unhappiness not escalate the tension and rhetoric online, on campus, and across Canada?

In the face of this encircling unhappiness, Jordan continued to offer a positive, encouraging message to his students. He had recently witnessed the opposite trend at a symposium of academics speaking on the environment,

> I've heard people say, human beings are like a cancer on the planet. . . . One of the professors who was a radical environmentalist . . . told the whole audience, they were all people about your age, that if they had any ounce of ethical, if they had any ethical standards whatsoever, they wouldn't reproduce. . . . I thought that's bloody pathological when you stand up in front of a whole bunch of young people who have their whole future in front of them, you say, well you know, you're such a horrid creature in your very core that it would be a moral violation for you to propagate.[15]

In spite of his typical crushing schedule of full-time professor, scientific paper researcher and publisher, clinical psychologist caretaker of twenty patients, architect of an online presence with tweets, videos, and online assessment tools, consultant for law firms, author and editor writing *Maps of Meaning*, assessment tools designer for Examcorp, and active parent of teenage son Julian and college student Mikhaila, Jordan had also been an activist for years in grassroots environmental politics with a group called Marine Life Advocacy. The group had addressed a letter to former prime minister Stephen Harper that began,

> June 1, 2014
>
> Dear Prime Minister Stephen Harper,
>
> Canadian oceans are still not being protected. Canada currently protects 1.1% of its oceanic territory while the United States of America protects 29.4% and Australia 27.9%(1). . . . The lack of oceanic protection is compromising the fishing industry, which currently employs 120,000 people(2) and exports $4.1 billion (CAD)(3) worth of goods every year.

Jordan spoke at events for the group with prominent environmental leaders including Dr. Arthur Hanson, an officer of the prestigious Order of Canada. In response to a question about how to change people's minds regarding the protection of Canada's oceans, Jordan encouraged direct political engagement:

> The only real effective means of changing individual behavior that I think would actually work is for people to write their MPs [members of parliament] and members of the cabinet because, believe it or not, politicians actually pay attention to letters. . . . Our political system actually does work. It's much more permeable than people really think. . . . You know most people don't really participate in the political system so it leaves it in the hands of the very small minority who do. But it's surprisingly permeable if you're interested in permeating it.[16]

He was also now speaking regularly to a national audience through the Canadian Broadcast Corporation (CBC) as well as appearing regularly to regional Ontario audiences on Television Ontario (TVO). He was known among national lawmakers for his occasionally controversial public statements as well as for his aforementioned online platform, now eliciting nearly one million YouTube views, and extremely popular Twitter, Quora, and Facebook accounts.

He addressed the emerging problem of political and civil violence such as the Columbine and Sandy Hook school shootings, the recent Jerusalem bus bombings, and the Charlie Hebdo killings on a CBC radio program called *A History of Violence: CBC Ideas.* This program was edited from the audio recording of his live appearance previously at the Stratford Festival in Stratford, Ontario. His statement on the causes of violence seems informed by his recent reading of the Christian Bible's New Testament and the book of Genesis regarding "the word":

> Chaos is transformed into order by the word and you are all speakers of the word. If you want chaos to be transformed into hell, then lie. If you want chaos to be transformed into heaven, then tell the truth. . . . I think if you want to fix the world, fix yourself. It's a lot harder than you think, right? It says in the New Testament it's harder to rule yourself than to rule the city, but why? Well, it turns out you're more complicated than a city. It also turns out that you're more important, in some sense, than a city.

His increasing references to Christian ideology were winning him no friends on the progressive, generally atheistic political left. The NDP already considered him a traitor. He was now an active public relations and political problem. A posted comment on the CBC page that carries the program gives a possibly representative atheistic response,

> Count me out of Jordan Peterson's imagined species. Fortunately, there's good archaeological evidence that early humans (not Paul, nor Cain and Abel) didn't "thirst" for violence, and that these behaviors stemmed from specific conditions like possessing fixed property, not Peterson's Western "archetypes". We do our species a disservice in believing we are worse than we are, and we endanger ourselves when we misidentify the

> causes of our real problems. Peterson's arguments obliterate the experiences of whole nations of humanity, and entire passages of history.
>
> It's gross and it's wrong. I usually enjoy Ideas, and I'm sad to hear airwaves clouded with misanthropy and straw-man intellectual dishonesty.

But Jordan's appearances on national media were not creating nearly as many problems for progressives as his online postings, particularly his tweets like, "University bans use of 'Mr.' and 'Ms.' in all correspondence."[17]

This was drawing fire directly toward Trudeau's Liberal Party and its continuing efforts to build public support for gender speech codes. Apparently, Jordan was ready to take them on. He continued to tweet and cite articles against the throttling of free speech,

> "Public university spends $16K on campaign to warn students to watch what they say"[18]
>
> "University of Missouri Police Ask Students to Report 'Hurtful Speech'"[19]
>
> "Microaggression, Macro-Crazy by Heather Mac Donald, City Journal Summer 2015"[20]
>
> "Canadian govt's online 'ethics' course offers its victims a 'happy face' each time they answer correctly."[21]

And finally, at the end of 2015, Jordan tweeted a change of pace, linking to a funny article in *The Onion* titled, "Woman's Parents Accepting Of Mixed-Attractiveness Relationship."[22]

He may have been weary of politics, or just lighthearted since witnessing a miracle in his own home. In November, after months of slow improvement, Mikhaila's depression of fifteen years lifted completely. In fact, all of her afflictions had disappeared. She had gradually stopped taking all her medications including the last to go, the SSRIs for her depression. After generations of the Peterson family suffering so desperately, she had returned from her hero's journey just in time for Christmas.

During her short lifetime of constant suffering, Mikhaila had proven that she was at least as tough-minded as her ancestors, early settlers on the frozen northern Alberta prairie. Her many undeserved punishments had not ruined her, made her bitter or self-pitying. Just the opposite. She had completely regained her sunny, fun-loving, and kindhearted disposition.

Mikhaila was free, but depression still clung to her father like a leech, draining his happiness and energy. He was skeptical of Mikhaila's all-meat diet and, for the moment, deaf to her pleas to try it. He hesitated, remaining vigilant against another relapse of her depression. It was November, a potentially deadly time for depressives.

A month passed and Mikhaila continued to enjoy life as a depression-free and symptomless twenty-three-year-old. She applied her new exuberant energy into hounding her father incessantly. He had to at least try the diet. Perhaps as a Christmas present, perhaps because he was just so overjoyed to see his precious daughter healthy again, he conceded and began her strictly carnivorous diet on December 21.

By the spring of 2016, Jordan was being pulled directly into the public debate over gender. The previously unimaginable idea that gender, including gender-specific behavior and psychology, was a social construct, had gained widespread credibility. TVO responded with a program on *The Agenda* series called "Gender and the Brain" that featured Jordan, Dr. Daphna Joel from Tel Aviv University, and Dr. Margaret McCarthy of the University of Maryland School of Medicine. Jordan appeared a bit trimmer and overall healthier as compared to recent appearances and sported a short haircut with his hair straightened and combed forward, a style never seen before. Perhaps he was covering the thinning hair that remained on his front left hairline.

After hearing the current scientific evidence on the unique

electrical patterns in the brains of men and women (horizontal across brain hemispheres for women, and vertical front to back within hemispheres for men), Dr. Joel argued the progressive, political line on gender differences relating them to racism,

> I think we should not be obsessed by the question. Are we obsessed by the question of whether there is an essential difference between people with light skin color and dark skin color? Are we obsessed with this? This is not politically legitimate to even ask this question, is it?
>
> So why is it legitimate to ask the question whether males and females are fundamentally different? And I think the only reason to ask this question, and this is why we are obsessed with it, is we want to say that there are natural differences because this justifies the different treatment of males and females in our society.[23]

Dr. McCarthy calmly argued against Joel's claim that it was not even politically legitimate to ask about the differences between men and women, saying that there were many legitimate reasons to ask the question and pursue the answers. Steve Paikin, the host, took Jordan off on a discussion of recent research showing marked differences in male and female children's play, long before any socialization could be applied. But Jordan was drawn back immediately afterward to the political question raised by Joel,

> First of all, I don't think there are politically illegitimate domains of scientific inquiry, there's just scientific inquiry. I mean, with racial differences for example, it's the case that the causes of elevated blood pressure, for example, in black Americans versus white Americans are not the same.
>
> Black Americans tend to be more salt sensitive than white Americans and that actually happens to be an important thing if you're a black American with high blood pressure.[24]

He then went on to cite examples of important differences in the biology of many groups of people, including Jewish people and more specifically European Jews, like Dr. Joel. He then politely attacked her ideological argument and subtly insulted her for inserting her politics about gender into the discussion without any scientific or sociological evidence:

> But part of the reason you want to get it right is because people take their guesses about gender differences which are usually ideologically informed and so they're global and not specified and usually not based on any data, and then they make political decisions that are predicated on them.[25]

He then zeroed in on Joel to cite the precisely relevant scientific data that defeated her position. He also indicted her for promoting political coercion, all in the quiet tones of professional discussion, continuing,

> In Scandinavia for example, the presumption has always been that the reason that there are more female nurses than male nurses is because of socialization differences. And then the consequences [of that]. You might say, so what? But the consequence of that is that there are continual movements by people who are obsessed with equality of outcome to ensure that that stops being the case and you can think of that as a form of coercion.[26]

Host Paikin recognized the political drift of the conversation and pulled the discussion back to gender differences. Dr. Joel ignored the discrediting Scandinavian example and referred instead back to a previously mentioned study about babies and face recognition. She dismissed this facial recognition study as flawed allowing her to reassert her "mosaic" or genderless theory, and the discussion falls back again into the minutiae of scientific nitpicking.

Dr. McCarthy spoke at length about various studies that confirmed the clear role of testosterone in aggressive male behavior, and Jordan cited several more studies of specific male behaviors related to dominance and why men and women at different points in life have particular behaviors. Dr. Joel, an Israeli, dismissed both sets of scientific fact in slightly fractured English: "I think this is [*sic*] very nice stories but there is no good evidence. I mean it's very descriptive but it doesn't show that this is nature or biological."[27]

The camera does not show the reactions of her two disparaged colleagues. She goes on to cite a study with chimpanzees and bonobos showing cooperative child rearing among primates who have multiple sexual partners—a sort of nursery collective—and suggested this was a wise peacekeeping adaptation that humans should employ.

Jordan was included in a split screen and appeared at first pensive and paying close attention. His reaction of disbelief built as Dr. Joel continued to admire the wisdom of monkeys. Jordan wagged his head and slowly looked down, his head coming to rest in his hand as if he's just witnessed something very disheartening. Dr. Joel continued in a conflicting postmodern thrashing of language that left Jordan momentarily stunned with head in hand, "I'm assuming that the way our society is apparently built is a result of evolution and, necessarily, the only possible result of evolution. Again, it's a political argument. It's not . . . nothing makes it a scientific argument."[28]

Host Paikin saw Jordan rally from his discouragement, take a drink of water, and prepare to go back at Joel. He said, "OK, Jordan, I know you want to get back in here, but we've got fifteen minutes left . . ."

Paikin directed the discussion toward "the most significant debate of the last twenty years on this issue" that was started by the president of Harvard, Lawrence Summers, when Jordan was there in 2005. Paikin read a quote as a graphic of Summers's quote appeared on screen:

> "There is relatively clear evidence that whatever the difference in means, which can be debated, there is a difference in the standard deviation and variability of a male and female population."
>
> That was Lawrence Summers . . . on why he thought men were better at math than women. And of course, when he said that, female professors at Harvard were extremely disappointed and upset and I think some walked out on his speech when he said that.[29]

Paikin was correct. After the women walked out on President Summers, they led a movement that convinced him to leave before he got thrown out. Jordan referred again to the Scandinavian research confirming males indeed differed widely in a variety of ways from females, particularly and against expectations, in a gender-neutral political environment like Scandinavia. Dr. McCarthy added confirmation of gender differences personally as a wife and mother of two children, stating categorically, and from personal observation rather than statistics, that men and women had distinct natural tendencies to behave as either fathers or mothers.

Again, Dr. Joel did not believe or chose to ignore what her colleagues had just said. She continued to insist that gender was entirely determined by society, not biology, saying, "So the problem is again our social structure which reinforces and creates these differences. Whether in a gender-neutral society we will still have these differences, no one knows."[30]

Except people actually did know, and Jordan had just explained the science twice that said so. Clearly, the argument for Dr. Joel and presumably many other progressives was beyond rational discussion. It was now apparently a matter of quasi-religious faith, and as in President Summers's case, an effective weapon of political coercion.

The NDP had been promoting the same belief in nonbiological gender for years.

In 2014, they distributed a public brochure that outlined legalistic concepts they planned to use in a future bill in parliament. It read,

> Harassment (of non-binary gendered people) is a form of discrimination. It can include sexually explicit or other inappropriate comments, questions, jokes, name-calling, images, email and social media, transphobic, homophobic or other bullying, sexual advances, touching and other unwelcome and ongoing behaviour that insults, demeans, harms or threatens a person in some way.[31]

In the final language of the bill, phrases like "other inappropriate comments" would be struck as too broad, the word *jokes* would be struck as likely to draw resistance from free speech advocates, and "behaviour that insults" would be changed to "behaviour that disrespects" as a concept more grounded in law. Again dismissing biology and medical science for "deeply felt" feelings, the NDP floated the concept in the brochure that "Trans people can have their name or sex designation changed on identity documents and other records. The criteria and process should not be intrusive or medically based."[32]

Again, science had no place in their argument. The NDP would define what gender was. They planned to control what could and could not be said about it. And they, through their acolytes in the OHRC, would punish the wicked and the profane.

Jordan apparently did his research work during the first semester of the school year, September through December. This included writing up the research for peer review. It could take several months before these papers were reviewed and published in various scientific journals.

The first to be published in 2016 was called "Openness to Experience and Intellect Differentially Predict Creative Achievement in the Arts and Sciences." Published in April, it concluded, "We confirmed the hypothesis that whereas Openness predicts creative achievement in the arts, Intellect predicts creative achievement in the sciences."

This topic was a line of inquiry he had been working on for years, ever since he moved from the study of alcoholism in late 1990s. But what was notable this year was the predominance of politically oriented research. Two of the four papers published this year were concerned with politics.

The first, "From Dispositions to Goals to Ideology: Toward a Synthesis of Personality and Social Psychological Approaches to Political Orientation" was published in May, then "Ideological Reactivity: Political Conservatism and Brain Responsivity to Emotional and Neutral Stimuli" was published in December. The remaining fourth paper had to do with the performance of new researchers, unrelated to creative artists or political personalities. His research could almost be read as a psychic roadmap for the coming year.

On January 12, 2016, he introduced a new course at the University of Toronto, designated as Psychology 230, that he had designed to include his most current research. He titled the course 2016 Personality Lecture. There were thirteen lectures in the series, and all of them were recorded on a single camera from a stationary position to his left and below, creating an odd, frankly amateurish, low-angle profile view. Yet, the first video in the series eventually gathered an extraordinary 223,997 views strictly from word of mouth. The series ended on March 29. Within weeks it had driven his YouTube channel to over 1 million views. He was then a bona fide internet phenomenon.

The first lecture in the thirteen-part series was called Openness and Intelligence, referring to Jordan's most recent research on the dominant personality traits of artists versus scientists. He introduced the course,

> This course is in fact wide-ranging. It brings in elements of cultural history, elements of moral philosophy, and then elements that I would consider are almost completely biological.

> And it does that in order to provide you with a multidimensional view of what it means to be a human being.

This was a fair description of Jordan himself at this point, his eclectic approach from philosophy to history to culture to biology, and finally, to his eternal quest after what it meant to be a human being.

Through the three months of this series he appeared healthy and energetic. His mood was arguably a bit lighter. His hair was again naturally wavy and combed back. His alopecic thinning hair was unnoticeable. He was beginning to experience some very odd effects of Mikhaila's carnivore diet.

First, his legs got jumpy. He thought it might be restless leg syndrome. For about twenty years, a four-inch-wide strip on the sides of each leg from the knee to the thigh had been numb. Tammy had massaged the areas and brought some feeling back but not very much. A few days after the jumpiness started, he woke up in the morning and the numbness was gone. Both legs were calm, the jumpiness was also gone.

He noticed he was losing the big belly he'd carried in recent years, and his weight was dropping. Throughout his life he'd never really felt drowsy before sleep; he'd just suddenly fall asleep, often from exhaustion. But now, he noticed as he was reading at night that he was getting sleepy and could drift off easily.

The floaters in his eyes caused by his frequently inflamed lower eyelids disappeared. Symptoms of antidepressant overdosing suddenly appeared. The nerve endings in the tips of his fingers itched, making him want to rub them against his palms. He then cut his antidepressants in half; in midwinter, the itching stopped and he suffered no additional depression. He had no scientific explanation for any of it.

In April, he and Mikhaila appeared again on TVO's *The Agenda* to discuss what had happened. Their segment was called "Digesting Depression." It was broadcast and also viewed 366,474 times on YouTube, drawing 1,768 comments. When pressed by host Steve Paikin, Jordan said he would not and was not recommending dietary changes for his depressed clients. He simply didn't know enough about it. Yet, he was amazed by the remarkable changes in Mikhaila, particularly the fact that she no longer slept seventeen hours a day. He instead deferred to Mikhaila's expertise on the subject, mentioning that she'd read over three hundred papers on related subjects such as the relationship between inflammation and depression and the production of neurological chemicals by certain types of gut bacteria. He simply threw up his hands and declared, "So it's a, it's a new bottomless pit of mystery."

As expected, Canadian prime minister Justin Trudeau introduced his more aggressive version of C-279 on May 17, 2016. It was written by his attorney general Jody Wilson-Raybould to resurrect and broaden the proposed gender protections of C-279. Wilson-Raybould kept the old name, An Act to Amend the Canadian Human Rights Act and the Criminal Code, but dropped the old parenthetical description (Gender Identity). It was designated for the new session of parliament as C-16. In summary, it read,

> This enactment amends the Canadian Human Rights Act to add gender identity and gender expression to the list of prohibited grounds of discrimination.
>
> The enactment also amends the Criminal Code to extend the protection against hate propaganda set out in that Act to any section of the public that is distinguished by gender identity or expression and to clearly set out that evidence that an offence was motivated by bias, prejudice or hate based on gender identity or expression constitutes an aggravating circumstance that a court must take into consideration when it imposes a sentence.

Also in May, the University of Toronto semester ended. New graduates, shaken by manufactured rumors of rape and hate speech on campus, moved on toward their adult lives. They faced diminishing career and job prospects. In the United States, many faced mountains of unforgivable student debt. To make this depressing reality even less tolerable, there were no safe spaces to run to or sympathetic faculty to protect them if something went wrong. And things were about to go very, very wrong.

The internet shuddered with fear and rumors of violence. Then the progressive world recoiled in horror. On June 16, 2015, golden-haired Donald Trump glided down to earth on his own golden escalator. He was everything the progressive world despised: rich, white, male, straight, disrespectful, and married to a much younger trophy wife. He announced his intention to become president of the United States and those who could manage, laughed. Donald Trump then spoke,

> The US has become a dumping ground for everybody else's problems. [*Applause.*] Thank you. It's true . . . When Mexico sends its people they're not sending their best. . . . they're sending people that have lots of problems and they're bringing those problems with [*sic*] us. They're bringing drugs, they're bringing crime, they're rapists and some, I assume, are good people.[33]

To some, this was pure racism wrapped in hate speech. At the very least it showed intolerable disrespect. In Canada among the NDP, the candidacy of Donald Trump was a potentially useful crisis, more fuel for the brushfire they now had burning in the Canadian legislature. But, if by some horrible curse he actually was elected, the OHRC would need to provide legal protection for Canada's many classes of vulnerable citizens.

As if to confirm he was truly the evil one, a braggart and a bully, Trump continued, "The theme for the new campaign is, it's going to be Make America Great Again, which is probably and possibly, the greatest theme in the history of politics."[34]

Fear and loathing began to stalk his campaign trail while Western civilization seemed to be coming apart. President Obama would later confirm the new crisis, saying,

> The one thing we do know is that we have a pattern now of mass shootings in this country that has no parallel anywhere else in the world. We should never think that this is something that just happens in the ordinary course of events because it doesn't happen with the same frequency in other countries.[35]

Mass shootings in America, involving four or more people per incident, were happening at the rate of almost one a day. A June headline of the British newspaper *The Guardian* read, "1,000 Mass Shootings in 1,260 days: This is What America's Gun Crisis Looks Like" and began, "Sunday's attack on the Pulse nightclub in Orlando, Florida was the deadliest mass shooting in American history—but there were five other mass shootings in the US during that weekend alone."[36]

Legislation to mute America's second amendment was hastily being drafted in Washington. Restrictions on gun ownership were in process in several states. Gun violence spread into the general population in the United States where police shootings of young black men were televised daily and the organization Black Lives Matter marched, mostly peacefully, in cities across America and Canada.

In Toronto, the emphasis was different. Black Lives Matter Toronto (BLM-TO) was not marching against gun violence or police shootings of young black men, since Canada had only one mass shooting that year and apparently none of police shooting black men. They were marching to assert black intersectionality. In the spirit of the season, BLM-TO stopped (Gay) Pride Toronto from completing their annual march through downtown Toronto and instead presented them with a list of demands. Alexandra Williams, cofounder of BLM-TO told the CBC that they wanted to hold Pride Toronto accountable for "anti-blackness":

> It's always the appropriate time to make sure folks know about the marginalization of black people, of black queer youth, black trans youth, of black trans people.
>
> We are not taking any space away from any folks. When we talk about homophobia, transphobia, we go through that too. . . . It should be a cohesive unit, not one against the other. Anti-blackness needs to be addressed and they can be addressed at the same time, in the same spaces.[37]

Shortly after BLM-TO was accommodated with a signed agreement, the parade continued but paused at three p.m. to honor those killed in the Orlando nightclub shooting. A float commemorated the 49 lives lost. The parade organizers did not think to respect any of the 121 people reportedly killed in mass shootings since then, or all the victims since the crisis began. Even grief had become political.

The real problem with the mass shooting crisis was that, like the rape crisis and the gender identity crisis, it didn't actually happen. The tragedy of Orlando and other mass shootings was indeed real and deserved intense public attention, they just weren't part of a crisis. President Obama would eventually be proven wrong again on the facts, but not before gun ownership had been somewhat restricted in the United States.

The truth about the gun crisis surfaced eventually from the Crime Prevention Research Center, a nonprofit, nonpartisan education and research organization:

> By our count, the US makes up less than 1.1% of the mass public shooters, 1.49% of their murders, and 2.20% of their

> attacks. All these are much less than the US's 4.6% share of the world population. Attacks in the US are not only less frequent than other countries, they are also much less deadly on average.
>
> Out of the 97 countries where we have identified mass public shootings occurring, the United States ranks 64th in the per capita frequency of these attacks and 65th in the murder rate.[38]

The Canadians at least had the good sense not to denounce the gun crisis for which they had no facts, but fell hard for another: the gender identity crisis, for which they had only deeply felt feelings.

Canadian minister of justice and attorney general Jody Wilson-Raybould had completed her mandate from Prime Minister Trudeau in May by introducing bill C-16. On first reading it received several minor edits and a warm welcome by the Honorable Ginette Petitpas Taylor who said,

> Mr. Speaker, today is International Day Against Homophobia, Transphobia and Biphobia. Please join me in celebrating equality for all Canadians. Today, I encourage all my colleagues to reach out to one another and promote individuals to be their true selves, regardless of sexual orientation or gender identity.
>
> I had the pleasure of working with different organizations in my riding [district], such as UBU Atlantic, a group that is working hard to help support our community by helping students and adults in understanding their journey, easing into transitioning, and supporting their families.[39]

MP Taylor's wonderfully positive and encouraging sentiments were graciously received without comment in parliament. The bill was scheduled for a second reading in October.

There was virtually no public comment other than from fringe conservative groups like the Christian Heritage Party, that had never earned a seat in parliament in its twenty-nine-year history up to this point. Its past president, Ron Gray, a former journalist and prolific commentator, had been investigated by the Canadian Human Rights Commission for the past two years in regard to a complaint, later dropped, that he had posted writings on the internet alleged to have exposed homosexuals to hatred or contempt. To Gray, it may have seemed the linguistic noose was tightening as the OHRC scrutinized his writings for "incitement of hatred." And certainly, he risked another lengthy investigation by posting this disturbing scenario of C-16's possible effects on the day of its introduction:

> Well, let's look at C-16 in action. Suppose a skinny-as-a-rake girl looks into the mirror and thinks, 'Ugh! I'm so FAT!' In such a case, we would probably say that she may be suffering from anorexia nervosa, and should be offered psychotherapy. But if that same girl looks into the mirror and thinks she sees a boy, C-16 says to her, 'That's OK, little guy; we're on your side. Be whoever you wanna be!' . . . It will soon be illegal for anyone to even suggest that she should seek counseling. No, instead she'll become eligible for massive doses of hormones that are at war with her DNA, and possibly for radical surgery to remove perfectly healthy body parts.

Gray had almost no support in discussing the possible effects of male/female confusion. He had not even begun to contemplate the hailstorm of confusion just on the horizon. Back in 2014, Facebook, the world's most popular forum, had already formulated a list of fifty-eight possible gender distinctions. More would be coming.

Facebook identified the following types of gender identities available at that time to its customers (a partial list)[40]:

Agender	Cisgender Female	Genderqueer	Trans*	Trans* Woman
Androgyne	Cisgender Male	Intersex	Trans Female	Transfeminine
Androgynous	Cisgender Man	Male to Female	Trans* Female	Transgender
Bigender	Cisgender Woman	MTF	Trans Male	Transgender Female
Cis	Female to Male	Neither	Trans* Male	Transgender Male
Cisgender	FTM	Neutrois	Trans Man	Transgender Man
Cis Female	Gender Fluid	Non-binary	Trans* Man	Transgender Person
Cis Male	Gender Nonconforming	Other	Trans Person	Transgender Woman
Cis Man Cis Woman	Gender Questioning Gender Variant	Pangender Trans	Trans* Person Trans Woman	Transmasculine Transsexual

Late in July 2016, Jordan started a fund-raising effort on Patreon, an online donation platform, in order to hire a professional video company to record his lectures and a website production company to upgrade his website at jordanbpeterson.com. Patreon and his social media integrated website were, in effect, Jordan's war chest and armory. In August, his first month on Patreon, he received about $1,000 in donations, not much of a war chest considering he was intending to skewer not only C-16, but the University of Toronto's human resources department and large parts of the school's administrative staff, the Ontario Human Rights Commission, the NDP and Liberal parties, the government of Canada, and the global progressive movement. By September, with what was left of his $1,000, his professional videos and social website in place, he ventured beyond the walls of his fortress like St. George and attacked the dragons of chaos.

His opening gambit included three videos, the first with the innocuous title "Professor Against Political Correctness: Part 1," unleashed a maelstrom of global hatred against him, a private citizen not seeking office or personal notoriety, that was probably unprecedented in human history. He began humbly,

> So I've been informed about a couple of things this week that have really been bothering me and I thought that . . . I wasn't sure what to do about it. I've been communicating with some of my friends and colleagues about it, but that wasn't enough. . . . There are continually things happening including in the administration here [University of Toronto] and in the broader political world that make me very nervous. I like to attribute that to the fact that I know something about the way that totalitarian and authoritarian political states develop and I can't help but think that I'm seeing a fair bit of that right now.

Disappointment was in his voice. Having worked his entire life against the ideologies of totalitarianism, he saw them at work now in his own university and at the highest levels of his government. He noted that 20 percent of professors in the social sciences now identified themselves as Marxists. He got specific, continuing,

> So I got wind of two events this week, one actually dates from last [*sic*] May . . . a bill called C-16, which is an attempt to alter the Canadian Bill of Human Rights, is tangled up with another organization . . . called the Ontario Human Rights Commission. And as far as I can tell, what happens at the Ontario Human Rights Commission is rapidly turned into policy in multiple provinces across Canada and perhaps increasingly at the federal level.[41]

Once he acknowledged the method by which this perceived diseased ideology had spread, he delivered more bad news. He wasn't offering an inspiring call to arms or a battle cry. It was more like a personal cry for help:

> So I'm making this video because I don't really know what else to do.
>
> The changes to the law scare me because they put into the legal substructure of the culture certain assumptions about basic human nature that not only do I believe to be untrue, I think they're also dangerous and ideologically motivated. I also don't think that the reason for the legal changes is the stated reason. . . . The doctrines behind the laws scare me. . . . There's a body of thought that's associated with a body of interpretations that are associated with it, that flesh out the law.[42]

He took the first swing of his sword:

> A lot of this seems to me to be driven by human resources departments which I think are generally the most pathological elements of large organizations and I say that because I've actually had fairly extensive experience dealing with human resources departments. I think HR training is very politically correct like many disciplines.[43]

That first swing drew blood and would prompt a counterstrike when the university's HR department issued a letter of warning and reprimand to him. He slashed again and cut even more deeply,

> The people behind the doctrines also scare me. I think that generally they're a very bad combination of resentful and uninformed. I also think that their aims are destructive rather than constructive. They claim constructive aims but of course everyone claims constructive aims. . . . The claims are always for equality and diversity and that kind of thing and those words are very easy to say but a lot harder to put into practice.[44]

He then assessed his precarious position by citing the unnerving comments of his colleagues. It seemed clear that he was very much on his own and held faint hope for any sort of help in this fight.

> I'm scared by the response of my colleagues at the university. A number of them are unnerved by the continual move towards political correctness and I'm going to tell you a couple of responses that I've gotten recently from people that I think are quite brave, by the way, but worried about making a statement, putting their careers on the line, worried about being tortured to death by people online, worried about administrative over-response.[45]

He then posted on the screen a few of their comments. The most telling of which was,

> I actually find myself censoring things that I'd normally say to students and I'm not sure how to stop that self-censorship. The censorship leads to me not truly educating them in a manner that will let me feel like I've done my job well. It's not as much from the administration yet as it is from the students.[46]

For this professor the culture had already turned from a free and open society to something closer to 1970s East Germany where one in three citizens was an informant for the Stasi, the murderous federal police. No one, especially not students, could be trusted. Under this quote was another even more chilling one from Jordan's colleague at a California university. It read, "The personal consequences of objecting are huge. The effect of my objection on society is miniscule. The risk isn't worth it. We should have acted ten years ago."[47]

Jordan then referenced his work as a clinical psychologist outside of the university where the real world effects of the political climate were having a significant and destructive impact. It is hard to imagine how, with this preponderance of evidence against him, Jordan had committed to and continued to carry out his attack. How could he risk everything he'd built and everyone he loved in this quixotic battle that seemed certain to fail? Yet, he pressed on. The stakes were too high. Jordan said, "I'm a clinical psychologist. This is starting to affect my clients. I've had three clients in the last two years who have been driven near the point of insanity by politically correct occurrences at work."[48]

One of Jordan's distressed clients was a bank employee who was involved in a lengthy discussion within the bank about the racism inherent in using the term *flip chart*, "flip" being a slur for Filipino. The bank decided to no longer use the term flip chart for the large pad of paper they used for demonstrations. The level of social confusion that this small incident implied seriously undermined her confidence in an orderly world. Everything, even the smallest, most innocent things, were suddenly trembling with chaos.

Jordan's second seriously disturbed client was a human resources professional, and the third was social worker. All of them were small cogs inside the massive clockwork of a society that was beginning to shudder under the force of political correctness. As a psychologist, Jordan could help them manage this vague threat, but finally, it was his own personal problem as well. He felt the same threat:

> I'm nervous about doing this lecture and I've also become nervous about some of the things that I'm teaching. . . . I think that some of the things that I say in my lectures now might be illegal. I think that they might be, I think that they might even be sufficient for me to be brought before the Ontario Human Rights Commission under their amended hate speech laws and that scares me.[49]

The series of three one-hour videos went on to examine the political threat in minute detail. What Jordan hoped the videos would accomplish, other than formalizing his arguments, was never clearer in this first video than, "I don't really know what else to do." He had read and discussed the proposed law carefully with his council of four or five advisors, colleagues, and family, including Tammy, sister Bonnie, and brother-in-law Jim Keller. But a distant alarm was ringing that may have unsettled him as much as any immediate concern for himself. A particular history was repeating itself.

In 1935, the Nuremberg Laws of Nazi Germany mandated that a citizen must demonstrate "by his conduct that he is willing and fit to faithfully serve the German people and Reich." It meant that political opponents could be stripped of their legal rights and their citizenship. The laws were passed a few months after the nationwide burning of offensive books, similar to the progressive nationwide purge of books by "old white men" like Shakespeare, Jung, and Chaucer from universities.

With growing anxiety, Jordan devoted weeks to creating his three videos. But at some point on September 27, 2016, the true moment of decision arrived. It was his moment in the garden of Gethsemane, before his certain crucifixion. He could walk away, stop his preaching, and save himself. No one would know and none would blame him. His finger hovered over the ENTER key on his computer. He was risking everything including the future of his family. This was a direct attack on hundreds of thousands of unknown, ruthless, and powerful enemies.

He pushed the key. It was now out of his hands. Far out on the horizon, storm clouds twisted. The winds of war came for him like greyhounds, pushing him far out to sea in his tiny, new boat.

CHAPTER FOURTEEN
RETALIATION

Every time you tell yourself a lie and every time you act out a falsehood, you disturb the pristine integrity of your nervous system, and the reports it'll give you about the nature of the world will be distorted as a consequence of that. So yeah, you have a moral obligation to follow the dictates of your conscience but you also have a moral obligation to make sure that your life is straight enough so that you can rely on your own judgment and you can't separate those things.

—JORDAN PETERSON, REALITY AND THE SACRED LECTURE

The reaction to his videos was swift. Howls of disgust and fury were posted on blogs and social media, in newspapers, and on broadcast radio and television. A protest rally rocked the University of Toronto campus. The *Toronto Star* carried the story,

> Rally co-organizer Cassandra Williams said education was an important part of the event.
>
> "Obviously, there's just a lot of people who aren't very well-informed about these things but Peterson is spreading misinformation to people who just don't know any better. . . . We wanted to correct a lot of the information," she said. The rally was also "calling out" U of T, she added, "for supporting and

> enabling individuals who have caused tremendous harm to the trans community."
>
> Along with speeches decrying Peterson's video, protesters also handed out leaflets to passersby with titles like "Whose gender is it anyway?" that explained gender spectrum and trans, intersex and non-binary identities.[1]

A group called Egale Canada Human Rights Trust posted on their website a highly sophisticated cartoon-style presentation called the The Genderbread Person using the child-friendly motif of a gingerbread man diagrammed to show gender identity, attraction, and sex as parts of gender expression. It featured a friendly cartoon man putting on makeup and a cartoon woman putting on a necktie. Their storybook explanation of C-16 dubbed the bill the Gender Identity Bill, rather than the popular derogatory name of the Bathroom Bill, saying, "Previously known as bill C-279, the Gender Identity Bill was created with the aim to provide human rights protections for transgender and gender diverse people in Canada."[2]

According to Egale, the only opposition to the bill was because people thought it was unnecessary. Against the global condemnation, many of Canada's leading journalists supported Jordan's position. The Postmedia Network, parent company to 140 of Canada's newspapers, came to his support. Suddenly, he was not alone on the barricades. Comments on Jordan's first video showed that he'd struck a deep and very personal nerve. Someone with the username Black Market Goodness wrote,

> I had to quit my job last year because of these issues (I'm a psychotherapist and suddenly was inundated with mentally fragile teens stating they were transgender). I have been waiting for your thoughts on this matter and greatly appreciate your willingness to speak out—I kid you not—I listen to your lectures day and night the last few months—my daughter listens to them too and passes them on to her friends—the reason I love

> your lectures is because you seem to be a dying breed—you speak your mind—your freedom [to] do so has literally been keeping me from going insane—you have been preserving my coherence—and what you said about being made into a tool for ideologues really nailed this dilemma—we are no longer valued for thinking but instead for offering our own minds up in the service of what? I will pass this on to others.[3]

This first video gathered 438,464 views and 1,968 comments.

An early YouTuber named Gad Saad, a PhD contributor to the magazine *Psychology Today,* professor of marketing at Concordia University, and author, was the first to conduct a video interview with Jordan after the launch of the three videos. Jordan had reached out to him as part of his campaign to build public opposition to C-16 and shield himself in the process.

Saad was not familiar with C-16 and asked Jordan to explain the issue. Jordan began with the examples of patients in his clinical practice, like the panicked bank employee, whose lives were severely disrupted by political correctness gone mad.

He then explained how, a few weeks before posting the videos, he'd gotten emails about C-16 and about the University of Toronto's HR department making anti-racism and anti-bias training mandatory for the HR staff. He gave his personal background to set his reactions to this news in context,

> My fundamental line of research, by the way, is on authoritarianism and ideology and the deep roots of ideological belief and the role that belief plays in structuring people's emotions and motivations, so [I] have a number of reasons for being interested in this.[4]

He recalled his surprise to the overwhelmingly positive reaction the videos received and how the lesser but vehemently negative, even threatening reactions, such as the small riot at his Smith Hall speech, prompted the chairman of UT's psychology department to call him and remind him that he was responsible for following UT's internal policies and the law. A written reminder followed.

Jordan characterized UT's communication as "rubbish," because something was in the air, a problem that needed to be discussed. There was no animosity in his comment. He clarified that he was grateful for his affiliation with the university, and that it had been very good to him over the years "in every possible way."

Saad dove into the social psychology of the issue from one of his own books, reading,

> Some theorists propose that heterosexuality is an imposed norm. In other words it is argued that heterosexuality should not be construed as an innate orientation. Interestingly, when it comes to a homosexual orientation many gay lobbyists posit that they were born with their same sex preference, hence by amalgamating these two premises one ends up with the "facts" that heterosexuality is not innate but homosexuality is; this is indeed quite an extraordinary worldview for sexually reproducing species.[5]

Jordan saw a serious potential publicity problem with Saad's comment. He didn't need any more claims of homophobia coming his way. He jumped in to clarify his as yet incompletely refined argument,

> People on the Left have accused me of or even pointed out that I'm throwing the baby out with the bathwater, and that we shouldn't forget about all the positive things left oriented political movements have done over the last fifty years. And you know people on the radical right are trying . . . to incorporate or identify me perhaps as one of their acolytes . . . a person who holds that kind of worldview and so I have to be very careful to differentiate that all out.[6]

Jordan, live on air, carefully worked through his basic dilemma. Was it the cultural conversation or the political activity around the conversation? He framed the issue mythologically as two monsters. His problem was, Which was the more dangerous of the two? It was clear this was not settled in his mind and so his way forward was muddled. He seemed to come down on the cultural conversation as the larger of the two problems. It was the source of all problems.

They diverted into studies on political motivation regarding personality. This was exactly what Jordan has been researching recently. Saad brought up his discovery of research on the correlation between physical strength and tendency toward conservatism. Jordan related this to a dominance display and expounded on his own research showing radical egalitarianism as it related to agreeableness, conscientiousness, and orderliness. These last two were normally predictors of "right-wing authoritarianism" but, "In fact the relationship between . . . verbal cognitive ability and the proclivity to hold viewpoints that were desirous of language control was higher than the relationship between verbal ability and academic grades."[7]

In other words, people with higher verbal cognitive ability wanted very badly to control what was said. The subtext here seems clearly to implicate women, the more "agreeable" and the more verbal of the two sexes by Jordan's previous research. It could be, and certainly would be, gleaned from this that, in promoting radical egalitarianism, the desire for fairness and equality, women were leading the charge. In summary, it wasn't right-wing authoritarians, but women who most wanted to control speech.

This may be a misreading or overly broad interpretation of Jordan's data and position. But a decisive split of male supporters and female detractors quickly formed around Jordan. At some level, women seemed to have gotten a misogynistic message and reacted with outrage.

Saad interjected his theory on male and female roles among social justice warriors:

> Are you familiar in zoology with the, this is the actual term so you'll forgive if it's crass, the Sneaky Fucker Strategy? Do you know what that is?
>
> It happens across many species, typically often in fish species, but in others as well where there are, if you like, two main phenotypes of males; one is sort of a dominant male that's very territorial, that's making sure that no other males infringe on his territory. And then there's another phenotype where males actually look like females, so that when they sort of approach this dominant male he is tricked into sort of letting them through and then, hence the Sneaky Fucker Strategy. Then they can access the females.
>
> So I've taken that idea and I've argued that male social justice warriors are ultimately pursuing some manifestation of the Sneaky Fucker Strategy.[8]

Jordan laughed and added,

> Every Seth Rogen movie has that sort of idea at its basis, right? . . . All those movies about guys who haven't grown up are all about guys who use "being on your side" with regards to . . . Yeah, that's the friend mating strategy.[9]

Jordan added details to Saad's theory on the male and female elements of social justice warriors:

> Women are higher in agreeableness than men and that's true in Scandinavia too for all you people listening who think that all those sorts of things are only cultural constructs which they most certainly are not. And the data on that is clear.
>
> So, disagreeable people . . . if you're negotiating with a disagreeable person it's more for them than for you. And so if you go to the extremes of disagreeable you find men in prisons, but if you go to the extremes of agreeable you find social justice warriors, roughly speaking.[10]

Jordan revealed the male to female split in reaction to his videos,

> What I've experienced is 98 percent support, 95 percent of which was from reasonable people. And then I would say, within that group of supporters there's a full range of political affiliations slightly shifted to the right, but not so much as you might think.
>
> I have plenty of radical left people writing me and talking about their experiences being stifled in their freedom of expression by their compatriots. And also plenty who are concerned about premature closure of discussion surrounding human sexuality. It's not like all of this is going to be universally good for the people who are pushing it forward.[11]

He offered his psychoanalytic perspective. He began to speak more rapidly, more forcefully, as this brought up his fears for Western society,

> Underneath the surface, look, I mean, if you're talking to someone and you make a comment that they react to in a very emotional way, that's an indication from a psychoanalytic perspective of the existence of a complex underneath the surface and a complex, you might regard a complex as a mass of highly emotional undigested and unarticulated experience demanding expression so that it can sort itself out. Well, that's the situation we're in in this society.
>
> Because we are pushing very hard in the radical left direction on all sorts of fronts at every level of society and we're dangerously confusing large segments of the population who are having a difficult time articulating their perspective.[12]

He went on, becoming more animated as his current situation loomed in front of him,

> All of a sudden, bang, there's just noise everywhere, right? I mean it's crazy! It was national news on CTV and CBC and I think all the major newspapers, the national newspapers covered it in detail. And you know there's been sixty-five thousand views on the first video [in the first two weeks] and like, it's been a real explosion.
>
> The question there is, well, why? And I can tell you it's not because of pronoun usage in relationship to transgender people. Although it would be lovely if we could oversimplify the argument to that, define me as a bigot, and make the argument disappear. Well, that's not happening, it's not disappearing.[13]

And then he dropped into a serious tone, a confession, a statement of his core motivation,

> Anybody who knows my work knows that I live by that ethos, right? I mean, I take on issues that are much more dangerous to my own well-being and that of my children than simply that, transgenderism, right? So yes, there are much bigger monsters out there than the activism transgenderism. And yet I do it because my commitment to the truth, or at least as I'd like to perceive the truth to be, is more important than anything else and therefore my unique personhood compels me to act in the ways that I do . . . for me it's simple.[14]

Saad sat silently, listening intently as Jordan unburdened himself in a torrent of ideas, a stream of consciousness. He bounced from dreams to the miraculous resolution of "one very long-lasting crisis in my family," (meaning Mikhaila's health recovery by following a carnivore diet), to his destiny.

> My wife had a dream about this the other day that I'm actually going to post. Because I analyzed the dream about where we are in this debate. And her dream indicated that the door is

> still open to a peaceful solution to all of this, but that it's a lot later in the game than people think, which I also believe.
>
> I've talked a lot with my family about this over the last two weeks because, of course, we just happened to go through one very long-lasting crisis in our lives that we got resolved. And then I introduced all this.
>
> What I suggested to my wife was that, well, I can either have this fight now on my terms, or I can wait for five years and have it brought to me, right? . . . Sometimes you have two suboptimal choices, frying pan or fire.[15]

Finally, Jordan launched into his "killer idea." The excitement built in his voice until the force of it made Jordan bounce in his chair and made Saad laugh. It's the fully realized idea that Jordan had been writing, lecturing about, and researching for over thirty-five years. It was a revelation, a very pure, pristine vision of a pathway to heaven:

> Meaning is the biological instinct that tells you that you're properly situated on the line between explored and unexplored territory. And that's a good place to be because you have one foot in order, so you're stable, and you have one foot in chaos, so you're exploring, and so you get the benefits of being orderly and stable with the benefits of continually updating your knowledge. And you do that through clearly articulated speech. Now this is a killer idea, like seriously, it's a killer, right?
>
> Especially the idea that, you know, you're evolved. And I believe that explored and unexplored territory are the fundamental domains of existence. That's what you're evolved for! And your sense of meaning is the thing that orients you to proper position within those meta domains. Man! I tell ya, it's a killer idea![16]

Saad interjected, laughing and saying, "Too bad you're not passionate when you speak!"

Jordan chuckled at the joke at his own expense, but rolled right on,

> Well, let me add one more thing to that. So look here, here's another profound religious truth. Life is suffering. It's the fundamental Buddhist dictum, the Jews know all about it, the Christians know all about it. That's why the crucifix is the central symbol, right? Life is suffering, okay? So fine. And that can make you resentful and it can fill you with hate and no wonder, buddy.
>
> But here's the counter proposition. You need something to counteract the suffering of life and what you need to counteract the suffering of life is meaning, and you need a meaning that's so profound that you say, the suffering that's a precondition for all this is worth it; it's worth it so that makes being itself worth it. Well, you find that in the forthright articulation of truth; there's nothing more meaningful than that and that's the antidote to suffering. Safety is not the antidote to suffering, there is no safety in life. Truth is the antidote to suffering so [hopefully] . . . [17]

Saad interrupted again, "So no trigger warnings, right?" Jordan laughed and nodded in agreement, then stopped and said, "No," then continued,

> So you speak forth your being properly. And that orients you in a world of suffering. And that stops you from becoming resentful and hateful as well, and we don't want that. And that, you know, that's what I see happening on the radical right.[18]

Saad, having failed twice to slow Jordan down with jokes, finally pulled the plug in the interest of time. Jordan was clearly cut off, but nodded in deference to his host, bowing out gracefully. Saad acknowledged he'd just experienced something closer to a sermon than an interview. He said,

> Keep speaking the truth, brother. Great job, real pleasure talking to you. Stay on the line, I will be posting a link to your website and also to your YouTube channel so that people can watch your excellent recent series. Thank you.[19]

A few days later, after the first protesters on the UT campus had accused Jordan of "causing tremendous harm to the transgender community," Jordan found his first supporting volunteer organization, The Rebel Media, an Ontario-based, online, conservative news and advocacy publisher led by self-proclaimed "rebel commander" Ezra Levant. The group organized Jordan's global media debut on the same spot that the protesters used in front of Sidney Smith Hall on the UT campus.

They sent their Millennial reporter Lauren Southern and a camera crew to cover the event.

At Smith Hall, about one hundred students and faculty gathered in a semicircle as the Rebel Media camera turned toward Jordan, standing alone at the center of the crowd holding a microphone in one hand. In the crowd was also a young man, a YouTuber with the online name genuiNEWitty, who began recording as well.

Jordan raised the mic to speak and his introduction to the world began with protesters chanting, "Shame! Shame! Shame!" Supporters in the crowd responded by chanting, "Peterson! Peterson! Peterson!" Jordan said, "Okay," to quell the crowd.

Immediately, blaring, amplified white noise drowned out any chance of hearing him. The white noise sputtered.

GenuiNEWitty's camera panned over and caught a young man in a green sweater pulling the audio line out of the amplifier and arguing with a young red-haired woman about it. The noise stopped. Jordan began with a mild rebuke,

> Well, as you can see, the opponents of free speech are capable of making a lot of inarticulate noise. Alright, so I want to tell you a couple of things about what this is all about as far as I'm

> concerned. I'm not going to talk about sexual politics, it's not my primary concern. What I'm going to talk about is freedom of speech. . . . I've been thinking about this very carefully over the last two weeks, partly because of the videos that I made.[20]

White noise blasted over him again, and he lowered his head in frustration. Again, genuiNEWitty's camera followed the action to the young red-haired woman and a person of indeterminate sex with multiple facial piercings standing by the white noise amplifier, guarding it. A young man in a blue bandanna marched out of the crowd and pulled the audio lead from the back of the amplifier, knocking it over in the process. Green Sweater again grabbed the lead from Blue Bandanna and this time retreated into the crowd with it. Blue Bandanna respectfully righted the knocked-over amplifier and yelled at the crowd, "We need some men here, people! We need some men here who can stop this nonsense! He's brilliant!"[21]

Blue Bandanna returned to the crowd receiving a smattering of applause. Jordan lowered his microphone and clasped his hands behind his back. He was going to speak without amplification. He began to stride like a general reviewing his troops. His voice boomed, "Alright. So there's a reason I'm defending free speech . . ." Small applause from the crowd. He stopped midstride and turned to face the front of the crowd. He suddenly launched into a snarling, furious tirade, teeth bared as he paced like General George Patton accusing his troops of cowardice, of quailing in the face of the enemy, "and the reason for that is quite *straight-forward*! The reason I'm defending freedom of speech is because *that's* how people of different opinions in a *civil* society *settle* their differences!"[22]

Massive applause and whoops of enthusiasm broke out. The veins stood out on his neck as he continued to shout and pace, fully in command. He stabbed an extended forefinger at the ground, punctuating his delivery,

> *Now!* Here's what's happened with bill C-16 and the surrounding legislation. *Free* speech is the mechanism by which we keep our society functioning. The consequence of free speech is the ability to *speak* so people can put their *finger* on problems, articulate what those problems are, solve them and come to a *consensus*! And we risk losing that![23]

The crowd fell completely silent. He throttled back his fury but his voice remained a shout.

> Now! You can say there should be reasonable restrictions on free speech. And that's the case. You shouldn't be allowed to yell "Fire!" in a crowded theatre. And reasonable people can discuss and debate what those restrictions should be. But you can't debate the fact that putting restrictions on free speech is something dangerous beyond comprehension. And that's what we're faced with. . . . It's the first time in our legislative history that people are attempting to *make us speak their language*![24]

Jordan's hands, down at his side, shook from the effort of emphasizing his words. He'd gone a bit too far; a violent argument broke out in back of him, and ended. He continued to rail about the left seeking to turn the argument into an argument about sexual politics, but he insisted it was about "language that is designed to control our freedom of expression!" General applause and cheers went up. He continued, citing his many friends and colleagues who had been criticizing him for what he said. He admitted, "No wonder, I don't speak perfectly. And my arguments aren't perfectly formulated. And neither are anyone else's."[25]

He turned away from the far crowd and paced directly toward genuiNEWitty's camera, his voice rising again until it broke into a full bellow of fury, his face contorted into an openmouthed mask of rage. His body was fully tensed, fists clenched, directing all his power into his words, "And we have to say what we have to say *badly*! Or we won't be able to think at all! And I know where that leads. I've studied totalitarianism for four decades and I know how that starts!"[26]

Jordan paced back to the far end of the crowd. His words were lost to genuiNEWitty's camera but he shouted his final words, his open hands slapping against his thighs in exertion. A general cheer went up from his supporters as fans of C-16 shouted against them.

The Rebel Media's camera caught people pushing each other, shouting in each other's faces, and fighting. The person with multiple facial piercings attacked them and knocked down their camera. A young lady in a yellow knit watch cap standing close by spoke to Southern, saying glibly, "I didn't see anything. I didn't see anything that happened."[27]

The Rebel Media's coverage cut to Jordan being interviewed by Lauren Southern. The riot had dissipated, as she reported, after police arrived. Jordan had regained his composure. He said,

> Free speech is the alternative to violence. And there are lots of people who would like violence and are waiting for the opportunity to use it. And I'm hoping we can talk our way out of it. . . . People have commented, and they did today too, on my bravery and that isn't really how I see it. I see that I'm taking the path of least resistance.
>
> And that's how frightened I am of the alternative. And it's real. There are ugly things brewing. There are ugly things brewing.[28]

Jordan's fire-breathing speech and the small, bitter riot it caused flashed across the internet via YouTube. The genuiNEWitty video got 620,813 views and 3,632 comments. The Rebel Media's video gathered 995,719 views and 9,347 comments.

Within days, the human resources department at the University of Toronto issued Jordan a warning letter suggesting that he stop speaking publicly on the matter. To hopefully settle things, the office of David Cameron, dean of the faculty of arts and science at UT, set the date of November 21 for a mediated, public debate to be livestreamed on the internet about C-16. The debate featured Jordan against Dr. Brenda Cossman, professor of law and director of the Mark S. Bonham Centre for Sexual Diversity Studies at UT, and Dr. Mary K. Bryson, professor of language at the University of British Columbia and chair of the Vice Presidential Trans, Two-Spirit and Diversity Task Force.

Condemnation continued to rain down from progressive and liberal sources as Jordan's online following grew by the tens of thousands, and public support grew exponentially. His remaining two videos gained him another 240,686 views. He had now over 100,000 YouTube followers, while donations on Patreon, in the two weeks after his videos posted, jumped from $1,000 per month to over $2,500. By the time of the university debate in November, they were over $7,600.[29]

At 3:35 p.m. on October 18 in the House of Commons, regarding passage of bill C-16 for a second reading, Speaker Geoff Regan announced, "I declare the motion carried. Accordingly, the bill stands referred to the Standing Committee on Justice and Human Rights."

The vote was 248 in favor, 40 opposed. C-16 looked unstoppable. An overwhelming majority coalition of NDP, Liberal, Bloc, and Green Parties were behind it.

Jordan's longtime target of derision, the NDP-controlled Ontario Human Rights Commission, was emboldened by the level of support C-16 now had in parliament. It had been eleven years and seven failures since the NDP first introduced the law. Now with the OHRC fully infiltrated and a majority in the government in hand, it was not about to let a loudmouthed professor dash its plans. The OHRC issued a veiled threat to Jordan through its new director Renu Mandhane speaking to the *Toronto Sun* that was reporting on the Peterson/C-16 controversy. The *Sun* asked, "Is it a violation of the Code to not address people by their choice of pronoun? And if so, in what setting?"[30]

Mandhane replied,

> Refusing to address a trans person by their chosen name and a personal pronoun that matches their gender identity, or purposely misgendering, is discrimination when it takes place in a social area covered by the Code (employment, housing, and services like education).[31]

But added an unusual flourish for an experienced lawyer,

> The OHRC recognizes the right to freedom of expression under the Charter. However, lawmakers and courts have found that no right is absolute. Expression may be limited where it is hate speech under criminal law; or amounts to harassment, discrimination, or creates a poisoned environment under the Code.[32]

If Jordan was unnerved by the OHRC's veiled and incredibly broad threat concerning "a poisoned environment," he didn't show it publicly. But privately, it was time to seek the best legal counsel he could find.

Jared Brown, a private Toronto attorney specializing in business litigation, was disturbed by what he saw in the burgeoning C-16 debate, particularly in Jordan's comments and videos. He began to investigate. In the relevant case law he found two cases settled before the Supreme Court of Canada that seemed to contradict the intentions of C-16, stating,

> Anything that forces someone to express opinions that are not their own is a "penalty that is totalitarian and as such alien to the tradition of free nations like Canada even for the repression of the most serious crimes." National Bank of Canada v. Retail Clerks' International Union et al. (1984) SCC; Slaight Communications Inc. v. Davidson (1989) SCC.[33]

Brown would become Jordan's most important legal ally and would appear with him before parliament to object to the law. He posted on his blog shortly after the proposed law was referred for a second reading,

> Some might perceive the compelled speech requirements inherent in the [Human Rights] Code, and Bill C-16 as minor, particularly given the widely held opinion that a failure to follow the compelled speech stipulations will not result in serious criminal sanction.
>
> This opinion may very well be correct, but not because the legislation lacks the ability to bring forward serious criminal sanction. In fact, breaches of Human Rights Tribunal orders can and have (at the federal level) resulted in imprisonment. Further, the Hate Speech provisions of the Criminal Code can result in increased sentences for those found guilty.
>
> Focusing on the Human Rights Tribunals, and particularly the OHRT, the path to prison is quite straight-forward.[34]

At the first livestreamed debate about the law sponsored by his university, Jordan was calmly alert and dressed casually in a yellow button-down collar shirt, sleeves rolled up, and blue jeans. He was thin again, having lost most of his unhealthy fifty extra pounds.

Dean David Cameron introduced the debate by acknowledging and giving thanks for use of the historic native tribal land that the university occupied. He then introduced Dr. Mary Bryson, who was sporting a close-cropped, military-style haircut, a man's sport coat, and collared shirt, commenting on the many accomplishments of her gender-oriented work outside of the university. He commented on Dr. Brenda Cossman's awards and her books concerning feminism and law. He introduced Jordan and his many accomplishments, awards, and books.

Jordan began by asking all of the women in the audience to stand up, then all the men. He invited them to then sit. He spoke calmly and without notes.

> Thank you. It's about two to one males in here and I thought I'd point that out because it's kind of interesting to me because I'm a personality psychologist. And this debate is about ideas. There's a personality trait called openness which is associated with intellect and creativity. And there are pronounced gender differences in openness such that men are higher in intellect which encompasses interest in ideas, and women are higher in aesthetics which encompasses interest, in, well, in art and literature and that sort of thing.[35]

He moved on to his opening point,

> I just wanted to point out that there was a natural gender divide that occurred automatically and without compulsion in this particular case, in the case of this debate. And that the more our society enforces its increasingly absurd demands for equity upon everyone, the less likely it is that such natural divisions will be able to manifest them and manifest themselves in our society in keeping with the pronounced and deep differences between the genders.[36]

Boom, there it was. His opening move, complete with the insult of absurdity leveled at what was likely the focus of his opponents' lives' work. It got worse.

> I've been keeping an eye on political correctness for a long time and I was also very upset with the human resources and equity department's decision to make anti-racism, so-called anti-racism, anti-bias training, mandatory for their staff which I regard as an unacceptable intrusion into their staffs' right to their political opinion.

> As well as noting that there's absolutely no evidence whatsoever that mandatory anti-racism and anti-bias training has the impact that is claimed. In fact, the empirical evidence suggests quite the contrary. When you mandate that sort of thing, you actually make people more prejudiced. It's also based on what I would say is a rather pernicious form of pseudoscience that's been promoted by social psychologists, a group that I have a fair bit of trouble with. And that's been transformed into a kind of educational fascism that has no grounding whatsoever in the empirical literature.[37]

It was a full-frontal assault of facts, insult, and ridicule. Whatever fear he once had about starting a war was obviously gone. There would be no consensus, no collegial niceties. Having accused his opponents of being members of an absurd, pseudoscientific, fascistic cabal of misguided educators, he clearly expected there would be no mercy either. He continued,

> So what the hell's going on here exactly? And why are we damn near at each other's throats? Look at what happened in the United States a week and a half ago [the election of Donald Trump, rioting, and the Women's March].
>
> There's some things to talk about here and I started to try to talk about them, and I would say that my freedom to do so was rapidly infringed upon, my career was put at risk, and I find this absolutely unacceptable.[38]

He referenced the first of two letters that would eventually be sent to him from the university administration warning him that he may be in violation of the Canadian Human Rights Code. The letter suggested that he apologize to offended groups and essentially shut his mouth about the issue. By his opening remarks, it was now clear that that was not going to happen.

He rolled on to acknowledge the tsunami of publicity his videos caused, stating that about 140 articles had been published about him in the last two months, dozens of radio and television interviews and demonstrations had happened, while millions of people had been following the melee online.

He elaborated on his tirade in front of Smith Hall that stressed the importance of being allowed to speak badly, make mistakes, receive unfiltered feedback, and so naturally correct one's skewed thinking:

> I don't believe that freedom of speech is just another value. I think that's preposterous. I think that if you claim that, then you know nothing about Western civilization. . . . It's the mechanism by which we keep our psyches and our societies organized and we have to be unbelievably careful about infringing upon that because we're infringing upon the process by which we keep chaos and order balanced. . . . And if chaos and order go out of balance . . . then all hell breaks loose. . . . Thank God the university agreed to have this debate, you know, because there's things to talk about. And if we don't talk about them, then we're going to fight.[39]

He referenced the issues at hand, the "hyper-repressive order of radical right and the absolute devouring chaos of the radical left."[40] He suggested society had become unmoored, lost its way, and the only thing that could save it was the dialogue he was talking about. He said the issues were about inclusion versus bigotry, the left wing versus the right wing, who's free to choose the words they use and the degree of respect they afford to others. He got to the nub of the threat as he saw it, and elaborated on its mythological identities,

> Implicit in bill C-16, and I'm telling you there is an assault on the idea of objectivity itself, an assault on the idea of biology itself, and if the university thinks that the sciences are going to be immune from the ideological doctrine that's embedded

> in these pieces of legislation, they better think again, because there is trouble coming. . . . We noticed that Ken Zakhar got hounded out of his job just a few years ago even though he was an entirely credible scientist and clinician. . . . There's a mother versus father thing going on here too . . . you kind of saw that with Hillary Clinton versus Donald Trump. I would say that was the overprotective Devouring Mother versus the tyrannical father.[41]

Bringing the discussion back to the issue, he concluded,

> I think at the moment that we're in, we're embroiled in a war on every single one of those dimensions and several others that I haven't had time to list. And the evidence that we're in that sort of war is precisely the fact that this has attracted so much attention.
>
> I mean, I just sat [in] my bloody office at home and threw up a couple of amateurish videos more or less attempting to articulate my feelings about a couple of policies, and it's like all hell broke loose. And why? Well, because that hell is right underneath the surface. I'm done.[42]

Dr. Cossman argued that,

> Hate speech provisions in the criminal code have a very, very high threshold. The Supreme Court of Canada has repeatedly defined hate speech as only including the most extreme forms of speech. The court has said over and over again and I quote, "the unusually strong and deep felt emotions of vilification and detestation." The court has said it is not disdain, it is not dislike, it is not offence. Plus something that's often lost, hate speech criminal charges cannot be laid without the approval of the attorney general.[43]

Dr. Bryson began with a comment suggesting her disgust toward Jordan,

> To make sense of what it means to be here today, I found myself going back frequently to the 1989 debate at Western [University of Western Ontario] on the subject of race and IQ between Philippe Rushton and David Suzuki. The stakes then and now are very familiar. To borrow David Suzuki's opening words on that day, quote, "I do not want to be here. I do not want to dignify this man and his ideas in public debate," end quote.[44]

Bryson attacked Jordan by reading her edited transcript of his words in his first video, leaving out his qualifying and clarifying phrases for provocative effect:

> "Bill C-16 scares me," lectures Dr. Peterson, "the Ontario Human Rights Commission is a particularly pathological organization, social justice warrior types are overrepresented and I can't help but think it's because our current premier is a lesbian and that in itself doesn't bother me one way or another, I don't think it's relevant to the political discussion. . . . The LGBT community has become extraordinarily good at organizing themselves and has a fairly pronounced and very, very sophisticated radical fringe. . . . Gender identity and gender expression are not valid ideas, they're not true, there's no evidence for it. There's an idea that there's a gender spectrum but I don't think that that's a valid idea. I don't think there's any evidence for it."[45]

Dr. Bryson went on to reference a body of scientific data, but did not quote anything that might support her position or refute Jordan's claims. She closes with another reference to Dr. Suzuki's noxious opinion of another scientist, inferring Jordan should be tarred with that same disdain.

Jordan replied by ignoring Bryson's calls for his investigation, her personal disgust, and selective editing of his words. He instead summarized the harmful principle in C-16 and cited scientific research that refuted the idea of a pervasive gender spectrum:

> I want to tell you a little bit about what the law does, and this is with regards to its interpretation from the policy guidelines. It instantiates social constructionism into our legal system. You have to understand what that means . . . it makes this legal doctrine that biological sex, gender identity, gender expression, and sexual orientation vary independently, and they don't. Now the reason they don't is because 98 percent of people, it's 99.7 percent of people by the way at least with regards to the most credible statistics, have a gender identity that's essentially identical with their biological sex. And almost everybody who is male and female, by biological sex and gender identity, dresses that way and that's what a gender expression essentially is.[46]

Dr. Cossman rebutted, saying that social constructs in law were common and gender expression was simply one of them. Her comments went on at some length about similar previous laws, and claimed that C-16 ultimately could take all of a violator's assets but could not put that person in jail. No doubt this was little comfort to Jordan or to the audience members who were advised to read Solzhenitsyn's account of innocuous-sounding "social constructionist" laws destroying millions of lives in recent history.

Dr. Bryson returned to inject an apparently postmodernist, quite incomprehensible or thrashed, interpretation of scientific experimentation regarding gender,

> Actually it comes down to the fact that science, about causality, about in essence sex being linked and producing gender, requires us to move outside of the current realm. All that we

> have in this realm is quasi-experimentation. We can't actually do studies where we manipulate the chromosomal or the hormonal environment, and so since we can't remove sexism and misogyny from the production of gender. We can actually reach conclusions about what we take to be gender differences.[47]

Apparently, Jordan's debate performance convinced exactly no one. At least not colleagues close to him who were most liable to be directly affected. He received a petition signed by nearly two hundred UT professors and faculty members urging him to resign. It was a shock and a depressing blow to his confidence. He thought he'd made at least a reasonable case.

At home, Julian, now an independent twenty-two-year-old musician and hockey fan with many friends, had stopped by. Jordan shared his burden with him. Jordan would later laugh as he told this story,

> Jesus, Julian, you know, like two hundred people, faculty members . . . petitioned the Faculty Association, and then they sent a petition to the administration to get me fired. It was the Faculty Association, that's my union! They didn't even contact me.[48]

Julian said, "Don't worry about it, Dad. It was only two hundred people."[49]

Jordan had finally lost all fifty pounds he'd gained in recent years. He was again rail-thin; his energy, always high, was now steady and almost inexhaustible. He no longer needed his daily nap. His menu was now meat, a little salt and water, three meals a day. All autoimmune symptoms had disappeared, and antidepressants remained at half dosage, even though it was the cusp of winter coming onto Christmas. In spite of the pressure and threats coming from all directions, his mood remained positive, at least by his video appearances.

Tammy prepared for the coming holiday as a parent and foster parent, making their home, now filled with Soviet and native tribal art, welcoming and restful. She also remained at her post as Jordan's most trusted advisor. Her valued counsel and even her dreams, in the native tribal custom, were a primary guidance for him.

A third story had been built on the house in the fashion of a native Kwakwaka'wakw tribal meeting place, primarily to hold Jordan's native art collection. All of it represented the dreams and visions of the artist and his friend Chief Charles Joseph.

His Soviet art echoed a horrific past, but hopefully the chief's carvings gave him solace and hope for a more peaceful future.

But even in his restful home, away from the riot of warring ideologies outside, Jordan was hard at work. His new project, based on the refinements he'd made to *Maps of Meaning* and his lecture series Personality, was a more popular interest book tentatively titled *The 12 Most Valuable Things Everyone Should Know*. As always, he required complete, uninterrupted silence during his writing time. But with energetic Julian stopping by with friends, Mikhaila sorting out life with her boyfriend, Andrey Korikov, and Tammy's live-in foster child growing up, noise levels must have been an occasional topic of discussion.

Mikhaila was building an extensive online presence as her own and her father's consistent, positive results on the carnivore diet boosted her confidence. She became an outspoken advocate and posted pictures of herself with flawless skin and a trim figure on Instagram. She and boyfriend Andrey were apparently happy together now that she was reliably depression-free and in control of her urges to binge or experiment. She even allowed herself an occasional bourbon, as she claimed, with no ill effects.

The full Peterson house rumbled with the activity of children and friends. It was a safe harbor from the storm of Jordan's professional life. His Patreon online donations that were $7,600 per month in November were now over $12,000 in December. Things were about to get even a bit happier. Mikhaila was pregnant with his first granddaughter, Elizabeth Scarlett.

But it didn't help his situation that he was suddenly swept up in the wide-eyed panic surrounding Donald Trump's November election. Hillary Clinton had been defeated decisively and to make matters even worse, she had been ridiculed by Trump with the disrespectful nickname "Crooked Hillary" as his rallies thundered with *Lock her up!* Women around the world took this personally and swore revenge.

Accusations of racism, misogyny, and homophobia fell like hail on all deviants, like Jordan, attacking the left. The Women's March televised furious speeches and thousands of disgusted women demanding resistance to everything and everyone even remotely associated with conservative politics. The political divide in America and Canada had widened into an unbridgeable chasm.

Bill C-16 was now urgent, an absolute necessity to address the new crisis of rampant transphobia, bigotry, and racism. In fact, at Jordan's next scheduled live appearance at McMaster University in nearby Hamilton, Ontario, he was shouted down by young women. About one hundred crowded into a lecture hall where Jordan was scheduled to speak on a panel with three other panelists. One or two young men joined the ladies in ringing cowbells, blowing air horns, and chanting through a bullhorn and by shout, "Transphobic piece of shit! Transphobic piece of shit! Transphobic piece of shit!"[50]

The three other scheduled speakers apparently had second thoughts about appearing with Jordan. They never took their seats next to him. Jordan sat calmly at the front of the room, trying to speak through amplification to the seventy or so students seated quietly in tiered rows in front of him hoping to hear him speak. Though barely audible, he mentioned that one benefit of free speech was to expose intolerance and ignorance, indicating the protesters. The young ladies were not having that. A young lady with a bullhorn moved from the back to the front of the room. A professionally designed banner followed her that read, NO FREEDOM FOR HATE SPEECH, STAND UP, FIGHT BACK! with the modified biological symbols for sex indicating a third sex that combined the male and female symbols. Inside the central circle of the sex symbols was the Soviet and communist image of the clenched fist of revolution. Obviously, the ladies had been preparing for him. The banner crowded Jordan to his right; an air horn, used to warn boaters from a long distance, was blasted close enough to cause damage to the hearing of some of the audience. Angry reactions began to confront the protesters. The banner moved in front of Jordan, blocking him entirely from view.

A violent counter-chant erupted, "Free speech matters! Free speech matters! Free speech matters!"[51]

The seated audience of primarily young men began to stand up and join the chant. It overwhelmed the protesters as the recording camera of YouTuber eggplantfool was hit by the air pressure waves generated by the men. The picture shuddered with every *matters!*

Jordan stepped from behind the banner, continued to fight to be heard. The men stopped their chant to hear Jordan. He continued to make his points over the protesters' noise. The seated young men, and a few young women, applauded his points as they could hear them. An official or administrator walked to Jordan and said something. Jordan surrendered the microphone for a moment; it looked like the protesters were going to win. A cheer went up. Jordan saw the defeat coming and took back the microphone. He suggested that everyone move outside. It was an astute, tactical maneuver.

The last patches of snow were on the ground. Jordan managed to speak to the large surrounding crowd that now included dozens who had filled the hallways to the lecture hall. Many of these were nonprotesting young women. He spoke without amplification over the now distant and scattered cowbells and chants. The angry young ladies had been marginalized by the young men and women interested in free speech.

He showed none of the fire that had made his first public speech at Smith Hall so remarkable. Instead he spoke, again without notes, calmly but forcefully for another thirty minutes, even managing to take questions. He clearly won the day and delivered his message.

In a video he posted the following evening, he commented on and read a message that he had received after his appearance at McMaster from the president's Advisory Committee on Building an Inclusive Community. The video is Jordan, head and shoulders, rather dimly lit, sitting in a dark room, presumably his home office. He prefaced the reading of the message with his personal comment,

> I want to read it to you because it actually does irritate me half to death. I'll read it to you and you can make up your own mind. God, you can hardly read this.
>
> "There is nothing new about Dr. Peterson's position then. It is a position taken by multitudes of others before him. We anticipate that Dr. Peterson's talk will, and should result in public critical opposition to his ideas, including public opposition to how he has treated trans and gender non-conforming people, which may take the form of public protest.
>
> "In the present climate, proponents of free speech may try to paint such opposition as just another indicator that Dr. Peterson's freedom of speech is in fact under threat."[52]

He went on in his video to issue his reply and challenge,

> So, this is what I'll say about that. To the members of the PAC-BIC, President Advisory Committee on Building an Inclusive Community. If you would like to debate with me about the issue of gender and sexuality, I'm willing to do that with as many people as you want to put forward, at any time you want, at any place of your choosing. Hopefully sooner rather than later.
>
> And if you're not willing to do that, and you're gonna write cowardly little letters like this and make them public instead, I might suggest that if you're unwilling to defend your ideas in public, that you should just shut up and go away. And I might also suggest that you should stop teaching students the kind of nonsense that you are teaching them.

> Anyways, I don't have much more to say than that, except, I'll just repeat it. I have no problem defending my ideas about gender and sexual difference. And if you guys think that you know what the hell you're talking about, then why don't you come out and face me instead of sending your student proxies to complain about me when I come to your university to try to make a case.
>
> I think you're appallingly cowardly. And so I'm calling you out. Come and debate me, whenever you want.[53]

The video then shows a clip of Clint Eastwood in a gunslinger's face-off from the movie *The Good, the Bad and the Ugly.* The clip was titled, "Go ahead . . . make my day," mixing Clint Eastwood movie metaphors with *Dirty Harry,* but nonetheless it seemed Jordan was enjoying his victory.

Bill C-16 passed its second reading in the Senate on March 2, 2017, and was scheduled for its third and final reading on June 15. Jordan was scheduled to testify before the Senate on May 17. Attorney Jared Brown would attend with Jordan and act both as his counsel and also as a witness to testify specifically on the legal problems he found with the bill. In the meantime, Jordan used every opportunity, and there were many, to speak about his opposition to and potential defiance of the bill and its surrounding legislation.

A week later he spoke at the University of Western Ontario to a welcoming audience, primarily of young men, organized by Young Canadians in Action. His performance here was relaxed, even lighthearted.

It is possible that he was now aware of Mikhaila's pregnancy and his spirits were buoyed by it. Maybe that is why he began his lecture with a child's toy, a hand puppet of Kermit the Frog. Kermit spoke first while looking at Jordan from the end of Jordan's right arm. Kermit sounded exactly like Jordan, "Are there differences between men and women?"[54]

Jordan replied, to general laughter, "Yes, Kermit, there are."

Jordan had forgotten to use a Kermit voice and apologized for his low skill as a puppeteer. He put the puppet down and looked over his audience, saying,

> So the first thing I noticed, and I actually mentioned this at the University of Toronto debate which some of you probably watched, is that, and I've been thinking about this for quite a while, that there was an overwhelming majority of men in the room. And if you look around here today, you'll see that it's probably running, I would say, about ninety to ten, and that's pretty remarkable, because there are more women than men in universities now.
>
> And so it's been quite interesting to me to see that at the public talks the vast majority of people are men. Also the people that are looking at YouTube, it's about ninety/ten as well. And we're not exactly sure why that is, although I think maybe that nobody is actually speaking to men properly.
>
> Maybe I'm doing a bit of that and I would say, that's probably also pretty good for women because if men aren't doing very well, you can be sure that women aren't going to do very well. Because as it turns out, we actually need each other.[55]

He continued with the flaws of C-16. First among them was the fluid concept of gender expression as a protected group. Second, that the law was going to be interpreted by the biased Ontario Human Rights Commission. And finally,

> There's no reason whatsoever why your employer, no matter who they are, should be messing about with the fundamental perceptual structures of your psyche. Especially when they're looking at things that aren't even voluntary. So it's appalling on multiple dimensions.
>
> And one of the things I would seriously recommend to all of you is that if anybody starts to suggest that you need to

> undergo mandatory retraining through your unconscious racial biases, that if you go along with that, you're immediately admitting that you're the sort of bigot who needs to be retrained. And I would think very carefully about admitting that. . . . In fact if you were a clinical psychologist using tests of that sort to diagnose individuals, you'd be in violation of the statutes that are governing proper practice. So I have my reasons for objecting to these things.
>
> You know, what I really don't like about bill C-16 and its surrounding policies, is that it's putting into our law a sequence of presuppositions that actually happen to be false. And it was me pointing out that they were false that's got me in whatever trouble I've been in, and generated the accusations of such things as transphobia and racism because of the insane individuals who are running Black Lives Matter in Toronto.[56]

By taking on race as well as gender, he was clearly hammering at the foundations of the better world progressives were building. In public and online, they descended from disgust into hatred. Logical argument broke down into deaf superstition.

Anonymous online haters struggled to find new curses. They sent emails, left phone messages, and mailed letters full of the worst images and accusations they could imagine. He was called alt-right, Nazi, and fascist, as well as a "transphobic piece of shit." He was made responsible for various depravaties and evils.

It was not water off a duck's back, particularly the contentious live interviews and events like the McMaster University assault. He admitted these type of things affected him for two to three days afterward. He would never get used to it. Confrontations would always remain upsetting to him.

Yet he maintained discipline and continued to attack. He considered the race and gender antagonists one unified, deceitful mob who deserved no mercy. And while it was still, thankfully, a battle of ideas and words, his best weapon for these attackers was their own words against him. It was his duty then to suffer the impact of their words.

He spoke to the Young Canadians in Action for the next hour and ten minutes without pause, showing a fluidity and continuity in his arguments and a mastery of the material ranging from biology to psychology, to politics, law, and social science. He was like a prize fighter in training, conducting a sparring exhibition for his fans.

Whatever was coming next, he seemed as prepared as he could possibly be.

He brought a professional video crew with him everywhere now, afforded by his Patreon donations that were now just under $31,000 a month. Again, like an athlete in training, he scoured the videos of these practice bouts for weaknesses in his technique. As well, almost everything he posted now was jumping to the top trending videos on YouTube. The Young Canadians lecture would eventually gather 272,666 views. The potential reach and impact of each new view could not be estimated, so he posted the Young Canadians video with links to relevant personality studies including, "Gender Differences in Personality Across the Ten Aspects of the Big Five[57]; "Gender Differences in Personality Traits Across Cultures: Robust and Surprising Findings"[58]; "Gender Differences in Personality and Interests: When, Where, and Why?"[59]; and "Cross-Cultural Studies of Personality Traits and their Relevance to Psychiatry."[60]

Through April 2017 he spoke wherever he was asked to appear while managing to maintain a full teaching schedule consisting of his twenty-two lectures in his series now called, simply, Personality. These lectures were professionally recorded, edited, and posted with an animated, professionally designed logo and pop-up icon that linked to his Patreon donation site. He was now fully in the business of online content production. He continued teaching and consulting while preparing to testify on May 17 before the Canadian Senate.

He continued to alienate and enrage the left, particularly the radical feminist left, while emboldening the political right. On May 9, just over a week before his Senate appearance, Jordan appeared on *The Joe Rogan Experience* podcast. Rogan appeared, in the current fashion of many successful web entrepreneurs, completely informal in a logo-emblazoned black hoodie, unshaven, and tattooed. Jordan maintained the relaxed, but more traditionally formal version of the Baby Boomer academic in sport jacket, T-shirt, and clean shaven.

They spoke for three hours, first about C-16 and the antagonism Jordan was receiving.

In particular, Rogan cited a large research grant Jordan had recently been denied, assuming the cancellation was an attack and public denunciation of Jordan from the left. Jordan couldn't say for sure, but ventured, "I can't help suspect that the fact that the grant application concentrated on delineating the personality characteristics of politically correct belief might have had something to do with it."[61]

They moved on to the gender argument that had progressed in Canada to include elementary school education materials like the sexually amorphous Genderbread Person. Jordan pointed out even more disturbing government sanctioned material:

> Look up *the gender unicorn*. . . . The gender unicorn is this little happy symbol that's being marketed to children you know, in elementary school, describing to them the fact that biological sex, gender identity, gender expression, and sexual proclivity vary independently, which of course they don't, by any stretch of the imagination.[62]

Jordan dominated the conversation going into the corruption of Black Lives Matter, some of the male feminists who demonstrated with activist feminists that he described as, "they've kind of got cold eyes like a codfish," the "sterile and chaotic" philosophy of the young progressives, and the "pathological postmodern professors who are hiding behind them."[63]

They ventured into Jordan's core philosophy of meaning as the key to a less tragic, more successful life. They had a good laugh about the mythological monster that Rogan, a comedian, became while making fun of the Kardashians and Caitlyn Jenner.

Jordan diverted into the symbolic meaning of the Virgin Mother in Christianity. He returned to the utter stupidity of those attempting to restructure society with no understanding of what they were destroying. He spoke appreciatively of the people who now stopped him on the street to thank him. It wasn't about the fame of being recognized; he spoke about the warmth and compelling stories of these people.

Rogan signed off after two hours and fifty-seven minutes of continuous conversation saying, "It was awesome. I could I say it was my favorite podcast of all time. . . . I think you touched on some things that made me think in a very unique way today, so thank you very much for that. I'm gonna listen to this one a couple of times."[64]

The YouTube video of this podcast received over four million views. Jordan's Patreon donations were now at $38,474 per month and would soon exceed $60,000 per month.

Conservatives in the United States had been incredulous and deeply outraged by an event at Evergreen State College in Washington State on March 16, 2017, eight weeks before C-16 was due before the Canadian parliament. In a spasm of overt racial bigotry, Professor Bret Weinstein was accosted by Evergreen students demanding that he leave the campus for the day along with all other white people. Weinstein refused.

A *day of absence* had been observed at Evergreen for years. A particular minority of students and faculty were invited to take a day off campus, one day a year. This was done to invite everyone who remained to acknowledge and celebrate that missing culture's unique contribution to the school and society. But in 2017, Professor Weinstein felt the exclusion of white people from campus for a day, *because* of their skin color, was not a celebration of a relatively obscure culture, but instead a denigration of the predominate white race. He wrote a letter to the Evergreen administration and was denounced for his effort. He wrote, "On a college campus, one's right to speak—or to be—must never be based on skin color."[65]

In May 2017, Weinstein's letter led to massive demonstrations on

Evergreen's Olympia, Washington, campus. Online threats flooded in. Like Jordan, Professor Weinstein was suddenly a global media phenomenon garnering international headlines. Campus police told the professor that they could not protect him. They advised him to stay away from campus. Dutifully, Professor Weinstein retreated to Sylvester Park in downtown Olympia to teach his biology class. It soon became clear that he could never return safely to his classroom, or set foot again on campus.

By September 2017, the settlement of a lawsuit against the university for failing to properly protect him and his wife made Weinstein and his wife $500,000 richer but unemployed. They had sought $3.8 million in damages from their former employer.[66]

Following his resignation from Evergreen, Weinstein manned the barricades with Jordan and dozens of other professors and intellectuals defending free speech and attacking grievance studies, nonbiological gender diversity, intersectionality, and the hoary old chestnut of white privilege. He made the rounds online appearing on Joe Rogan's and Sam Harris's podcasts several times. He started his own YouTube channel and became an online content producer like Jordan and many others.

The entire episode was disorienting because the progressives, like territorial chimpanzees, turned against one of their own and tore him to pieces. Professor Weinstein had been a lifelong liberal and outspoken defender of civil rights for years. Yet they came for him, the raging, disrespectful children of his colleagues, and eventually his feckless colleagues as well. They called him a racist and much worse. Weinstein's brother, Eric Weinstein, a noted mathematician and managing director of Thiel Capital, was quoted regarding the persecution of his brother,

> If you had asked me who is one of racism's most powerful foes, I would have said Bret Weinstein. . . . There's something sort of *Twilight Zone* about one of the most thoughtful commentators on race, at one of the most progressive schools in the country, getting called a racist.[67]

Eric offhandedly also coined the term the *intellectual dark web* to identify a loose group of academics and media personalities that included his brother Bret, Jordan, Ayaan Hirsi Ali, Sam Harris, Heather Heying, Claire Lehmann, Douglas Murray, Dennis Prager, Maajid Nawaz, Steven Pinker, Joe Rogan, Dave Rubin, Ben Shapiro, Lindsay Shepherd, Michael Shermer, Debra Soh, and Christina Hoff Sommers. Eric explained,

> You have to understand that the IDW emerged as a response to a world where perfectly reasonable intellectuals were being regularly mislabeled by activists, institutions and mainstream journalists with every career-ending epithet from "Islamophobe" to "Nazi." Once IDW folks saw that people like Ben Shapiro were generally smart, highly informed and often princely in difficult conversations, it's more understandable that occasionally a few frogs got kissed here and there as some IDW members went in search of other maligned princes.[68]

Bret Weinstein would come to testify before the US Congress, like Jordan in Canada, that an ascendant conspiracy to destabilize and destroy foundational Western principles was afoot. His testimony was nearly point by point confirmation of the progressive agenda and tactics that were also deployed in Canada.

The live televised hearing for C-16 in the Canadian Senate began on May 17, 2017, with Senate president Bob Runciman speaking,

> Good afternoon and welcome colleagues, invited guests, and members of the general public who are following today's proceedings of the standing Senate Committee on Legal and Constitutional Affairs.
>
> Today we continue our consideration of bill C-16, An Act to Amend the Canadian Human Rights Act and the Crim-

> inal Code. With this our last day of hearings on the bill, we will move to clause by clause consideration tomorrow. With us today for the first hour, are Jordan B. Peterson, professor, psychology department at the University of Toronto, and from the D. Jared Brown Professional Corporation, D. Jared Brown, lead counsel. Thank you gentlemen for being here. You both have up to five minutes for opening statements.[69]

Jordan began calmly, without notes, elbows on the table, fingers interlaced in front of him,

> So I think the first thing I'd like to bring up is that it's not obvious, when considering a matter of this sort, what level of analysis is appropriate. If you're reading any given document you can look at the words or the phrases or the sentences or the complete document. Or you can look at the broader context within which it is likely to be interpreted.
>
> And when I first encountered bill C-16 and its surrounding policies, it seemed to me that the appropriate level of analysis was to look at the context of interpretation surrounding the bill, which is what I did when I went and scoured the Ontario Human Rights Commission webpages and examined its policies.[70]

His voice began to rise in rate and volume, and he unclasped his fingers and began rubbing his palms with his fingertips, perhaps a reflexive reaction to stress that mimicked the antidepressant overdose reaction. He quickly stopped and resumed his hands-clasped position.

> I did that because at that point the Department of Justice had clearly indicated on their website, in a link that was later taken down, that bill C-16 would be interpreted within the policy

> precedents already established by the Ontario Human Rights Commission. So when I looked on the website I thought, well, there's broader issues at stake here, and I tried to outline some of those broader issues in the initial, you may or may not know, I made some videos criticizing bill C-16 and a number of the policies that surrounding [*sic*] it.[71]

He looked down at his notes, continuing,

> And I think the most egregious elements of the policies are that it requires compelled speech. The Ontario Human Rights Commission explicitly states that refusing to refer to a person by their self-identified name and proper personal pronoun, which is [*sic*] the pronouns that I was objecting to, can be interpreted as harassment. And so, that's explicitly defined in the relevant policies. So I think that's appalling.
>
> First of all, because there hasn't been a piece of legislation that requires Canadians to utter a particular form of address that has particular ideological implications before, and I think that it's a line that we shouldn't cross.[72]

He began to flex his hands. He looked up from his notes and addressed the Senate as he would address his own classroom,

> Then, I think that the definition of identity that's enshrined in the surrounding policies is ill-defined and poorly thought through, and also incorrect. It's incorrect in that identity is not and will never be something that people define subjectively, because your identity is something that you actually have to act out in the world as a set of procedural tools which most people learn. And I'm being technical about this. Between the ages of two and four it's a fundamental human reality, it's well recognized by the relevant developmental psychological authorities.

> And so the idea that identity is something that you define purely subjectively is an idea without status as far as I'm concerned.[73]

He spoke to Senator Runciman directly,

> I also think it's unbelievably dangerous for us to move towards representing a social constructionist view of identity in our legal system. The social constructionist view insists that human identity is nothing but a consequence of socialization. . . . And there's an inordinate amount of scientific evidence suggesting that that happens to not be the case.
>
> And so the reason that this is being instantiated into law is because the people who are promoting that sort of perspective, or at least in part, because the people who are promoting that sort of perspective know perfectly well that they lost the battle completely on scientific grounds.[74]

He began to tick off the reasons C-16 should be defeated on his fingers without breaking stride, cramming as much information as he could into his remaining two minutes:

> It's implicit in the policies of the Ontario Human Rights Commission that sexual identity, biological sex gender, identity gender expression, sexual proclivity all vary independently and that's simply not the case. It's not the case scientifically, it's not the case factually, and it's certainly not something that should be increasingly taught to people in high schools, elementary schools, and junior high schools, which it is.[75]

He picked up and showed a printout of the Gender Unicorn, saying,

> And it is being taught. I include this cartoon character that I find particularly reprehensible, aimed obviously . . . at children

> somewhere around the age of seven, that contains within it the implicit . . . claims as a consequence of its graphic mode of expression, that these elements of identity are first, canonical and second, independent. And neither of those happen to be the case.[76]

The video cut to a wide shot from behind Jordan and Jared Brown to show the thirteen attending legislators of the committee, then returned to Jordan, front view.

> I think that the inclusion of gender expression in the bill is something extraordinarily peculiar given that gender expression is not a group, and that according to the Ontario Human Rights Commission, it deals with things as mundane as how behavior and outward appearance, such as dress, hair, makeup, body language, and voice, which now as far as I can tell, open people to charges of hate crime under bill C-16 if they dare to criticize the manner of someone's dress, which seems to me to be an entirely voluntary issue.[77]

He raised a glass of water to drink, but put it down and continued to his summation,

> So I think that the Ontario Human Rights Commission's attitude towards vicarious liability is designed specifically to be punitive in that it makes employers responsible for harassment or discrimination, including the failure to use preferred pronouns; they have vicarious liability for that whether or not they know it's happening, whether or not the harassment . . . was intended or unintended. And so I'll stop with that. Thank you.[78]

Attorney Jared Brown was called upon next. He testified as to the increase he saw in claims of discrimination in every employment-related court claim. He said his phone "now rings weekly with

Human Rights Tribunal matters." He then offered a very disturbing observation:

> In August of last year I became aware of Dr. Jordan Peterson. He was discussing what he saw as a problematic law, poorly written. That's when I observed the oddest thing happening.
>
> Lawyers, academic lawyers, important people, began to say that he had the legal stuff wrong, nothing unusual about this bill. And they also said you don't get to go to jail if you breach a Human Rights Tribunal order. What was happening was they weren't defending the law, but downplaying its effects.
>
> Now as a practicing lawyer, any time a lawyer and particularly an academic says, "Look away, there's nothing to see here," it gets my antennae way up. So I did some research which could be found in the brief that I filed in advance of today. It sets out the path to prison on this.[79]

He went on to say that, as a commercial litigator, he knew that anyone could end up in jail if they breached a Tribunal order. The issue was, then, what about the fundamental freedoms of thought, belief, opinion, and expression written in Canada's founding charter? He asked,

> What if rather than restricting what you can't say, the government actually mandated what you must say? In other words, instead of legislating that you cannot defame someone, for instance, the government says when you speak about a particular subject, let's say gender, you must use this government approved set of words and theories? . . . In Canada the Supreme Court has enunciated the principle that "anything that forces someone to express opinions that are not their own is a penalty that is totalitarian and as such alien to the tradition of free nations like Canada."[80]

Brown went on to cite case law and recorded legal opinion that showed that C-16, if passed, would be left to the federal Human Rights Commission to fill in the details of how the law was to be enforced, exactly as it had been by the Ontario Human Rights Commission. It could, and very likely would, include prosecution for vague, catchall terms like, "creating a poisonous environment," as had been publicly stated by OHRC director Renu Mandhane in her veiled warning to Jordan via the Toronto *Star* newspaper.

The committee thanked Attorney Brown and went to the question and answer period. Instead of asking questions, the first committee member, Senator George Baker, reminded Jordan and Brown that all nine provinces of Canada already had laws like C-16. It went downhill from there.

The next committee member, Senator Donald Neil Plett, questioned Jordan on how he treated his students currently. Jordan responded in part,

> You don't meet people, generally speaking, in a mutual display of respect. You generally meet people in a mutual display of alert neutrality, which is the appropriate way to begin an interaction with someone, because respect is something that you earn as a consequence of reciprocal interactions that are dependent on something like reputation, which is also a consequence of repeated interactions.
>
> And so the notion that addressing someone by their self-defined self-identity isn't necessarily an indication of basic human respect for them. I think it's an entirely spurious argument, especially given that there's no evidence that moving the language in a compelled manner in this direction is going to have any beneficial effect. We're supposed to assume that just because, hypothetically, the intent is positive, that the outcome will be positive, and any social scientist worth his or her salt knows perfectly well that that's rarely the case.[81]

The questioning and responses continued for the next thirty to forty minutes before the committee adjourned. The committee convened the following day, May 18, to consider, possibly amend, and vote on the future of the bill. Jordan posted the complete recording of the hearing to his YouTube account that same day with a note under the video window, "Update: on May 18, C-16 sailed through the Canadian Senate with no amendments."[82]

He had failed to stop or even slow it down. The following month, on June 15, 2017, parliament voted to adopt the bill. It received royal assent on June 19 and immediately became law. For progressives in Canada, their long legal fight to control speech in Canada was over. For Jordan, it was just beginning. He braced for retaliation.

The media reaction was fevered since almost all had picked a political side to support, and this was a defining moment in the struggle for dominance. Jordan charged ahead, spinning headlines for them, instead of laying low and hoping to avoid a summons from the Ontario or Canadian Human Rights Commission. He used the summer recess from university to continue to press his case.

His YouTube subscribers were now approaching two million, he had nearly one million Twitter followers, and his Patreon account donations shot up to $61,417 per month.[83]

He was a global celebrity, a default member of the intellectual dark web and ground zero for the detonation of all-out war between the political left and right. He had drawn the war fever of progressives by appearing to support long-suppressed conservatives jubilant from the recent election of Donald Trump.

Jordan found the publisher Penguin Books for his new book, formerly *The 12 Most Valuable Things Everyone Should Know,* now retitled *12 Rules for Life: An Antidote to Chaos.* The phone rang and Creative Artists Agency, one of the most powerful talent brokers in the world, made a successful pitch to represent him. They introduced him to Rogers & Cowan, one of the most powerful public relations firms in the world, who also won Jordan's publicity contract. On

August 7, his granddaughter, Elizabeth Scarlett, was born. Soon he was holding her in his arms.

Perhaps then, if even for a moment, the extraordinary stresses of his personal war might have lifted. It had been an interesting summer vacation. He'd have plenty to tell the freshmen class in the fall.

The first widely publicized victim of C-16 was twenty-two-year-old graduate student and teaching assistant Lindsay Shepherd at Wilfrid Laurier University, about fifty miles west of Toronto. In early November 2017, four months after C-16 became law, Shepherd was alleged to have committed the crime of showing her communications class an edited clip from Jordan's debate with Dr. Nicholas Matte about the new law.[84]

Shepherd was hauled in front of an emboldened tribunal from the Diversity and Equity office at the university. The office's tribunal members were Professor Nathan Rambukkana, an assistant professor of communication studies; Herbert Pimlott, associate professor of communication studies; and Adria Joel, acting manager of the Diversity and Equity office. Rambukkana took the lead, telling Shepherd that showing a clip of Jordan "basically was like . . . neutrally playing a speech by Hitler."[85]

He never explained the problem with playing a speech by Hitler, but went on to explain to Shepherd that she was "legitimizing" Peterson and his harmful views, some of which were now deemed illegal. After all, he had publicly refused to use state-sanctioned multigender pronouns.

Rambukkana said that students had complained about her presentation. He wouldn't say exactly how many, but implied it was several. He said Shepherd had created "a toxic climate." For her punishment, she was told from then on she must submit her lesson plans to Rambukkana in advance, he may choose to sit in on her next few classes, and she must "not show any more controversial videos of this kind."[86]

Oddly, Shepherd and her accusers mainly shared the same political views. She was a liberal, a vegetarian, and pro-choice. She supported universal health care and was a dedicated environmentalist.[87]

She had earned her master of arts degree in cultural analysis and social theory at Wilfrid Laurier, so these were her senior colleagues. The only difference between them seemed to be that she supported free speech absolutely and she wisely recorded the meeting on her hidden cellphone.

Shepherd challenged her accusers,

> The thing is, can you shield people from those ideas? Am I supposed to comfort them and make sure that they are insulated away from this? Like, is that what the point of this is? Because to me that is so against what a university is about, so against it. I was not taking sides, I was presenting both arguments.

Rambukkana responded,

> So the thing is, about this is, if you're presenting something like this, it, ah, you have to think about the kind of teaching climate that you're creating. And this is actually, these arguments are counter to the Canadian, um, Human Rights Code ever since and I know that you talked about C-16.
>
> Ever since this passed, it is discriminatory to be targeting someone due to their gender identity or gender expression. So bringing something like this up in class and not critically. And I understand that you're trying to, like—
>
> Shepherd: It was critical. I introduced it critically.
>
> Rambukkana: How so?
>
> Shepherd: Like I said, it was in the spirit of debate.
>
> Rambukkana: Okay, in the spirit of the debate is slightly different than being like, okay. This is, this is, like, a problematic idea that maybe we want to unpack.
>
> Shepherd: But that's taking sides.
>
> Rambukkana: Yes.[88]

Yes. Her superiors were ordering her to take sides; antithetical to teaching her students how to think, she was being ordered to tell them what to think. The Socratic method of education was now replaced by the Soviet method.

They were telling her that politics was more important than education. They were accusing her of violating the new law. They were saying that she must promote their political views or be denounced to the OHRC for a federal crime. They were silencing her.

She was incredulous and soon fighting back tears of shock and rage. It probably seemed like an Orwellian nightmare come true, but she fought on. To make her inquisition before the tribunal even more disorienting, Rambukkana thrashed the language with Orwellian newspeak, "Okay, so I understand the position that you are coming from, and your positionality, but the reality is that it has created a toxic climate for some of the students."

Shepherd replied, "Who? You know, how many? One?"

"Yeah . . . may I speak?" The professor was not agreeing that one student complained; he was acknowledging her concern. Rambukkana was evasive and seemed unsure of himself, but was extremely committed to this Big Brother reality. Shepherd started to lose it. Her voice cracked as she continued to interrupt, "I have no concept of, like, how many people complained, like what their complaint was. You haven't showed me the complaint."

He apparently didn't have to show her anything. He was telling her the Diversity and Equity office's decision. He dodged her questions about the number of students who had complained and what exactly they had complained about. Rambukkana went on, "Yes, I understand that this is upsetting but there's also confidentiality, confidentiality matters."

"The number of people is confidential?" Shepherd asked.

"Yes. Do you see how this is not, it's not something, like, that's intellectually neutral, that is kind of 'up for debate'? This, I mean, this is the Charter of Rights and Freedoms." Rambukkana replied.

The professor lied about the number of people being confidential.

He warned her that she may have violated Canada's constitution. That too was a lie, and Shepherd was having none of it, going further, "But it *is* up for debate."

The professor hissed in exasperation, "But, I mean, you're perfectly welcome to your own opinions but when you're bringing it into the context of the classroom, that can become problematic and that can become something that is, that creates an unsafe learning environment for students."

Shepherd replied, "But when they leave the university they're gonna be exposed to these ideas. So I don't see how I'm doing a disservice to the class by exposing them to ideas that are really out there. And I'm sorry I'm crying. I'm stressed out because this to me is so wrong, so wrong."

Office manager Adria Joel jumped in: "Can I mention the Gendered Violence, Gendered and Sexual Violence Policy?" But Rambukkana ignored her, intent on pursuing Shepherd, continuing, "Do you understand how what happened was contrary to, sorry, Adria, what was the policy?"

"Gendered and Sexual Violence Policy," said Adria.

Shepherd then appealed to Joel to present the evidence against her, "Sorry, what did I violate in that policy?"

Joel was stuck for an answer. She stumbled into one: "Um, [*pause*] so, gender-based violence, transphobia in that policy. Causing harm, um, to trans students by, uh, [*long pause*] bringing their identity as invalid. Or their pronouns as invalid."

Rambukkana interjected, "Or something like potentially—"

Joel cut him off, "Potentially invalid . . ."

"So I caused harm under the Ontario Human Rights Code?" Shepherd asked.

"Which is, under the Ontario Human Rights Code, a protected thing and also something that Laurier holds as a value," Joel responded.

"Okay, so by proxy, me showing a YouTube video, I'm transphobic and I caused harm and violence? So be it. I can't do anything to control that."

Rambukkana pounced on her defiance, “Okay, so that’s not something that you have an issue with? These are very young students and something of that nature is not appropriate to that age of student because they don’t have—”

“Eighteen?”

“Yes.”

“They’re adults.”

“Yes, but they’re very young adults. They don’t have the critical toolkit to be able to pick it apart yet. This is one of the things we’re teaching them, and so this is why it becomes something that has to be done with a bit more care.”

Shepherd raised her voice, “In a university, all perspectives are valid!”

“That’s not necessarily true, Lindsay.”[89]

Not necessarily true. Opinion writer for the *National Post* Christie Blatchford described the entire meeting this way:

> In the 35-minute meeting, where she was outnumbered three to one, Shepherd vigorously defended herself, explaining she had been scrupulously even-handed and not taken a position herself or endorsed Peterson’s remarks before showing the video, and that her students seemed engaged by it, and had expressed a wide range of opinions.
>
> But that was part of the problem, she was told—by presenting the matter neutrally, and not condemning Peterson’s views as “problematic” or worse, she was cultivating “a space where those opinions can be nurtured.”[90]

Blatchford went on to describe the aggressively suspicious nature of Rambukkana and Pimlott,

> The two professors seemed suspicious that perhaps Shepherd was a plant of Peterson’s, and were alert to any hint that she

> was a closet supporter of the dread "alt-right" movement they both mentioned.
>
> Rambukkana asked her off the top if she wasn't from the University of Toronto, and Shepherd said no.
>
> "Ah," said Rambukkana, "so you're not one of Jordan Peterson's students."
>
> He then told her Peterson was "highly involved with the alt-right," that he had bullied his own students and asked, "do you see why this is not something . . . that is up for debate?"
>
> Pimlott seemed obsessed with scholarly qualifications—his own and Peterson's alleged lack of same—and at one point expressed amusement at the way Peterson characterized the left as being in power in academia and "you're going to be in prison" if you don't use people's preferred pronouns or profess loyalty to cultural Marxism.
>
> "Everyone is entitled to their opinions," Pimlott said, but the university has a "duty to make sure we're not furthering . . . Jordan Peterson."
>
> They were oblivious to the fact that they themselves were proving him [Jordan] right by holding the 2017 equivalent of the "struggle sessions" so beloved in Mao's China.[91]

After the meeting, Shepherd was shunned by her progressive peers. She was called transphobic and a hero of the alt-right to her face and in print. She then said she was "about 70 percent sure I will be leaving Wilfrid Laurier after this semester is over."[92]

Public clamor was growing as word leaked out about the incident. Under pressure, the university examined Shepherd's reprimand and found that the tribunal was wrong. There were actually no complaints from any of Shepherd's students. It was all a lie created by the professors and administrator Adria Joel based on a complaint from someone who had overheard something about the incident on campus. Yet, in spite of this recognition, the university did not punish the three inquisitors or offer Shepherd any apology or acknowledgment of the wrongdoing. They did not lift the sanctions imposed against Shepherd. Just the opposite.

President Deborah MacLatchy appeared on the TVO program *The Agenda* and defended the tribunal. She refused to admit that Shepherd had acted properly despite host Steve Paikin's repeated questions about this specific issue. Public outrage finally erupted in defense of Shepherd and against the university.

As public anger boiled over, MacLatchy and Professor Rambukkana issued contrite, nonapologies in press releases, with MacLatchy writing,

> Through the media, we have now had the opportunity to hear the full recording of the meeting that took place at Wilfrid Laurier University. After listening to this recording, an apology is in order. The conversation I heard does not reflect the values and practices to which Laurier aspires. I am sorry it occurred in the way that it did and I regret the impact it had on Lindsay Shepherd.[93]

She said an apology was in order. She said she was sorry for the way the incident happened. She even regretted the impact it had on Shepherd, but tellingly, she did not apologize to Shepherd. Rambukkana was even more slippery, writing, "I wanted to write to apologize . . . I was not able to do so due to confidentiality concerns. . . . Everything that has happened since the meeting has given me occasion to rethink not only my approach to discussing the concerns that day, but many of the things I said in our meeting as well."[94]

Out of the public eye, there were also no apologies and no accommodation to make amends for Shepherd's ordeal. There was no punishment for the three accusers. Shepherd was shunned and made a pariah at Wilfrid Laurier. The sanctions barring her from speaking freely to her students remained in place.

By the following spring, Shepherd had had enough. It was obvious that her academic career was effectively over at the age of twenty-two. In June, she sued her three accusers; the university; and the graduate student from the Rainbow Centre, the campus LGBTQ support community, who had overheard a discussion of Shepherd's tribunal and filed a complaint against her at the office of Diversity and Equity. So this someone, apparently one of the many peevish and resentful progressives on campus, had complained about Shepherd's class. They just hadn't actually been there to witness it.

Shepherd sued the group and each individual for $500,000 for the tort of harassment, $500,000 for intentional infliction of nervous shock, $500,000 for negligence, $100,000 for constructive dismissal, $500,000 for aggravated damages, $500,000 for general damages, and $1 million for punitive damages—a total of $3.6 million.

Jordan took this opportunity to expose and denounce the entire incident in detail. He read his lengthy complaint in a thirty-seven-minute video.[95]

He was suing Wilfrid Laurier for "injurious falsehood and punitive damages." The amount was $1.5 million.

The university issued another ill-considered press release. Perhaps they could no longer restrain their peevish resentment of this transphobic leader of the alt-right.

The press release on August 31 stated that Jordan's lawsuit was "being used as a means of unduly limiting expression on matters of public interest, including gender identity."[96]

Whoops! Jordan's attorney, Howard Levitt, disagreed: "[Laurier] thought issuing a press release would help them, and instead they libeled him again."[97]

Jordan punished the university with a second lawsuit for defamation. This time the amount was $1.75 million. The university was now facing $6.85 million worth of lawsuits.[98]

Instead of retreating after his defeat over C-16, Jordan launched a series of counterattacks, the one against Wilfrid Laurier being only the latest. Instead of being over, the battle for Western civilization was now near full fury. The big guns were being moved into position.

BBC moderator Cathy Newman never knew what hit her. It was all attack and parry, "so what you're saying is," trying to put words in Jordan's mouth until it came to that one disarming, friendly response. She asked why he had the right to offend trans people. He said because she had the right to offend him and he was fine with that. Dead air, she sat, face twisted in thought, clearly puzzling over a retort that just would not hang together. Then she sputtered a bit for time to recover. Channel 4 News, the most popular news program in England, was not amused—bad show my dear. Jordan then struck the coup de grace, "Ha! Gotcha!"[99]

He continued,

> You get my point. . . . You're doing what you should do which is digging a bit to see what the hell's going on. And that is what you should do but you're exercising your freedom of speech to certainly risk offending me and that's fine. I think, more power to you, as far as I'm concerned.[100]

Her heated argument, that he shouldn't have the right to offend people, particularly transgender people, hung in pieces around her ears.

It was lights out for Cathy Newman for a while. The network later claimed that she'd been threatened by Jordan's supporters, engendering sympathy for Newman. It was good television though, eventually gathering over 17 million views on Channel 4's YouTube channel and over 130,000 comments. Unfortunately many, perhaps most, of the comments were not helpful for Cathy.

For Jordan, it was a total victory. He had blunted Newman's attack and turned it into an embarrassing rout. He had defeated, live on international television, one of the most vocal and publicized thought leaders of the progressive movement.

And to the victor went the spoils of war. Fame, power, and wealth rained down on him. It seemed that everyone in the world suddenly wanted to speak to him. They were jockeying for position in the queue. Large black cars whisked him from breakfast to interview to meeting to lunch and home to a hotel in some city, getting farther and farther away from Toronto.

Increasingly, Tammy and Mikhaila were managing the duties of reception and the back office. Tammy was also making sure Jordan's only food, beef, was organic, top quality, and cooked perfectly. Jordan discovered he could add sparkling water to his three-ingredient menu. It was an unbelievable treat with his meat and salt. Mikhaila's carnivore diet was rapidly becoming the most boring miracle he could imagine. The sheer boredom of it made sure he never overate. At one year on the diet, he had his complete blood work done which found everything to be in perfect working order, medically. The test results may have kept him interested, certainly the menu didn't.

Mikhaila and tiny Elizabeth Scarlett eventually joined the caravan with Tammy and sometimes Julian, as invitations took Jordan all over Canada and the United States. It was fun at first, then a bit scary as strangers increasingly approached Jordan on the street, in elevators, and in airports. Without exception, the strangers turned out to be friendly fans, many with heartrending stories of how his lectures had improved and in some cases saved their lives. Jordan always took time to listen. He was touched deeply, often to the point of tears. For all the fighting and strife, he still carried an extremely tender healer's heart. To some, he had become a messiah.

But that was January. By May, Jordan was done. Finished. Cooked. Just when his fame was cresting and his chaotic life was smoothing out into a daily routine, *The New York Times* called for an interview. It seemed like this was the moment.

America's premier newspaper would portray Jordan for many millions of English-speaking people around the world. He was entering history.

Reporter Nellie Bowles came to Toronto and spent two days befriending Jordan.

He extended a warm invitation to her, welcoming her into his home, sharing his thoughts with her, allowing her to listen in on business calls and join him at a local speaking engagement. A pleasant and productive two days passed, and they said a friendly goodbye.

Nellie returned to New York, consulted her editors, and reviewed her notes. Then she gently thrust a journalistic stiletto between Jordan's ribs. It was an act of pure, unrepentant treachery, the likes of which Jordan had only read about in fairy tales. But there it was, in black ink with a splash of poison. His friend wrote,

> Most of his ideas stem from a gnawing anxiety around gender. "The masculine spirit is under assault," he told me. "It's obvious."
>
> In Mr. Peterson's world, order is masculine. Chaos is feminine. And if an overdose of femininity is our new poison, Mr. Peterson knows the cure.
>
> Hence his new book's subtitle: "An Antidote to Chaos."[101]

It wasn't dripping with poison; Nellie was too clever for that. It was just enough to sicken, and it did. The word was out, Jordan Peterson was a brute and misogynist just like Trump—same guy, different accent. Objective reporting had taken a holiday, and Cathy Newman was avenged.

> Mr. Peterson's home is a carefully curated house of horror. He has filled it with a sprawl of art that covers the walls from floor to ceiling. Most of it is communist propaganda from the Soviet Union (execution scenes, soldiers looking noble)—a constant reminder, he says, of atrocities and oppression. He wants to feel their imprisonment, though he lives here on a quiet residential street in Toronto and is quite free.[102]

The New York Times had spoken. There was no appeal. He was finished. But that was May. This was September. Jordan's *12 Rules for Life: An Antidote to Chaos* had sold over two million copies.[103] It had topped international bestseller lists for months. Oddly, it never appeared on *The New York Times* bestseller list. They claimed it was because it had been published in Canada.[104] He was touring the world with his family and selling out theaters and lecture halls consistently. Dave Rubin, a popular comedian, podcast host, and pillar of the IDW, toured with the show as Jordan's opening act. Rubin was somewhat in awe of Jordan's stamina and mental powers on stage, saying,

> He's amazing. I've never seen him give the same performance twice.
>
> Every night is unique, completely, since he never works from notes. Spontaneous. He gives 100 percent fresh perspectives, every night. I've never seen anything like it.[105]

Paid attendance was approaching two hundred thousand people, and audiences were uniformly attentive and welcoming. There were virtually no disruptions. Even outside the venues where protests might be expected, they were extremely rare.

Hundreds of ticket holders paid an additional $200 or so to have a picture taken, a fifteen-second chat, and participate in a group question-and-answer period with Jordan after each show. The live audiences, unlike his YouTube channel and Twitter feed that were generally 90 percent men and 10 percent women, were approximately 70 percent men and 30 percent women.

Eight p.m. performances, if they weren't traveling the next day, often lingered to nearly midnight. After all the photos had been taken, Jordan sat on the stage apron patiently chatting and answering questions while Mikhaila, the show's road manager, was in the wings or seated in the back of the audience, patiently waiting until the last person was finished talking. She was responsible for supervising the stage crew in wrapping up and shipping the set, consisting of a small area rug, a chair, and an end table, to the next destination.

Mikhaila sometimes opened the show when Rubin wasn't available, sharing her friendly, unassuming take on the whirlwind of fame surrounding her family now. She took questions, mostly about her carnivore diet, sometimes about her father. There was no hint of nervousness or performing for the audience. She was just friendly, humble Mikhaila.

In spite of the rumors of his death by publicity in *The New York Times,* his power and influence continued to grow. On a break from the tour, back in Toronto, he boldly tweeted to Ontario premier Doug Ford another attack on the Ontario Human Rights Commission and a second target: "The faster the Ontario Human Rights Commission is abolished, the better @fordnation. There isn't a more dangerous organization in Canada, with the possible exception of the Ontario Institute for Studies in Education: [link] j.mp/2C7nuhf."[106]

This was in response to Renu Mandhane's appearance on CBC's radio program *Metro Morning with Matt Galloway* that same day, October 10. Mandhane discussed the OHRC's intention to intervene in support of a lawsuit that sought to inject the new theories of gender diversity and the rights of LGBTQ students into elementary school curriculum in the province. Eight days after his tweet, Jordan had a secret meeting with Premier Ford. It was discovered months later by the CBC through a Freedom of Information petition that "Ford met with Peterson 'to discuss free speech on Ontario's university and college campuses,' the premier's press secretary said Friday in an email to CBC News."[107]

Even with the direct provocation of OHRC's Mandhane and inflammatory public appeal to Ontario's Premier Ford, it was obvious that the OHRC was not prepared to go after Jordan for his many insults and challenges to gender diversity theory. It was also obvious that Jordan had been spoiling for a fight from the very beginning. He'd stated clearly, many times, in many ways,

> I think that the Ontario Human Rights Tribunal is obligated by their own tangled web to bring me in front of it. If they fine me, I won't pay it. If they put me in jail, I'll go on a hunger

> strike. [*Emphatically*] *I'm not doing this. And that's that.* I'm *not* using the words that other people require me to use. Especially if they're made up by radical left wing ideologues.[108]

Yet the OHRC remained mute and immobile. Why? With all the new power afforded by C-16, logically they would want to use it to defeat antagonists like Jordan Peterson. Their reticence was possibly because gender diversity theory and the laws surrounding it could not withstand a challenge before Canada's Supreme Court, and experienced lawyer Mandhane knew it. And she knew Jordan and Jared Brown were itching to see the OHRC there.

Legally, the OHRC was stymied by Canada's charter that guaranteed freedom of speech and by the new Freedom of Speech law sponsored by Premier Ford's office. Ironically, it was the Canadian universities who identified the practical defeat of C-16 in the real world. TVO host Steve Paikin, who had interviewed Jordan for over ten years, wrote on March 4, 2019,

> Some universities are concerned that the new campus freedom-of-speech policy will lead to Charter challenges going forward: students may claim that a speaker's free-speech rights have been violated by protesters and, ultimately, by their university's administration. The province has also threatened universities with unspecified funding cuts should they fail to adhere to the new freedom-of-speech policy.
>
> "Even if the Charter challenges are unsuccessful, it could cost millions for us to defend ourselves," says one university rep, who asked not to be named.[109]

It appeared that Jordan's private chat with Ontario premier Doug Ford had ultimately defeated C-16 for most practical purposes. Once Premier Ford's Freedom of Speech law threatened university funding cuts, C-16 collapsed. There would be no additional prohibited speech or compelled speech in Ontario and by extension, throughout

Canada. Jordan had won. For now. This didn't mean the OHRC had been entirely defanged. They would occasionally snare a working person like Lindsay Shepherd or a small business owner who could not afford a lawsuit against the government. Jordan would issue tweets in their defense and post many incidents on his website.

On April 14, 2019, Jordan's book tour for *12 Rules* took him to the Beacon Theatre in New York City. Mikhaila opened the show with her amusing thoughts on what it was like to be Jordan Peterson's daughter. She introduced her father. He entered to a standing ovation.

In his one-hour presentation, he paced comfortably across stage and back, occasionally stopping to check his words. He'd become even more careful than usual in using precise language. Many friends and supporters of the OHRC were scrutinizing every publicly spoken word. He moved fluidly across the themes in the various chapters of his new book, saying,

> It is a moral responsibility to put yourself together. . . . Solzhenitsyn felt his time in the gulag was atonement for his role in World War II. . . . When you fall in love, you see what the other could be. . . . The discovery of the future forestalls gratification. To payoff [delayed gratification] in the future is the discovery of time itself. . . . The resentful will complain to God even if they don't believe in him. . . . [Biblical] Cain's resentment is the root cause of the degeneration of civilization. . . . It is the failure of the individual, at the moral level, that perpetuates the horrors of the world. . . . The ability to speak the truth stabilizes the world. . . . People aren't lining up at the border to escape the United States. . . . The individual is charged with the responsibility for the world. . . . You don't get away with anything, ever. . . . In Genesis, God uses truth to create the world. . . . Something divine confronting potential creates something good. . . . Lies make life worse. . . . Older people regret missed opportunities mostly, not what they did. . . . If

> you're true to yourself, at least you get the adventure of your life. . . . You have a responsibility to play a role in constructing the reality of the world. If you don't, you leave a hole in the structure of the world. . . . We are all doomed sailors on the stormy seas. All we can do is chart a course by the stars. . . . Virtue is the combination of many virtues. . . . Study the cartoonist R. Crumb and you will understand the motivation of a rapist.[110]

He recommended five books: *The Gulag Archipelago, Crime and Punishment, The Road to Wigan Pier, Affective Neuroscience,* and *The Neuropsychology of Anxiety.*

He thanked the audience and bowed his head. The reaction was spectacular. The audience rose as one and applauded, whistled, and yelled, "Woo-hoo!" The commotion continued, he bowed again. It continued further, seeming to go on for minutes, never diminishing in energy. He bowed a third time. Then he stood, smiling, broadly looking into the balconies and across the mezzanine. Finally, he raised his arms in victory and exited.

Mikhaila came out and instructed the people who had purchased a photo with Jordan and participation in the question-and-answer period to line up in the stage-right aisle. A photographic backdrop was brought to the front of the audience. For the next hour or so, over two hundred people had their picture taken with Jordan. He shook hands and chatted briefly with each one. He clearly enjoyed meeting them; each chat varied in length and tone by his expressions. As each person finished, they were directed to the front of the center section of the orchestra seating.

The backdrop was taken away. Jordan climbed back onto stage and crossed to center. He stood for a moment, smiling, savoring the assembled committed fans. He moved downstage to the apron and sat down, legs dangling over the edge. He was part of them now, among them. For the next hour and a half, even though the show was scheduled to travel the next day, he patiently and thoughtfully answered every question. One had to imagine that he'd heard some of these questions hundreds of times recently, but none got a blunt or thoughtless answer. Mikhaila waited quietly, sitting on the steps to the stage-left fire exit in the middle of the house, while her father spoke freely about his thoughts and concerns.

EPILOGUE

The day before his Beacon Theatre appearance, I met Jordan in a little coffee shop on Sixth Avenue in Manhattan. He greeted me with his customary broad, closed smile and a curt nod. It was a friendly presentation and I very much wanted to appear as a friend to him, not a pushy or nosy biographer.

We sat together across a small table. I had my tea and croissant, he went to the counter to order a bottle of water while I reviewed my few notes. I wanted this to be a casual get-to-know-you, a personal encounter, no pressure. He returned and we traded small talk about New York since I'd lived there for almost twenty years, and he was new to it.

An older lady was attempting to get by Jordan to a lone seat along the far wall.

She balanced her coffee and roll in one hand while guiding her aluminum walker with the other. Jordan didn't notice, so I asked him to please excuse her, to let her pass.

He got up immediately and excused himself, clearing a path for her. Schoolgirls near her intended seat suddenly plopped down their piles of school books on it. She was stranded. I invited her to sit with us. Jordan smiled at the thought and she accepted.

I told her we were just having a business chat, and it would be pretty boring for her. She shrugged, unwrapped her roll from a napkin, and said, "Whatever. I can't hear anyway."

Jordan and I were amused at the typical New Yorker response.

Our chitchat resumed and in a moment our introduction was over. A pause, and then Jordan asked, "What questions do you have for me?"

He leaned back and his eyes narrowed, parsing my body language. His hands came up and clasped in front of his mouth. His body language was telling me he was about to be very careful with his words. That was not what I wanted at all. I knew I had months of research in front of me and there was not much sense going into detail or seeking usable quotes at this first meeting. I had prepared a few general questions but just wanted to get to know him, as a guy, a man in an unusual situation of sudden worldwide fame and great wealth. I had already written the first draft of the first chapter of this book in order to sell the idea of it to the publisher. I asked him, "Before we start, I thought you might like to read a little bit of the book, the first page. See if you like it."

Slowly, his hands came down from his mouth and he nodded in agreement. My editor had told me pointedly and repeatedly not to do this. If it backfired, it could end the entire project. I may have inherited a gambler's mind-set from my father, a notorious and highly successful long-shot gambler. I also had too much respect for Jordan and his work. If I was off base, if he hated my writing, I wanted to know right then. I could always get another job selling insurance.

As you have already read, the first chapter, especially the first page, was the most personally intrusive about Jordan, revealing him as a young man on the edge of madness and violence. He read carefully, nodding in approval, and eventually looked up at me with a final nod of acknowledgment, perhaps approval. I pushed, "Is that an approval?"

He was hesitant, still cautious, "Well, yes."

With the dice thrown and my point made, he returned to interview stance. He wanted to know if I had questions for him.

"With your new power and position, how will you avoid becoming corrupt?" I asked.

"Well, I have about thirty people now, watching me. Checking everything I'm doing," he responded.

"You should have them with you, like a posse, big gold chains and running suits. You'd look cool."

He laughed a bit. I really didn't want to get into an interview. I just wanted to chat, get a feel for him, see if we could work together. I asked a few more general questions, like his thoughts on the media, giving him an oblique shot at me if he wanted one. He predicted the "death of the mainstream media" and "of academia." They'd gone too far, according to him, they were killing themselves. I didn't sense any animosity at all toward me. Obviously, I wasn't an investigative reporter, and maybe I wasn't a friendly assassin either, like *The New York Times* reporter. He asked, "How long have you been doing this [writing]?"

The answer took me a moment to calculate. "Forty-two years."

He nodded again; his face registered respect for the commitment. I asked, risking a bit, "How are you doing with your depression?"

"Not bad, not too bad," he responded.

Why the hell did I say that?! I quickly stumbled on, sharing my own family's history with depression, including a current family member who had started with the earliest medications, even before SSRIs. I mentioned how I thought it had made him erratic, seemingly calm and pleasant one moment, angry and frustrated the next. I suppose I may have slumped or lost eye contact with Jordan for a moment, lost in my own dull pain. I looked up and he was staring at me with tears in his eyes. I thought, *Now I've really done it. I've hit his most vulnerable spot and hurt him.*

This was quickly becoming a disaster. I pressed on, "I know you've paid a terrible price, with people coming at you from all directions. Not knowing who to trust. It's gotta be tough. Me too, in a way, I've had to pay a lot to speak and think the way I do."

I meant my conversion to conservative, traditionalist philosophy, coming from a liberal, progressive family and background. He was calmly curious, "What have you paid?"

Now I was under the microscope. I could see the book, my big moment, my reputation all going down in flames when I revealed how weak and hopeless I was. The truth was, I was an emotional wreck. My wife of twenty years had recently passed away, and I was as isolated and depressed as I'd ever been in my life. I looked at him, took a moment, and said, "I've lost my friends and family."

He looked away, waved off my concern as if I'd lost my grandmother's recipe for butter cookies, and said, "Oh, that."

It was funny! Gallows humor. We were condemned men, heads down on the chopping block, making fun of the executioner's shoes. He knew exactly what I was talking about.

A young woman in her late thirties stopped at our table. She stared at Jordan for a moment. He smiled at her and said hello.

"Excuse me, Dr. Peterson. I just wanted to tell you how much you've helped me, really helped me."

Suddenly, her eyes filled with tears. Jordan watched her, head nodding slowly in acknowledgment as she went on about the terrible rifts in her family, crushing disappointment in love, and how listening to him brought her back from the edge of harming herself. She was brave, telling her story to the point of breaking down completely, even among strangers in a coffee shop.

I looked to Jordan. He was engrossed in her story, his eyes also filled with tears.

He reached his hand out to her. They held hands briefly and then he shook hers slowly, comforting her. She excused herself to me, then to Jordan, and dried her eyes. She said, "Thank you so much."

With that, she turned and walked out of the shop. Jordan turned to me, eyes about to spill over. He shrugged and shook his head slowly, at a loss for words.

Our time was up. Jordan mentioned his next appointment. We stood and shook hands and he smiled kindly. I didn't know what to say. There was just too much to grasp in the moment we had left. I was worried for him; he seemed emotionally fragile, but I knew I had to let him go.

"See ya," I said.

"Bye," he responded.

He walked out onto busy Sixth Avenue. He stopped to check his phone for his next address and walked away. I was shaken by the whipsaw of emotions that had overwhelmed us in our half hour together, but I was more seriously concerned for Jordan. His depression must be much worse than he let on. I thought to myself, *How in the world is he going to be able to manage? How will he get through everything he has to deal with if any stranger can make him cry?*

I had survived but it was a troubling start. I walked a few blocks to the Pierre Hotel, sat alone in the empty dining room, and ordered an outrageously expensive early lunch. I waited for my food quietly, not checking my email, expecting no one, decompressing. It slowly dawned on me. I hadn't wounded Jordan with my intrusive question about the state of his depression, he was reacting to my depression like he reacted to the young lady's story.

It seemed like he had no filter to shield him from the suffering of others, even strangers in a coffee shop, even me. He had been crying for me.

ACKNOWLEDGMENTS

Thank you, Roxanne Baker, my friend, copyeditor, and researcher, and Susie Newton, a selfless, tireless, and brilliant researcher. I couldn't have done this book without you two. To Marc Resnick, the kindest, most insightful editor I've ever worked with. You understood the importance of Dr. Peterson immediately, when others in your position were unsure. You kept faith with my occasionally unorthodox attempts to bring his achievements to life. May you always reign supreme.

To my oldest friend, David Fallon, and his family, to newer friends John Paxson, Peter Fallon, and Joey Barquin. Having friends who actually read and care about my work is a blessing and favor I'll never forget. Thank you.

To my loud and proud Jewish, Irish, Ghanaian, Czech, Italian American, gay, and straight family—Chip, Mike, Billy, Jim Kodlick, Johanna, Susannah, Anthony, Mick, and forever closer-than-a-brother cousin Daniel Zoller. To Terry, Lacey, Dave, Allotey, Olu, Elizabeth, and all the cousins and all the beautiful children in the family, Aku, Sena, Duki, Akushika, Akiode, Luci, Elise, Zack, Tim, Zoe, Noah, Ethan, Eric, Gia, and Jack. To Sue, Rachel, and Dee. You are always with me in my heart and my thoughts. Forgive me. I love you. I hope this book may help us be together.

To Pastor Bill Hild, you loved me back to life and taught me about the healing promise of God and Jesus Christ. You showed me a path through the darkness. To Barre Yeager, a mountain boy and a savior as well. For the loving hearts at First Baptist Church of Sarasota. Y'all rock. To the phenomenal Barbara Deutsche who coined the term, "love him back to himself," a true friend when many stepped away.

To my pals forever, Dave Brady, Guy Polhemus, Vivianne Castanos, and special friend Anita Wise. You hold the memories of our most beautiful times. To the beautiful, extraordinary spirit Debi Frock and my goddaughter Comfort Johnson, you are my family too. I am blessed to have you.

To God and my many darlings in heaven. I'm running a bit late. Don't wait up.

NOTES

CHAPTER ONE: DESCENT INTO HELL

1. "Jordan Peterson talks about Socialism at UBC," The Challenger, Jan. 12, 2019, https://youtu.be/9eZRkWx5SYw?t=872.
2. Pete Earley, *Comrade J: The Untold Secrets of Russia's Master Spy in America After the End of the Cold War* (New York: G. P. Putnam's Sons, 2007), 167–77.
3. Jordan B. Peterson, Preface to *Maps of Meaning: The Architecture of Belief* (New York: Routledge, 1999), xiii.
4. http://jsomers.net/vonnegut-1970-commencement.html.
5. https://www.youtube.com/watch?v=mqSV72VNnV0.
6. Jordan B. Peterson, Preface to *Maps of Meaning: The Architecture of Belief* (New York: Routledge, 1999), xiv.
7. https://torontolife.com/city/u-t-professor-sparked-vicious-battle-gender-neutral-pronouns/.

CHAPTER TWO: THROUGH THE UNDERWORLD

1. https://www.thestar.com/news/insight/2018/03/16/jordan-peterson-is-trying-to-make-sense-of-the-world-including-his-own-strange-journey.html.
2. Ibid.
3. https://en.wikipedia.org/wiki/Alexander_Luria#Books.
4. https://www.newscientist.com/article/dn13708-life-changing-books-the-mind-of-a-mnemonist/.
5. Jordan B. Peterson, Preface to *Maps of Meaning: The Architecture of Belief* (New York: Routledge, 1999), xiii.
6. Ibid.
7. Friedrich Nietzsche, *The Gay Science: With a Prelude in Rhymes and an Appendix of Songs*, translated, with commentary, by Walter Kaufmann (New York: Vintage Books, 1974), Kindle edition, Location 1443.
8. Jordan B. Peterson, Preface to *Maps of Meaning: The Architecture of Belief* (New York: Routledge, 1999), xiv.
9. Friedrich Nietzsche, *The Will to Power* (New York: Random House, 1968), Kindle edition, Location 5834.
10. Nietzsche, *The Gay Science.*
11. https://youtu.be/AR-86T8jpuQ?t=1795.

CHAPTER THREE: INTO THE BELLY OF THE BEAST

1. C. G. Jung, *Memories, Dreams, Reflections,* recorded and ed. Aniela Jaffé, trans. Richard and Clara Winston (New York: Random House, 1963), v.
2. Ibid.
3. Ibid.
4. William Bechtel, Robert C. Williamson, and E. Craig, eds. *Vitalism. Routledge Encyclopedia of Philosophy* (New York: Routledge, 1998), doi:10.4324/9780415249126 Q109-1.
5. Jordan B. Peterson, Preface to *Maps of Meaning: The Architecture of Belief* (New York: Routledge, 1999), xvi.
6. *The Collected Works of C. G. Jung,* vol. 7, *Two Essays on Analytical Psychology,* trans. R. F. C. Hull, Bollingen Series XX (Princeton, NJ: Princeton University Press, 1967), xvi.
7. Peterson, *Maps of Meaning,* xvi.
8. James Joyce, *Ulysses,* Classic Books Edition, Not So Noble Books, Kindle location 744.
9. Peterson, Preface to *Maps of Meaning,* xvi.
10. Jordan B. Peterson, *12 Rules for Life: An Antidote to Chaos* (Toronto: Random House Canada, 2018), Kindle edition, p. 249.
11. Peterson, Preface to *Maps of Meaning,* xvi.
12. Ibid.
13. Ibid.

CHAPTER FOUR: RETURN OF THE HERO

1. Jordan B. Peterson, *12 Rules for Life: An Antidote to Chaos* (Toronto: Random House Canada, 2018), Kindle edition, p. 235.
2. Yuri Bezmenov, TV interview, https://youtu.be/bX3EZCVj2XA?t=40, 1984.
3. "Resolution on Certain Questions in the History of Our Party Since the Founding of the People's Republic of China," adopted by the Sixth Plenary Session of the Eleventh Central Committee of the Communist Party of China on June 27, 1981; *Resolution on CPC History (1949–81),* (Beijing: Foreign Languages Press, 1981), 32.
4. Peterson, *12 Rules for Life,* 247.
5. Ibid.
6. Ibid.
7. Jordan B. Peterson, *Maps of Meaning: The Architecture of Belief* (New York: Routledge, 1999), 472.
8. Amos Zeichner and R. O. Pihl, "Effects of Alcohol and Behavior Contingencies on Human Aggression," *Journal of Abnormal Psychology* 88 (1979): 153–60.
9. Leo Tolstoy, *A Confession and Other Religious Writings* (Neeland Media LLC.), Kindle edition, p. 12.
10. https://youtu.be/4GcU9LjuVOo?t=5509.
11. https://youtu.be/6c9Uu5eILZ8?t=59.
12. Peterson, *12 Rules for Life,* Kindle edition, p. 251.
13. https://youtu.be/6c9Uu5eILZ8?t=98.
14. https://youtu.be/6c9Uu5eILZ8?t=64.
15. https://youtu.be/6c9Uu5eILZ8?t=525.

CHAPTER FIVE: SAVAGERY

1. *Pravda,* March 27, 1983.
2. Michael Harrington, *The Other America: Poverty in the United States* (New York: Macmillan, 1962).
3. Herbert Mitgang, "Michael Harrington, Socialist and Author, Is Dead," *New York Times,* Aug. 2, 1989, https://www.nytimes.com/1989/08/02/obituaries/michael-harrington-socialist-and-author-is-dead.html.
4. Ibid.
5. http://archive.wilsonquarterly.com/sites/default/files/articles/WQ_VOL8_SU_1984_Review_08.pdf.
6. Ernesto Guevara, *Che Guevara Reader: Writings by Ernesto Che Guevara on Guerrilla Strategy, Politics & Revolution,* ed. David Deutschmann (Melbourne, Australia: Ocean Press, 1997).
7. https://youtu.be/fEi4_HcOcLA?t=17.
8. https://youtu.be/fEi4_HcOcLA?t=120.
9. https://youtu.be/fEi4_HcOcLA?t=153.
10. Jordan B. Peterson, J. M. Rothfleisch, Philip Zalazo, and Robert O. Pihl, "Acute Alcohol Intoxication and Cognitive Functioning," *Journal of Studies on Alcohol* 51, (Dec. 1990): 114–22, doi:10.15288/jsa.1990.51.114.
11. Jordan B. Peterson, *12 Rules for Life: An Antidote to Chaos* (Toronto, CA: Random House Canada, 2018), Kindle edition, pp. 254–55.

CHAPTER SIX: TEMPTATION

1. David Horowitz, *The Black Book of the American Left,* vol. 2, *Progressives* (Sherman Oaks, CA: David Horowitz Freedom Center), Kindle edition, Location 442.
2. Paul Hollander, *Discontents: Post-Modern and Post-Communist,* op. cit., 281; cf. two typical collections with the same name: *After the Fall: The Failure of Communism and the Future of Socialism*, ed. Robin Blackburn (London: Verso, 1991), and, *After the Fall: 1989 and the Future of Freedom*, ed. George Katsiaficas (New York: Routledge, 2001).
3. Interesting Times, op. cit. Cf. also Geoffrey Wheatcroft's review of the autobiography in *New York Times,* Sept. 5, 2003, entitled "Still Saluting the Red Flag After the Flag Pole Fell."
4. Henry F. Myers, "Thinkers Who Shaped the Century," *Wall Street Journal,* Eastern edition; New York, NY November 25, 1991: PAGE A1.
5. *After the Fall: The Failure of Communism and the Future of Socialism,* ed. Robing Blackburn (London: Verso, 1991), 122–23; Interesting Times, 280.
6. Gerda Lerner, *Fireweed, A Political Autobiography* (Philadelphia: Temple University Press, 2002), 369.
7. Ibid.
8. Edward S. Shapiro, *Crown Heights: Blacks, Jews, and the 1991 Brooklyn Riot* (Waltham, MA: Brandeis University Press, 2006).
9. William Saletan and Avi Zenilman, "The Gaffes of Al Sharpton," *Slate,* Oct. 7, 2003, retrieved Oct. 20, 2007.
10. William McGowan, "Race and Reporting," Summer 1993, Manhattan Institute, *City Journal.*
11. https://www.amazon.com/Race-Traitor-Noel-Ignatiev/dp/0415913934/re/-sr_1_3? Keywords-race+traitor&gid-1573514882&sr-8-3.
12. Jordan B. Peterson, *12 Rules for Life: An Antidote to Chaos* (Toronto, CA: Random House Canada, 2018), Kindle edition, p. 91.

13. Ibid., 354.
14. Ibid.
15. Ibid., 351–52.
16. Ibid.
17. Jordan B. Peterson, *Maps of Meaning: The Architecture of Belief* (New York: Routledge, 1999), 340.
18. Eric Harris's Journal, transcribed and annotated by Peter Langman, Entry, April 10, 1998, p. 26,005, https://schoolshooters.info/sites/default/files/harris_journal_1.3.pdf.
19. Jordan B. Peterson *Maps of Meaning,* p. 340.
20. Jordan B. Peterson, Preface to *Maps of Meaning: The Architecture of Belief* (New York: Routledge, 1999), 344.
21. Jordan B. Peterson, *Maps of Meaning,* p. 312.
22. Peterson, *12 Rules for Life,* Kindle edition, p. 383.

CHAPTER SEVEN: A COMFY NEST OF VIPERS

1. Jordan B. Peterson, Preface to *Maps of Meaning: The Architecture of Belief* (New York: Routledge, 1999), 1.
2. https://www.thecrimson.com/article/1995/4/26/jordan-peterson-pharvard-students-may-know/?page=single.
3. Ibid.
4. Ibid.
5. Ibid.
6. Ibid.
7. David Horowitz, *The Black Book of the American Left,* vol. 2, *Progressives* (Sherman Oaks, CA: David Horowitz Freedom Center), Kindle edition Location 1408.
8. https://www.nationalreview.com/2019/04/harvard-uprising-protests-1969-radicalism/.
9. Ann Coulter, *Demonic: How the Liberal Mob Is Endangering America* (New York: Crown, 2011), Kindle edition, p. 172.
10. Horowitz, *The Black Book of the American Left,* vol. 2, *Progressives,* Kindle edition, Location 3302.
11. Ibid, Location 3309.
12. Noam Chomsky, *What Uncle Sam Really Wants* (Berkeley, CA: Odonian Press, 1992), 32.
13. Dave Zirin, "Howard Zinn: The Historian Who Made History" *Huffington Post,* Jan. 28, 2010.
14. Jordan B. Peterson, Preface to *Maps of Meaning,* xv.
15. Ibid.
16. "Sad but funny story about Jordan Peterson and his wife, trying to feed a child from another family," Pragmatic Entertainment, March 18, 2018, https://youtu.be/4baRTivL_fQ.
17. Ibid.
18. Jordan B. Peterson, "Maps of Meaning Lecture 01a: Introduction (Part 1)," Jan. 7, 2015, https://youtu.be/4tQOlQRp3gQ?t=3951.
19. Ibid.
20. Ibid.
21. Ibid.
22. Jonathan A. Lewin, "Tension High at Faculty Meeting," *The Crimson,* May 3, 1995.
23. Ibid.
24. Stephen Marglin, "Why Is So Little Left of the Left?" *Z Papers,* October–December 1992.

25. Jeffrey C. Milder, "At Harvard, Marxism Quietly Goes Out of Style," *The Crimson,* Oct. 31, 1994.
26. Horowitz, *The Black Book of the American Left,* vol. 2, *Progressives,* Kindle edition, Location 473.
27. Editor's response, *Race Traitor,* PO Box 499, Dorchester, MA 02122, 1993.
28. Jordan B. Peterson, "Identity Politics and the Marxist Lie of White Privilege," https://youtu.be/PfH81G7Awk0?t-296, Nov. 13, 2017.
29. "Modern Times: Camille Paglia & Jordan B Peterson," October 2017, https://youtu.be/v-hIVnmUdXM?t=1720.
30. Ibid., https://youtu.be/v-hIVnmUdXM?t=344.
31. Excerpt from the documentary film *Derrida,* https://youtu.be/vgwOjjoYtco, Sep. 6, 2008.
32. Peggy McIntosh, *Working Paper 189,* Wellesley Centers for Women, Wellesley, MA 1988.
33. University of British Columbia Free Speech Club, November 13, 2017, https://youtu.be/PfH8IG7Awk0.
34. Phone interview with Jim Proser, Gregg Hurwitz, May 17, 2019.
35. Lan N. Nguyen, "The Faculty Feuds Over the Politics of Scholarship," *The Crimson,* June 6, 1991.
36. National Association of Scholars, "Is the Curriculum Biased?," www.nas.org, What We Are Doing, Statements, November 8, 1989.
37. Kimberlé Crenshaw, "Demarginalizing the Intersection of Race and Sex: A Black Feminist Critique of Antidiscrimination Doctrine, Feminist Theory and Antiracist Politics," University of Chicago Legal Forum, 1989.
38. Judith Butler, Preface to *Gender Trouble: Feminism and the Subversion of Identity* (New York: Routledge, 1990), viii.
39. Ibid., 3.
40. Peterson, *Maps of Meaning,* 271.
41. Katy Bennett, "Jordan Peterson Criticizes Cambridge's Decision to Rescind Fellowship Offer," *Varsity,* March 21, 2019.
42. Email from Gregg Hurwitz to Jim Proser, May 18, 2019.

CHAPTER EIGHT: CHILD'S PLAY

1. Jordan B. Peterson, *Maps of Meaning: The Architecture of Belief* (New York: Routledge, 1999), 468.
2. "Depression: A Family Affair," *The Agenda with Steve Paikin,* TVO, May 9, 2012, https://youtu.be/KqXZY3B-cGo?t=209.
3. Peterson, *Maps of Meaning*, 461.
4. https://www.researchgate.net/post/How_many_papers_are_people_expected_to_publish_a_year.
5. Sherry H. Stewart, Jordan B. Peterson, and Robert O. Pihl, "Anxiety Sensitivity and Risk for Alcohol Abuse in Young Adult Females," *Journal of Anxiety Disorders* 9 (July–Aug. 1995): 283–92.
6. Jacob B. Hirsh, Colin G. DeYoung, Xiaowen Xu, and Jordan B. Peterson, "Compassionate Liberals and Polite Conservatives: Associations of Agreeableness with Political Ideology and Moral Values," *Personality and Social Psychology Bulletin* 36 (May 2010): 664–65.
7. Xiaowen Xu, Ramond A. Mar, and Jordon B. Peterson, "Does Cultural Exposure Partially Explain the Association Between Personality and Political Orientation?" *Personality and Social Psychology Bulletin* 39 (Dec. 2013): 1497–1517, https://doi.org/10.1177/0146167213499235.

8. "Jordan Peterson: 'My Biggest Regret,'" Sept. 22, 2017, https://youtu.be/z86kVQxXt7g?t=180.
9. Bernard Schiff, "I Was Jordan Peterson's Strongest Supporter. Now I Think He's Dangerous," Toronto *Star,* May 25, 2018.
10. "Depression: A Family Affair."
11. Schiff, "I Was Jordan Peterson's Strongest Supporter."
12. "Depression: A Family Affair."
13. https://www.ratemyprofessors.com/ShowRatings.jsp?tid=32245.
14. Craig Lambert, "Chaos, Culture, Curiosity," *Harvard Magazine,* Sept. 1998, https://harvardmagazine.com/1998/09/right.chaos.html.
15. Aleksandr Solzhenitsyn, *The Gulag Archipelago, 1918–1956: An Experiment in Literary Investigation,* vol. 1, trans. Thomas P. Whitney (New York: Harper & Row, 1974), 39.
16. Jordan B. Peterson, "Neuropsychology of Motivation for Group Aggression and Mythology," in *Encyclopedia of Violence, Peace, & Conflict,* ed. Lester Kurtz (San Diego, CA: Academic Press, 1999), 1329–40.
17. Tom Bartlett, "What's So Dangerous About Jordan Peterson?" *Chronicle of Higher Education,* Jan. 17, 2018, https://www.chronicle.com/article/what-s-so-dangerous-about/242256.
18. Harvey Shepherd, "Meaning from Myths," *Montreal Gazette,* Nov. 11, 2003.
19. Bartlett, "What's So Dangerous About Jordan Peterson?"
20. Schiff, "I Was Jordan Peterson's Strongest Supporter."

CHAPTER NINE: ORDER AND CHAOS

1. Jordan B. Peterson, *Maps of Meaning: The Architecture of Belief* (New York: Routledge, 1999), 366.
2. Jill Dougherty, "How the Media Became One of Putin's Most Powerful Weapons," *Atlantic,* April 21, 2015.
3. Julia Ioffe, "What Is Russia Today?," *Columbia Journalism Review,* Sept./Oct. 2010.
4. David Horowitz, *The Black Book of the American Left,* vol. 2, *Progressives* (Sherman Oaks, CA: David Horowitz Freedom Center), Kindle edition, Location 477.
5. Jordan B. Peterson, "Maps of Meaning: The Architecture of Belief (Precis)," *Psycoloquy* 10 (Dec. 1999): 1–31.
6. Jordan B. Peterson and Colin G. DeYoung, "Metaphoric Threat Is More Real Than Real Threat," *Behavioral and Brain Sciences* 23 (Dec. 2000): 992–93.
7. Jordan B. Peterson, "Awareness May Be Existence as Well as (Higher-order) Thought," *Behavioral and Brain Science* 23 (Dec. 2000): 214–15
8. Bernard Schiff, "I Was Jordan Peterson's Strongest Supporter. Now I Think He's Dangerous," Toronto *Star,* May 25, 2018.
9. "List of genocides by death toll," Wikipedia, multiple supportive sub-references, https://en.wikipedia.org/wiki/List_of_genocides_by_death_toll#List_of_the_genocides.
10. "Depression: A Family Affair," *The Agenda with Steve Paikin,* TVO, May 9, 2012, https://youtu.be/KqXZY3B-cGo?t=268.
11. "Digesting Depression," *The Agenda with Steve Paikin,* TVO, April 20, 2016, https://youtu.be/A6g_geYeL4U?t=122.
12. Tarek A. Hammad, "Review and Evaluation of Clinical Data. Relationship Between Psychiatric Drugs and Pediatric Suicidal Behavior," Food and Drug Administration, Aug. 16, 2004, 42, 115.

CHAPTER TEN: THE DEVOURING MOTHER

1. Jill Ker Conway, *True North* (New York: Alfred A. Knopf, 1994), 67.
2. Ibid., 240.
3. Jordan B. Peterson, "Strengthen the Individual: Q&A Parts I & II," speech at Ottawa Public Library, March 12, 2017, https://youtu.be/CwcVLETRBjg.
4. Liberty University Convocation, March 29, 2019, https://youtu.be/aDepoPl1oEM?t=1132.
5. https://thecosmicmother.org/home/kali/.
6. Jordan B. Peterson, "The Devouring Mother: Understanding the Psychological Archetypes of Consciousness," Sagacious News, July 16, 2017, https://www.sagaciousnewsnetwork.com/the-devouring-mother-understanding-the-psychological-archetypes-of-consciousness/; https://www.youtube.com/watch?v=mSQ_pZCP1w8&feature=youtu.be.
7. "The Coddling of the American Mind: A First Principles Conversation with Dr. Jonathan Haidt," *Real Time with Bill Maher,* https://youtu.be/tKW3vKpPrlw.
8. Blaine Conzatti, "4 Reasons Suicide Is Increasing Among Young Adults," Family Policy Institute of Washington, May 19, 2017, https://www.fpiw.org/blog/2017/05/19/4-reasons-suicide-is-increasing-among-young-adults/.
9. Michael Jonas, "The Downside of Diversity," *Boston Globe,* Aug. 5, 2007, https://archive.boston.com/news/globe/ideas/articles/2007/08/05/the_downside_of_diversity/.
10. Ilana Mercer, "Greater Diversity Equals More Misery," *Orange County Register,* July 22, 2007, https://www.ocregister.com/2007/07/22/ilana-mercer-greater-diversity-equals-more-misery/.
11. Ben Shapiro, "Comedy & Tragedy, 2003–2004," Young America's Foundation, 2003; *Brainwashed* (Nashville, TN: Thomas Nelson, 2004).
12. Ibid.
13. "Genders, Rights and Freedom of Speech," *The Agenda with Steve Paikin,* Oct. 26, 2016, https://youtu.be/kasiov0ytEc.
14. Mark S. Bonham Centre for Sexual Diversity Studies, University of Toronto, http://sds.utoronto.ca/people/instructors/440-2/.
15. Ibid.
16. https://www.ratemyprofessors.com/ShowRatings.jsp?tid=32245.
17. https://www.ratemyprofessors.com/ShowRatings.jsp?tid=1292465.
18. Ibid.
19. "The Positive Space Campaign," Conference Board of Canada, Aug. 20, 2012.
20. https://independentsector.org/resource/why-diversity-equity-and-inclusion-matter.
21. "Jordan Peterson," *The Joe Rogan Experience,* #1070, Jan. 30, 2018, https://www.youtube.com/watch?v=6T7pUEZfgdI&feature=youtu.be&t=7534.
22. Jordan B. Peterson, "The Meaning of Meaning," *International Journal of Existential Psychology & Psychotherapy* 1, no. 2 (June 1, 2007).
23. Ibid.
24. A Psycho-ontological Analysis of Genesis 2–6. J. Peterson—Archive for the Psychology of Religion, 2007.
25. Ibid.
26. Ibid.
27. https://youtu.be/UGQNc1Nrvlo?t=128.

CHAPTER ELEVEN: REALITY AND THE SACRED

1. Jordan B. Peterson, "Reality and the Sacred" lecture, 5iF3R, July 14, 2010, https://youtu.be/AESMraB4qt4.
2. Ibid.
3. Ibid.
4. Ibid., https://youtu.be/2c3m0tt5KcE.
5. Ibid.
6. Ibid.
7. Ibid.
8. Ibid.
9. Ibid.
10. Ibid.
11. Ibid.
12. Ibid.
13. Ibid.
14. Ibid.
15. Ibid.
16. Ibid.
17. Ibid.
18. Ibid.
19. Ibid.
20. Ibid.
21. Ibid.
22. Ibid.
23. Ibid.
24. Ibid.
25. Ibid.
26. Slavoj Žižek, "Shoplifters of the World Unite," *London Review of Books,* Aug. 19, 2011, https://www.lrb.co.uk/2011/08/19/slavoj-zizek/shoplifters-of-the-world-unite.
27. Antoine Reverchon and Adrien de Tricornot, "*La rente pétrolière ne garantit plus la paix sociale,*" *Le Monde,* March 14, 2011.
28. List of Riots, Wikipedia and subsources, https://en.wikipedia.org/wiki/List_of_riots#.
29. The Wayback Machine, "Adbusters," "About Adbusters," Oct. 31, 2011, http://www.adbusters.org/about/adbusters.
30. The Wayback Machine, "The Culture Jammers Network," Aug. 17, 2000, http://adbusters.org/information/network/.
31. Derek Thompson, "Occupy the World: The '99 Percent' Movement Goes Global," *Atlantic,* Oct. 15, 2011, https://www.theatlantic.com/business/archive/2011/10/occupy-the-world-the-99-percent-movement-goes-global/246757/.
32. "Palin to GOP: 'Fight Like a Girl,'" Fox News, April 16, 2011.
33. Mark Bray, Introduction to *Antifa: The Anti-Fascist Handbook* (New York: Melville House, 2017).
34. Ibid, 47.
35. Peter Beinhart, "The Rise of the Violent Left," *Atlantic,* Sept. 6, 2017.
36. Gender Research Institute at Dartmouth, Mission Statement, http://www.dartmouth.edu/~grid/about/index.html.
37. "Jordan Peterson: The War on Masculinity," *Tucker Carlson Tonight,* Fox News, published on March 11, 2018 https://youtu.be/kn1q6GRnxx0?t=28.

38. Ben Shapiro, "And The Damned: Dartmouth's Worst," *Dartmouth Review,* Sept. 27, 2002; *Brainwashed* (Nashville, TN: Thomas Nelson, 2004).
39. Paul J. Fleming, Joseph G. L. Lee, and Shari L. Dworkin, "Real Men Don't: Constructions of Masculinity and Inadvertent Harm in Public Health Interventions," *American Journal of Public Health* 104, no. 6 (June 2014): 1029–35, doi:10.2105/AJPH.2013.301820.
40. Carlos Lozada, "The History, Theory and Contradictions of Antifa," *Washington Post,* Sept. 1, 2017.
41. Andreas Dorpalen, *German History in Marxist Perspective: The East German Approach* (London: I. B. Tauris, 1986), 384.
42. "Agenda Insight: Gender Forever," *The Agenda with Steve Paikin,* TVO, Jan 19, 2012, https://youtu.be/QOJaVL7N4G4.
43. Ibid.

CHAPTER TWELVE: THE INTELLECTUAL DARK WEB

1. Jason VandenBeukel, "Jordan Peterson: The Man who Reignited Canada's Culture War," *C2C Journal,* Dec. 1, 2016.
2. Joseph Brean, "Ontario Rights Commission Dismisses Complaint, Sort of," *National Post,* April 10, 2008.
3. Joseph Brean, "Rights Body Dismisses Maclean's Case," *National Post,* April 9, 2008.
4. "No to National Censorship Council," editorial, *National Post,* Feb. 12, 2009.
5. Jordan B. Peterson, "What Matters," TVO, March 30, 2013, https://youtu.be/A5216ZJVbVs.
6. Ibid.
7. Ibid.
8. Peterson, "What Matters," Comments.
9. Ibid.
10. "The Coddling of the American Mind: A First Principles Conversation with Dr. Jonathan Haidt," *Real Time with Bill Maher,* https://youtu.be/tKW3vKpPrlw.
11. Ibid.
12. Tadeusz Biernot, *Layers,* introduced by Jordan Peterson at Articsok Gallery, Oct. 11, 2013, https://youtu.be/GR-lwWS9mTo?t=478.
13. "Mikhaila Peterson—'Don't Eat That,'" Boulder Carnivore Conference, Low Carb Down Under, April 9, 2019, https:// youtu.be/N39o_DI5laI?t=310.
14. Emma Colton, "The Daily Caller Proudly Presents: The Dumbest College Courses for 2015," *Daily Caller,* Aug. 21, 2015, https://dailycaller.com/2015/08/21/the-daily-caller-proudly-presents-the-dumbest-college-courses-for-2015/.
15. Ibid.
16. Xiaowen Xu, Raymond A. Mar, and Jordan B. Peterson, "Does Cultural Exposure Partially Explain the Association Between Personality and Political Orientation?" *Personality and Social Psychology Bulletin* 39 (Dec. 2013): 1497–517, https://doi.org/10.1177/0146167213499235.
17. Sean Stevens, "Campus Speaker Disinvitations: Recent Trends (Part 1 of 2)," Jan. 24, 2017, https://heterodoxacademy.org/campus-speaker-disinvitations-recent-trends-part-1-of-2/.
18. Heather Sells, "Turning Point: Is the Youth Vote Really All That Liberal?" *CBN News,* April 28, 2016, https://www1.cbn.com/cbnnews/politics/2016/april/turning-point-is-the-youth-vote-really-all-that-liberal.
19. Julie Bykowicz, "This Boy Wonder Is Building the Conservative MoveOn.org in an Illinois Garage," Bloomberg.com, May 7, 2015, https://www.bloomberg.com/news/articles/2015-05-07/conservative-boy-wonder.

20. Lachlan Markay, "Exclusive: Pro-Trump Group, Turning Point USA, Has Finances Revealed," *Daily Beast,* June 28, 2018, https://www.thedailybeast.com/exclusive-pro-trump-group-turning-point-usa-has-finances-revealed.
21. Dominique Morisano Jacob B. Hirsh, Jordan B. Peterson, Robert O. Pihl, and Bruce M. Shore, "Setting, Elaborating, and Reflecting on Personal Goals Improves Academic Performance," *Journal of Applied Psychology* 95, no. 2 (2010): 255–64.
22. Colin G. DeYoung, Lena C. Quilty, and Jordan Peterson, "Between Facets and Domains: 10 Aspects of the Big Five," *Journal of Personality and Social Psychology* 93, no. 5, (2007): 880–96.
23. UCLA Professor Joshua Muldavin, Geography 5, Lecture, January 16, 2001; Ben Shapiro, *Brainwashed* (Nashville, TN: Thomas Nelson, 2004).
24. Yuri Bezmenov, TV interview, https://youtu.be/mqSV72VNnV0?t=3.
25. Julia Ioffe, "What Is Russia Today?," *Columbia Journalism Review,* Sept. 2010.
26. Simona Chiose, "Jordan Peterson and the Trolls in the Ivory Tower," *Globe and Mail,* June 2, 2017.
27. Ibid.
28. "Mikhaila Peterson—'Don't Eat That.'"

CHAPTER THIRTEEN: THE MAELSTROM

1. CBC Radio, "'I'm not a bigot' Meet the U of T Prof who Refuses to Use Genderless Pronouns," *As It Happens,* Sept. 30, 2016.
2. Simona Chiose, "Jordan Peterson and the Trolls in the Ivory Tower," *Globe and Mail,* June 2, 2017.
3. Laura Kane, "Sexual Assault Policies Lacking at Most Canadian Universities, Say Students," Canadian Press, March 7, 2016, https://www.cbc.ca/news/canada/british-columbia/canadian-universities-sex-assault-policies-1.3479314.
4. "Rape and Sexual Assault Victimization Among College-Age Females, 1995–2013," U.S. Department of Justice, Bureau of Justice Statistics, Dec. 2014.
5. Kane, "Sexual Assault Policies Lacking at Most Canadian Universities, Say Students."
6. Criminal Code, R.S.C. 1985, c. C-46, s. 319, https://laws-lois.justice.gc.ca/eng/acts/C-46/section-319.html.
7. https://openparliament.ca/bills/41-1/C-279/.
8. Ibid.
9. Valerie Straus, "Canada's New Leader, Justin Trudeau was a Schoolteacher," *Washington Post,* Oct. 20, 2015, https://www.washingtonpost.com/news/answer-sheet/wp/2015/10/20/canadas-new-leader-justin-trudeau-was-a-schoolteacher/.
10. "Jordan Peterson—Uncensored," *Valuetainment,* Oct. 18, 2018, https://youtu.be/dvBbxbjFRw4, 1:15:15.
11. Jordan B. Peterson, "Maps of Meaning: Object and Meaning" (Part 2) lecture, Jan. 14, 2015, https://youtu.be/6Rd10PQVsGs.
12. Ibid.
13. Ibid.
14. Caitlin M. Burton, Jason E. Plaks, and Jordan B. Peterson, "Why Do Conservatives Report Being Happier Than Liberals? The Contribution of Neuroticism," *Journal of Social and Political Psychology* 3, no. 1 (April 2015): 89–102, http://dx.doi.org/10.23668/psycharchives.1706.
15. Peterson, "Maps of Meaning: Object and Meaning" (Part 2) lecture.
16. Jordan B. Peterson, "The Death of the Oceans," Nov. 10, 2014, https://youtu.be/IrtEH5BYpmE, 1:48:03.

17. Alexandra Zimmern, "University Bans Use of 'Mr.' and 'Ms.' in All Correspondence," College Fix, Jan. 29, 2015, http://www.thecollegefix.com/post/21034.
18. "Public University Spends $16K on Campaign to Warn Students to Watch What They Say," College Fix, Feb. 9, 2015, http://www.thecollegefix.com/post/21174/.
19. Alex Griswold, "University of Missouri Police Ask Students to Report 'Hurtful Speech,'" Mediaite, Nov. 10, 2015, https://www.mediaite.com/online/university-of-missouri-police-ask-students-to-report-hurtful-speech/.
20. Heather Mac Donald, "Microaggression, Macro-Crazy," *City Journal,* Summer 2015, http://t.co/wrb9jEha4P?amp=1.
21. https://twitter.com/jordanbpeterson/status/578578554885144576/photo/1.
22. "Woman's Parents Accepting of Mixed-Attractiveness Relationship," *The Onion,* Jan. 14, 2015, https://t.co/PW6cxz3ZT6?amp=1.
23. "Gender and the Brain: When a Little Means a Lot," *The Agenda with Steve Paikin,* TVO, May 5, 2015, https://youtu.be/sSIEs1ngNiU?t=1023.
24. "Gender and the Brain; Differences Now?" *The Agenda with Steve Paikin,* TVO, May 5, 2015, https://youtu.be/sSIEs1ngNiU?t.
25. Ibid.
26. Ibid.
27. Ibid.
28. Ibid.
29. Ibid.
30. http://www.ohrc.on.ca/sites/default/filesGender%20Identity_Gender%20Expression%20Brochure_Accessible_English.pdf.
31. Ibid.
32. Ibid.
33. Donald Trump Presidential Campaign Announcement, June 16, 2015, FOX 10 Phoenix, https://youtu.be/MEqINP-TuV8.
34. Ibid.
35. Stephanie Condon, "Obama Responds to San Bernardino Shooting," *CBS News,* Dec. 2, 2015, https://www.cbsnews.com/news/obama-responds-to-san-bernardino-shooting/.
36. "1,000 Mass Shootings in 1,260 Days: This Is What America's Gun Crisis Looks Like," *Guardian,* June 13, 2006, https://www.theguardian.com/us-news/ng-interactive/2015/oct/02/mass-shootings-america-gun-violence.
37. "Black Lives Matter Toronto Stalls Pride Parade," Canadian Broacasting Company, July 3, 2016, https://www.cbc.ca/news/canada/toronto/pride-parade-toronto-1.3662823.
38. "Mass Public Shootings are Much Higher in the Rest of the World and Increasing Much More Quickly," Crime Prevention Research Center, Nov. 22, 2018, https://crimeresearch.org/2018/11/new-cprc-research-mass-public-shootings-are-much-higher-in-the-rest-of-the-world-and-increasing-much-more-quickly/.
39. Parliament of Canada, House of Commons, House Publications, 42nd Parliament, First Session, May 17, 2016, https://www.ourcommons.ca/DocumentViewer/en/42-1/house/sitting-57/hansard.
40. Russell Goldman, "Here's a List of 58 Gender Options for Facebook Users," *ABC News,* Feb. 13, 2014, https://abcnews.go.com/blogs/headlines/2014/02/heres-a-list-of-58-gender-options-for-facebook-users/.
41. Jordan Peterson, "Part 1, Fear and the Law," September 27, 2016, https://youtu.be/fvPgjg201w0.
42. Ibid.
43. Ibid.

44. Ibid.
45. Ibid.
46. Ibid.
47. Ibid.
48. Ibid.
49. Ibid.

CHAPTER FOURTEEN: RETALIATION

1. Jackie Hong, "Protesters Decry U of T Professor's Comments on Gender Identity," Toronto *Star,* Oct. 5, 2016, https://www.thestar.com/news/canada/2016/10/05/protesters-decry-u-of-t-professors-comments-on-gender-identity.html.
2. Egale, "What is Bill C-16," https://egale.ca/billc16/.
3. Jordan B. Peterson, "Part 1, Fear and the Law," September 27, 2016, https://youtu.be/fvPg-jg201w0.
4. Gad Saad, "My Chat with Psychologist Jordan Peterson," https://www.youtube.com/watch?v=Bpim_n0r0z0&t=565s.
5. Ibid.
6. Ibid.
7. Ibid.
8. Ibid.
9. Ibid.
10. Ibid.
11. Ibid.
12. Ibid.
13. Ibid.
14. Ibid.
15. Ibid.
16. Ibid.
17. Ibid.
18. Ibid.
19. Ibid.
20. "Jordan Peterson's First Protest at the University of Toronto," Oct. 11, 2016, https://youtu.be/HAlPjMiaKdw.
21. Ibid.
22. Ibid.
23. Ibid.
24. Ibid.
25. Ibid.
26. Ibid.
27. Ibid.
28. "Toronto Radicals Fight Free Speech," *Rebel Media,* Oct. 13, 2016.
29. "Dr Jordan B. Peterson," https://graphtreon.com/creator/user?u=3019121.
30. Antonella Artuso, "Human Rights Commissioner Weighs in on ze and hir," Toronto *Sun,* Nov. 13, 2016, https://torontosun.com/2016/11/13/human-rights-commissioner-weighs-in-on-ze-and-hir/wcm/0254ab55-ade7-40f4-b1f3-553b75b10842.
31. Ibid.
32. Ibid.

33. Jared Brown, "Bill C-16—What's the Big Deal?" *Perspectives on Commercial Ligigation* (blog), Dec. 24, 2016, https://litigationguy.wordpress.com/2016/12/24/bill-c-16-whats-the-big-deal/.
34. Ibid.
35. "University of Toronto Free Speech Debate," University of Toronto, Nov. 21, 2016, https://youtu.be/68NHUV5me7Q.
36. Ibid.
37. Ibid.
38. Ibid.
39. Ibid.
40. Ibid.
41. Ibid.
42. Ibid.
43. Ibid.
44. Ibid.
45. Ibid.
46. Ibid.
47. Ibid.
48. "Jordan Peterson," *The Joe Rogan Experience*, #1070, Jan. 30, 2018, https://www.youtube.com/watch?v=6T7pUEZfgdI&feature=youtu.be&t=7534.
49. Ibid.
50. Ibid.
51. Ibid.
52. Jordan B. Peterson, "Go ahead, make my day . . . ," March 18, 2017, https://youtu.be/0p1U-FiNiOek?t=112.
53. Ibid.
54. "Jordan Peterson," *The Joe Rogan Experience*, #1070, Jan. 30, 2018.
55. Ibid.
56. Ibid.
57. "Gender Differences in Personality Across the Ten Aspects of the Big Five," http://bit.ly/2bnlWUy.
58. "Gender Differences in Personality Traits Across Cultures: Robust and Surprising Findings," http://bit.ly/2ns6MhJ.
59. "Gender Differences in Personality and Interests: When, Where, and Why?" http://bit.ly/2ooh3R8.
60. "Cross-Cultural Studies of Personality Traits and their Relevance to Psychiatry," http://bit.ly/2nvcy31.
61. "Jordan Peterson," *The Joe Rogan Experience*, #1070, Jan. 30, 2018.
62. Ibid.
63. Ibid.
64. Ibid.
65. Bradford Richardson, "Students Berate Professor Who Refused to Participate in No-Whites 'Day of Absence,'" *Washington Times*, May 25, 2017, https://www.washingtontimes.com/news/2017/may/25/evergreen-state-students-demand-professor-resign-f/.
66. Susan Svrluga and Joe Heim, "Threat Shuts Down College Embroiled in Racial Dispute," *Washington Post*, June 1, 2017, https://www.washingtonpost.com/news/grade-point/wp/2017/06/01/threats-shut-down-college-embroiled-in-racial-dispute/.
67. Richardson, "Students Berate Professor Who Refused to Participate in No-Whites 'Day of Absence.'"

68. Ibid.
69. Jordan B. Peterson, "2017/05/17: Senate hearing on Bill C16," May 18, 2017, https://youtu.be/KnIAAkSNtqo.
70. Ibid.
71. Ibid.
72. Ibid.
73. Ibid.
74. Ibid.
75. Ibid.
76. Ibid.
77. Ibid.
78. Ibid.
79. Ibid.
80. Ibid.
81. Ibid.
82. Ibid.
83. "Dr Jordan B Peterson."
84. "Genders, Rights and Freedom of Speech," https://youtu.be/kasiov0ytEc.
85. Christie Blatchford, "Thought Police Strike Again," *National Post,* Nov. 10, 2017, https://nationalpost.com/opinion/christie-blatchford-thought-police-strike-again-as-wilfrid-laurier-grad-student-is-chastised-for-showing-jordan-peterson-video.
86. Ibid.
87. Ibid.
88. Jordan B. Peterson, "Secret Recording: Jordan Peterson Witchhunt with TA at Wilfrid Laurier University," Nov. 19, 2017, https://www.youtube.com/watch?v=usoID8zkUQM.
89. Ibid.
90. Blatchford, "Thought Police Strike Again."
91. Ibid.
92. Ibid.
93. https://www.w/v.ca/news/spotlights/2017/nov/apology-from-laurier-president-and-vice-chancellor.html.
94. https://www.w/v.ca/news/spotlights/2017/nov/open-letter-to-my-ta-lindsay-shepherd.html.
95. Ibid.
96. https://www.w/v.ca/news/spotlights/2018/aug//laurier-files-statement-of-defence-in-jordan-peterson-lawsuit.
97. https://www.the.record.com/news-story/8894891-jordan-peterson-doubles-down-on-laurier-lawsuit/.
98. "Jordan Peterson Doubles Down on Laurier Lawsuit," *The Record,* Sept. 11, 2018, https://www.therecord.com/news-story/8894891-jordan-peterson-doubles-down-on-laurier-lawsuit/?s=e.
99. "Jordan Peterson Debate on the Gender Pay Gap, Campus Protests and Postmodernism," *Channel 4 News,* Jan. 16, 2018, https://youtu.be/aMcjxSThD54.
100. Ibid.
101. Nellie Bowles, "Jordan Peterson, Custodian of the Patriarchy," *New York Times,* May 18, 2018, https://www.nytimes.com/2018/05/18/style/jordan-peterson-12-rules-for-life.html.
102. Ibid.
103. Guy Stevenson, "Straw Gods: A Cautious Response to Jordan B. Peterson," *Los Angeles Review of Books,* Oct. 1, 2018.

104. Deborah Dundas, "Jordan Peterson's Book Is a Bestseller—Except Where It Matters Most," Toronto *Star,* Feb. 9, 2018.
105. Jim Proser, telephone interview with Dave Rubin, May 28, 2019.
106. Tweet to Ontario Premier Doug Ford, https://twitter.com/jordanbpeterson/status/1050097390722699265.
107. "Doug Ford Met Jordan Peterson, Appointment Calendar Reveals," *Maharlika News,* Jan. 27, 2019, https://www.maharlikanews.com/2019/01/27/doug-ford-metjordan-peterson-appointment-calendar-reveals/.
108. "Genders, Rights and Freedom of Speech," *The Agenda with Steve Paikin,* TVO, Oct. 26, 2016, https://www.youtube.com/watch?v=kasiov0ytEc&feature=youtu.be&t=3087.
109. https://www.tvo.org/article/why-the-governments-campus-free-speech-policy-is-making-universities-nervous.
110. Jim Proser, contemporaneous notes at Beacon Theater, April 14, 2019.